Gardening for Acidic Soils

WORKING WITH NATURE TO CREATE A BEAUTIFUL LANDSCAPE

Gardening for Acidic Soils

WORKING WITH NATURE TO CREATE A BEAUTIFUL LANDSCAPE

TODD BOLAND and **JAMIE ELLISON**

BOULDER
BOOKS

Library and Archives Canada Cataloguing in Publication

Title: Gardening for acidic soils : working with nature to create a beautiful landscape / Todd
    Boland and Jamie Ellison.
Names: Boland, Todd, author. | Ellison, Jamie, author.
Description: Includes bibliographical references and index.
Identifiers: Canadiana 20220143978 | ISBN 9781989417492 (softcover)
Subjects: LCSH: Plants—Effect of soil acidity on. | LCSH: Plant-soil relationships. | LCSH: Garden
    soils. | LCSH: Soil acidity. | LCSH: Acid-tolerant plants. | LCSH: Gardening.
Classification: LCC S596.75 .B65 2022 | DDC 631.4/2—dc23

Published by Boulder Books
Portugal Cove-St. Philip's, Newfoundland and Labrador
www.boulderbooks.ca

Design and layout: Todd Manning
Editor: Stephanie Porter
Copy editor: Iona Bulgin

Printed in Canada

We acknowledge the financial support of the Government of Newfoundland and
Labrador through the Department of Tourism, Culture, Industry and Innovation.

Newfoundland
Labrador

Funded by the   Financé par le
Government   gouvernement
of Canada   du Canada   Canadä

CONTENTS

Acidic soils are often associated with foggy, wet climates.

Understanding soil preferences and soil-plant interactions can be daunting for any gardener, novice or seasoned. Terrestrial plant species have complex relationships with soil microbes and specific penchants for soil makeup, specifically the chemistry of soil and the availability of nutrients based on that chemistry. Soil pH plays an important role in nutrient availability, the plant's ability to assimilate nutrients, and the general health of the soil ecosystem. Acidic soils (pH <5.5) are widespread, especially in humid regions or areas with high precipitation. Approximately 30 per cent of the world's total land area, and fully a third of the soil in North America (the eastern half of North America and the Pacific Northwest), has a pH of 6 or lower and is considered acidic.

Very few, if any, publications are available on how to garden specifically on acidic soil; in fact, many books provide the opposite—advice on how to make acidic soil less so. We live by the saying, "If life gives you lemons … make lemonade." Work with nature, rather than trying to change it. A wide variety of ornamental plants, both native and exotic, thrive in acidic soil conditions or require them to survive. We hope to educate readers on how to develop a garden and gardening style that takes advantage of acidic soil conditions, a feature that has too often been considered a detriment to gardening.

An azalea-rhododendron garden.

This book concentrates on developing sustainable gardens that include a broad group of plants, both woody and herbaceous, that prefer acidic soil conditions. Classic acid-loving shrubs such as rhododendrons, mountain laurel, heaths, and heathers are described in the following pages, along with woody plants, including witch-hazel, *Magnolia*, and *Viburnum*. Among the herbaceous perennials featured are Japanese iris, gentians, and candelabra primroses. These fascinating plants have a myriad of ornamental attributes with specific survival strategies for acidic soil conditions.

WHAT IS pH?

Soil pH, a measurement of its alkalinity or acidity, is measured on a scale of 1 to 14, with 7 as the neutral mark. Soil below pH 7 is considered acidic, or sour, while anything above pH 7 is considered alkaline, or sweet.

The most common classes of soil pH are:

Extremely acidic 3.5–4.4

Very strongly acidic 4.5–5

Strongly acidic 5.1–5.5

Moderately acidic 5.6–6

Slightly acidic 6.1–6.5

Neutral 6.6–7.3

Slightly alkaline 7.4–7.8

Moderately alkaline 7.9–8.4

Strongly alkaline 8.5–9

Most plants prefer a pH between 6.2 and 7, or slightly acidic to neutral pH soils. This range optimizes the availability of essential nutrients for plants. Soil microbial activity, decomposition, and nutrient cycling are also at peak levels within this range. As soil pH increases or decreases, microbial diversity is affected and usually decrease, resulting in fewer benefits to the flora. Only flora adapted to these more extreme soil types can survive, usually by adapting to nutrient availabilities generally considered deficient and toxic. The next few pages elaborate on pH and adaptations to low pH and nutrient availability. The focus of this book is gardening within a pH 4.5 to 6 range, which is moderately acidic to strongly acidic soil.

ACIDIC SOIL REGIONS OF NORTH AMERICA

The acidic soil regions in North America are predominantly found in eastern North America as well as the Pacific Northwest. In eastern North America, many of the ecoregions and habitats are influenced by the parent material of igneous rocks like granites. Low-pH soils are the result of the weathering of these materials in association with high precipitation and the topography. The Appalachian Mountains, found in eastern North America, stretch from Newfoundland to northern Georgia. This old mountain system, once as tall as the Rockies, is comprised mainly of igneous rock which has been eroding for at least 400 million years. The surrounding soils in the region generally have a low pH, a consequence of the constant weathering of

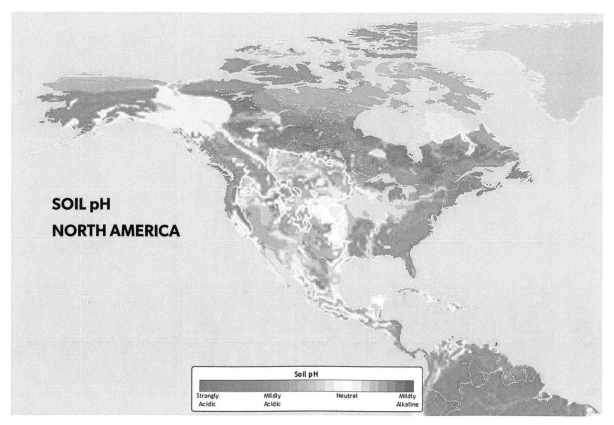

SOIL pH
NORTH AMERICA

Soil pH

| Strongly Acidic | Mildly Acidic | Neutral | Mildly Alkaline |

Soil pH map by permission of the Center for Sustainability and the Global Environment, Nelson Institute for Environmental Studies, University of Wisconsin-Madison.

A planting of acid-loving shrubs.

A typical fen featuring many sedges and grasses.

Barrens often have rocky outcrops.

this material and a high annual precipitation. The major biomes in the Appalachian region include the boreal forest to the north and deciduous temperate forests to the south. The forests of the Canadian Maritimes and the northeastern US, called the Acadian forest, are a transition between the two. Various peatlands, such as fens, bogs, and marshes, are also found within these ecoregions. Some habitats have specific soils that are nutrient-deficient and have a low pH. These include the cold, wet, peaty soils of northern bogs, thin peaty glacial tills along the coastal headlands, and inland sand barrens. Populations of acid-tolerant plant species populate these sites and form overstorey and understorey colonies. Ericaceous plants dominate in many of these habitats, forming heathlands.

In the Pacific Northwest, low-pH soils are found in areas with high precipitation and igneous parent material, including parts of British Columbia and Washington, Oregon, and northern California. Coastal and sea-level climates are benign in these regions compared to the eastern equivalent of the continent, but they feature similar plant communities, habitats, and soil types. The Pacific Northwest is characterized by temperate rainforests from coastal Alaska and British Columbia south to northern California. The excessively high precipitation in these areas contributes to and maintains the low-pH soils throughout this region.

The poor incorporation of the organic surface layer into the underlying mineral layer is one indicator of an acidic soil. Flora dominated by species from the Ericaceae (Heath) family is another.

THE CHEMISTRY OF ACIDIC SOIL, TOXICITY, AND NUTRIENT AVAILABILITY

Soil chemistry is a multifaceted interaction among several biotic and abiotic factors, including parent material (bedrock), local or regional climates, and natural vegetation. In some cases, soil management practices can affect soil pH. For example, the excessive application of high-nitrogen fertilizers can make soils more acidic.

The chemical composition of parent material and the weathering process of that material are perhaps the most important factors in determining soil pH. Soil acidification is a natural occurrence in areas that are humid or foggy or have high seasonal precipitation. Soils generally become acidic when basic pH elements such as sodium, calcium, magnesium, and potassium are replaced by hydrogen ions. When water combines with carbon dioxide in the air, it forms the weak acid carbonic acid. The more water, the more carbonic acid that forms. Parent rocks such as granite and sandstone are naturally low in basic pH elements. When they are exposed to high annual precipitation, the hydrogen ions in the carbonic acid leach the basic pH elements held in the soil, causing it to become acidic. Parent rocks high in these basic pH elements, such as limestone or dolostone, release calcium, which neutralizes hydrogen ions in the soil, thus resulting in neutral to alkaline pH soil. The leaching of basic pH elements occurs at a much lower rate when soils are formed under arid conditions; hence, deserts often have a neutral pH soil, even when the soil is derived from granite or sandstone.

Soil acidity can be a limiting factor for successful plant growth. It can restrict the availability of certain essential nutrients and render others toxic. Plant essential macronutrients, both primary and secondary, become less available or are rendered inaccessible to plants as the soil pH decreases. Nitrogen (N), phosphorus (P), calcium (Ca), and magnesium (Mg) become deficient as the pH decreases. Some elements, such as aluminum (Al), manganese (Mn), and iron (Fe), become more soluble and can reach toxic levels as soil pH lessens.

Aluminum toxicity can affect plant metabolism by interfering with the transport and uptake of some nutrients by the plants. Although aluminum is not an essential nutrient for plants, it enters the plant osmotically through the root system and high levels result in inhibited root growth. Lateral roots and tips become thickened and can show minimal branching. In extreme cases, root tips may turn brown, with a noticeable increase in more shallow root systems. This could inevitably affect the capability for nutrient procurement and potentially lead to drought stress due to inadequate root mass. Soil microbes, particularly beneficial bacteria, some crucial to the nitrogen cycle, could be negatively affected by the high aluminum levels that are linked with low soil pH.

In contrast to aluminum, the plant essential nutrient manganese is readily transported from roots to shoots. Symptoms of manganese toxicity first appear on shoots and leaves and include leaf cupping or crinkling. High levels of manganese in the soil also affect the uptake of other mineral plant essential nutrients such as calcium and magnesium, both of which can become deficient under such conditions.

Iron toxicity can also result from a low-pH soil. Too much iron can cause leaf spotting and stunted growth; it can also affect chlorophyll production and subsequently affect the rate of photosynthesis and negatively impact plant growth and health.

HOW PLANTS ADAPT TO ACIDIC SOIL CONDITIONS

Many plants are extraordinarily adaptable to various environmental and climatic conditions. Soil is the basis for success with terrestrial plants and is host to a complex system of mineral cycling, microbial activity, pH, and plant-soil interactions. This system is sometimes referred to as the "soil ecosystem" or the "soil food web." An incredible diversity of organisms comprises the soil food web: from tiny one-celled bacteria, fungi, algae, and protozoa, to more complex micro and macro fauna, including nematodes, earthworms, insects, miniature vertebrates, and plants. The ecosystem works with regular organic inputs, moisture, optimum temperatures, and cycling of nutrients through biotic and abiotic factions. Governing this system is pH. Technically, pH is a gauge of the hydrogen-ion concentration (potential hydrogen) in a substance. For the gardener's needs, it is enough to know if the soil is alkaline or acidic, because certain nutrients can only be accessed by plants when the soil pH falls within an acceptable range. No amount of fertilizer will improve their health until the pH has been adjusted.

How have plants adapted? Some plants can manage nutrient deficiencies in acidic soils via revisions to their root morphologies and

A conifer garden.

A garden featuring a mix of acid-loving plants.

rate of nutrient uptake and metabolism. One family of plants renowned for its success in adverse low-pH environments is the Ericaceae. Ericaceous plants, along with many other unrelated plants, have symbiotic relationships with beneficial fungi called mycorrhizae, or fungus root. These relationships are very old and involve the fungus inhabiting the root system both internally (endomycorrhiza) and externally (ectomycorrhiza). The plant provides nutrition to the fungus through the form of sugars, while the fungus provides nutrition to the plant via its ability to capture plant essential nutrients that are sometimes difficult to obtain by the plant itself. Studies have also shown that mycorrhizal liaisons can aid plants during droughts, combat harmful pathogens, and increase survivability in metal-rich soils, as low-pH soils can be. Ericaceous plants rely heavily on mycorrhizae and are successful colonizers of low-pH environments such as bogs and heathlands. Mycorrhizae is a general term—specifically, diverse fungal groups contain small factions of species that partner with their host plants. Ericaceae generally associate with ericoid mycorrhiza (an example of endomycorrhiza), which represent a significant adaptation to acidic and nutrient-poor soils, including in boreal forests, sphagnum bogs, and low-pH heathlands.

Ericoid mycorrhizae produce fungal coils that inhabit the epidermal cells of the fine hair roots typical of many ericaceous species. The fungi produce lax networks of hyphal strands around the outside of the roots. The hyphae infiltrate the roots and form densely packed coils inside the cortical cells, subsequently becoming nutrient- and carbohydrate-exchange sites.

Ericoid mycorrhizae appear to have degradative properties with an ability to break down complex organic molecules through specific enzymatic facilities, giving the plant access to organic forms of nutrients, such as nitrogen and phosphorus. These nutrients are in low quantities in environments typically inhabited by ericaceous plants. Studies reveal that, in addition to ericoid mycorrhiza giving this plant family a nutritional advantage in low-pH environments, ericoid mycorrhiza may harbour an exclusion mechanism to absorbing harmful elements in low-pH soils. This may relieve the plants of stress rather than tolerance of toxins in metal-rich soils. As mentioned previously, iron may be toxic in low-pH soils. Studies have indicated that ericoid mycorrhiza may have the ability to regulate iron consumption even at higher concentrations, giving ericaceous plants an advantage.

The ability of the mycorrhizal partner to process toxic metals and sequester plant essential nutrients from low-pH organic soils and/or poor, disturbed subsoil conditions contributes significantly to the success of Ericaceae under acidic soil conditions in their natural heathland environments.

WHAT ARE THE ERICACEAE?

The family Ericaceae was first described by Antoine Laurent de Jussieu in 1789. The name comes from the genus *Erica*, derived from Greek, loosely interpreted as heather. In 2002, families including Empetraceae, Epacridaceae, Monotropaceae, Priontaceae, and Pyrolaceae were made redundant and included under Ericaceae based on a combination of morphological, molecular, and embryological data. The plant family Ericaceae now consists of more than 124 genera and over 4,000 species. Generally, ericaceous plants are woody and vary in size from low ground covers to small trees. A few, like *Monotropa*, are herbaceous and lack chlorophyll. They obtain nutrients through myco-heterotropism, that is, they parasitize specific mycorrhizal fungi associated with photosynthesizing overstorey trees in woodland environments. While most ericaceous plants are terrestrial, some species of Vireya rhododendrons live as epiphytes on the branches of trees in the tropical ecosystems of Southeast Asia.

Ericaceae's flowers have fused petals. Most genera have the urn-shaped bells typically seen in *Vaccinium* and *Erica* species. Blossoms may be solitary or in large clusters, commonly referred to as trusses, in genera such as *Rhododendron* and *Kalmia*. Reproductive structures are generally in the form of fleshy fruit or dried capsules encasing an abundance of minute seeds.

Ericaceous plants have a shallow-spreading root mass found marginally below the soil surface. Roots are composed of fine, fibrous strands which lack root hairs. An evolutionary advantage to this root system is that moisture and nutrient absorption occurs very rapidly through the mass of delicate roots. The shallow thick root mass allows for relatively easy transplanting with most genera; however, the delicate, fine roots and the absence of root hairs require ample and consistent moisture during the growing season.

Many ericaceous plants are known as *calcifuges*, a Latin name meaning to flee

Heathers, dwarf ericaceae, and conifers.

from chalk. These plants do not tolerate high calcium in the soil. However, soils low in calcium are usually nutrient poor. To overcome this problem, ericaceous plants depend on mutualistic relationships with mycorrhizae to obtain sufficient nutrients from the surrounding soil. Some species from the genus *Pyrola* are labelled mixotrophic, suggesting that they take sugars as well as nutrients from their mycorrhizal surrogates.

Most Ericaceae will struggle in clay-based soils with poor drainage and low oxygen content, instead preferring soils that are moisture-retentive but well drained. There are some exceptions: some species in *Arctostaphylos*, *Arbutus*, *Corema*, and *Empetrum* are quite drought-tolerant, while *Chamaedaphne*, *Andromeda*, and a few *Rhododendron*, *Kalmia*, and *Gaylussacia* species can grow in extremely wet soils.

Most genera have evergreen foliage in endless varieties of shapes and sizes. The presence of evergreen foliage provides plants with a nutrient storage repository and lowers the energy costs involved in annually replacing the foliage. This presents plants with another strategy to deal with nutrient retention in unproductive soils. Many species have waxy cuticles, pubescent new growth, or indumentum on leaf undersides. These evolutionary adaptions protect foliage from insects, disease, moisture loss, and sunburn depending on the environment in which the plants are growing.

Ericaceae have a global distribution; they are absent only from Antarctica, the high Arctic, lowland tropics, and the most hostile parts of Australia and central Africa. Many are found in temperate climates and prefer locations that do not experience rapid changes in temperature or sites that exhibit extreme summer temperatures combined with low humidity. With few exceptions, precipitous changes between cold and damp to heat and arid are unwelcoming for most ericaceous plants. In northeastern North America, Ericaceae form extensive "heathlands," which are characterized by an abundance of Ericaceae and infertile acidic soils. Heathland habitats include coastal barrens, sphagnum and dry bogs, woodland understorey, and alpine tundra and can also include a diversity of plant species. In Europe, there is seemingly less diversity in their heathland equivalent, called "moors." Moors or moorlands are composed mainly of *Calluna vulgaris* and a few *Erica* species. In Australia and New Zealand, the genus *Epacris* (Australian heaths) form extensive diverse heathlands throughout. One of the most distinct and diverse heathlands is the "fynbos" in South Africa. The fynbos is possibly one of the most botanically rich heathlands on the planet and is home to over 700 species of *Erica* alone.

SIGNIFICANCE OF ERICACEAE

Ericaceous plants provide important environmental and economical services to

A garden of Ericaceous plants.

local economies and habitats. Plants such as *Rhododendron*, *Kalmia latifolia*, *Pieris*, and others are highly ornamental and have been cultivated and subjected to breeding regimes for at least a century. The genus *Rhododendron*, with over 1,000 species, now boasts at least 28,000 hybrids and counting, making it one of the most popular ornamental crops in horticulture. The range of plant habits, leaf shapes, and flower variation is virtually endless.

Heaths and heathers are also important ornamental plants, particularly in the UK and Europe. This group is composed mainly of low-growing hardy *Erica* species and varieties, and *Calluna vulgaris* cultivars. Some cultivars from tender *Erica* species and *Rhododendron indica* are popular seasonal plants and treated like disposable crops. *Erica gracilis* and cultivars and salal, *Gaultheria shallon*, are often included as cut flowers in the floral industry trade.

Globally, heathlands offer food and cover for many animal species. The extensive heathlands in North America provide environmental services such as carbon storage in plants and the peat media they inhabit. This storage helps to mitigate climate change. Thick carpets of heathland plants act as a filtration system; they also slow water movement and consequently decrease the potential for floods during rain events.

Ericaceae are economically important in the small-fruit industry in eastern North America, the Pacific Northwest, and, to a lesser degree, in South America. Blueberry and cranberry crops in Canada and the US are significant exports. These crops, often called "superfoods," have high vitamin content and are important sources of antioxidants. The neotropical Ericaceae of Central and South America are currently under research, with preliminary results indicating that the concentration of antioxidants in this group are significantly higher than in commercial blueberries.

In the UK and Western Europe, "heather honey" derived primarily from Scotch heather, *Calluna vulgaris*, has a distinct flavour and is a sought-after commodity. Heather honey, used in the production of liqueurs, is an integral ingredient of the famous Scotch liqueur Drambuie. In North America, an ericaceous tree, sourwood, *Oxydendron arboreum*, produces a rare honey that is rated as one of the best in the world. Due to its limited range and brief bloom period, sourwood honey is relatively scarce and commands a premium price.

WOODLAND GARDENS

Dealing with shade is a challenge to most gardeners. Such areas are not just low on sunlight but, especially if under conifers, will be highly acidic and potentially dry. If you are hoping for a garden full of large blooms under a tree, you are out of luck. Most shade-tolerant plants have small, exquisite flowers. Flowers are most often white to allow the blossoms to be more easily seen by the pollinators. Shade gardens must rely heavily on foliage to create interest. Fortunately, plenty of acid-loving plants have spectacular foliage.

The first step in planning a woodland or shade garden is to determine what type of shade is present—not all shade is created equal. The deepest shade is under evergreens, such as large conifers. Branches that sweep close to the ground will result in heavy or low shade. In the wild, the most common plants found in these conditions are mosses. The light levels might be too low to support much else. If the tree is limbed high with the lowest branches 3 metres or more above the ground, enough light might penetrate from the sides to allow ferns, hosta, and native woodlanders to grow. This is often called high shade.

Under large deciduous trees, such as maples, summer shade may also be very dense. Depending on the branch structure, the shade may be low or high. In spring, however, before the trees leaf, the ground may receive enough light to allow spring ephemerals to thrive. A walk in the Carolinian forests shows this very clearly. In April and May, the forest floor is a riot of blooms from trilliums, trout lily, Dutchman's-breeches, corn lily, and a host of other plants. Plenty of ferns are also visible. These plants need spring sun but tolerate deep shade in summer. Some simply go dormant and disappear if the shade becomes too intense.

If deciduous trees are large but well spaced, shafts of sunlight may reach the ground throughout the growing season, allowing for even a wider variety of plants. As well, if the trees have small leaves, such as birch, beech, or locust, then spots of sunlight create dappled shade. Gardens of intense beauty can be created under dappled shade conditions. Many acid-loving shrubs are ideal for a dappled shade garden. Witch-hazel, azaleas, mountain laurel, and hydrangea are but a few of note. These types of shrubs are often called understorey plants and, in the wild, typically grow in the shade of much taller deciduous trees.

Perhaps your shaded area is along the north side of the house. If the house is light-coloured, it can reflect some light onto the garden. If the surrounding area on the north side of the house is unobstructed, that is, there are no trees, it will also allow light. In mid-summer, this area may receive early morning and late evening sun. Generally, the north side of an unobstructed house is often called "bright shade" and, like dappled shade, can allow for stunning plant displays.

The east or west side of a building will receive either morning or afternoon sun. These areas are called partly shaded. Morning sun is not as intense as afternoon sun, so while shade-loving plants may thrive on the east side of a house, they may burn on the west. Most acid-loving perennials grow well in partial shade.

Several gardening styles are suited to gardening in shade. If you want to work with nature, you can recreate a typical eastern woodland scenario by planting a variety of native spring ephemerals. This is especially pleasing if the shade in your garden is created by taller trees. Native acid-loving perennials include *Asarum canadense, Arisaema triphylla, Clintonia borealis, Dicentra cucullata, Erythronium americanum, Maianthemum, Sanguinaria canadensis, Trillium, Tiarella,* and *Uvularia.* Native shrubs to combine with these perennials could include *Amelanchier, Calycanthus floridus, Corylus americana, C. cornuta, Diervilla, Itea virginica, Viburnum lantanoides,* and *Viburnum trilobum.*

A popular approach to shade gardening is to create a white garden. White flowers and white-variegated leaves brighten up dark areas in a garden. As noted earlier,

An early summer woodland garden.

A woodland garden featuring hosta, geum, astilbe, and ferns.

A spring woodland garden of ephemeral plants.

many shade plants have white flowers. Suggested acid-loving and shade-tolerant perennials include *Gillenia trifoliata*, *Cimicifuga*, *Pulmonaria* 'Sissinghurt White', *Primula denticulata* 'Alba', *Trillium grandiflorum*, *Aruncus*, white-flowered *Astilbe*, *Maianthemum*, and *Hosta* 'Royal Standard'. Among shrubs, *Amelanchier*, *Viburnum*, and *Hydrangea* can be used for their white blossoms. Complement white flowers with white-variegated plants such as *Cornus sericea* 'Ivory Halo' and/or 'Elegantissima', *Carex morrowii* 'Ice Dance' and/or 'Ice Ballet', and white-variegated *Hosta*.

Asian-style gardens are suited to shady locations, especially under the dappled shade of taller trees. Flowers are kept to a minimum, while foliage is prominent. *Acer palmatum* is a staple for Asian gardens and ideal for acidic soil circumstances. *Viburnum plicatum*, *V. sieboldii*, *Hamamelis*, *Skimmia*, *Sarcoccoca*, and azalea are other excellent woody subjects. Among ornamental "grasses" for shady Asian gardens are *Hakonechloa macra* cultivars combined with *Carex morrowii*, *C. oshimensis*, and *Ophiopogon*. Use *Athyrium nipponicum* and *A. vidalii* ferns as a strong foliage contrast. For subtle touches of floral colour, try *Brunnera* selections, *Astilbe*, *Anemone hupehensis*, and *Hosta*.

Perhaps the most popular approach to shade is to create a garden dominated by a variety in foliage forms, colour, and texture. If these plants produce flowers as well, that's a bonus. Suggested shade-tolerant perennials with noteworthy foliage are *Arisaema*, *Bergenia*, *Brunnera*, *Disporum*, *Epimedium*, *Hakonechloa*, *Hosta*, *Streptopus*, and ferns. To make an impact, you could strive to use larger-leaved plants to create a tropical effect. Bold foliage plants include *Aruncus*, *Ligularia*, *Podophyllum*, *Polygonatum*, *Matteuccica*, and *Dryopteris affinis*. Bottom line: don't let acidic soil and shade be a deterrent to creating a beautiful garden!

BOG GARDENS

Gardening with low-pH soil that is perpetually wet and low in nutrients can be challenging even for seasoned gardeners. In nature, such conditions develop into various types of wetlands, including bogs, mires, fens, swamps, and marshes. These diverse habitats are home to specialized plants. As swamps and marshes are seasonally flooded, most gardeners attempt to replicate a bog, mire, or fen, collectively referred to as a bog garden.

The characteristics of a true bog are specific and need to be emulated to have success with cultivating bog plants. The bog wetland is nutrient-poor (oligotrophic) and strongly acidic, with pH around 4.5. The woody vegetation of these sites can house a large concentration of ericaceous plants which can tolerate a low pH, as well as waterlogged and nutrient-poor conditions. Nitrogen is a plant essential nutrient which is always deficient in sphagnum bogs due to the anaerobic conditions. Therefore, it is not uncommon to see adaptations such as carnivory and plant groups with low nutrient requirements growing there.

Natural bogs receive most of their water and nutrients from precipitation and a slowly decomposing organic base composed primarily of sphagnum moss. This organic layer is generally more than 30 centimetres deep but can exceed 9 metres under ideal conditions. Natural bog areas are found throughout the globe, each with its own complement of specialized flora.

Soil with poor drainage, especially sites located in low hollows, are prime considerations for developing a bog garden. In nature, bogs are nestled into rocky depressions or adjacent to slow-moving streams, ponds, and lakes; incorporating bog gardens into rock gardens or adjacent to garden pond features can be fitting.

The key to a successful bog garden is mimicking the components found in a natural bog: poor drainage, low pH, and peat/sphagnum moss media that remains constantly moist. A sunken area with an underlying heavy clay soil can be a great asset. Most gardeners do not have these conditions and may use a PVC liner, the type used to create garden water features. In fact, construction of a bog garden is much the same as for a garden pool.

Select a site that receives at least 6 hours of direct sun per day—the sunnier the better. Dig a hole to your preferred dimensions, at least 60 centimetres deep. Place a 10-centimetre layer of coarse sand in the bottom of the hole, then the PVC liner, leaving about 30 centimetres of liner over the edge of the hole to allow for settling. Once settled, the exposed edges of the liner can be hidden by mulch or rocks. Poke holes around the edges of the liner about 30 centimetres below what will be the finished soil surface. These holes will allow excess water to drain from the upper 30 centimetres of the garden, but the deeper retained water will keep the upper soil moist enough to accommodate

A bog pool and garden.

A bog garden.

the requirements of the plants. Backfill the garden with a 60-40 mix of peat and coarse sand. Water well and allow to settle for a week or so before planting. You may need to add more media if it settles significantly.

For those in northeastern North America, natural bogs are readily seen and offer ideas about what types of plants will work best. Native bog plants suited to an artificial bog garden include exotic-looking species such as the pitcher-plants (*Sarracenia* species), *Platanthera* orchid species, and bog orchids such as *Arethusa*, *Calopogon*, and *Pogonia*. Natural bog wetlands can be carpeted with thickets of ericaceous plants such as

bog laurel, *Kalmia polifolia*; bog rosemary, *Andromeda polifolia*; and bog huckleberry, *Gaylusaccia bigeloviana*. Other woody plants in the mix are chokeberries, *Aronia* species, and conifers such as eastern larch, *Larix laricina*, and black spruce, *Picea mariana*. Any of these species can be incorporated into a bog garden if the conditions imitate their native habitats.

Plan for all four seasons. Starting with spring, introduce showy floral displays from species such as bog laurel, *Kalmia polifolia*, with its pink, open, cupped flowers or lavender purple drifts of Rhodora, *Rhododendron canadense*, and perhaps the white form *R. canadense* 'Alba'. For larger bogs, swamp azalea, *Rhododendron viscosum*, can fill a 2-metre space with white tubular flowers and a spicy scent. For autumn interest, choose plants with noteworthy fall foliage and fruit displays. Species such as bog huckleberry, *Gaylussacia bigeloviana*; purple chokeberry, *Aronia prunifolia*; dwarf birch, *Betula pumila* and *B. michauxii*; and dwarf cultivars of eastern larch, *Larix laricina*, produce incredible autumn displays of fiery oranges, reds, and golds. Cranberries, *Vaccinium macrocarpon*, produce persistent edible red fruit. Cranberry spreads rapidly and needs to be kept in check in smaller bog gardens; a dwarf form such as 'Hamilton' may be a good choice. Also with persistent winter fruit is winterberry holly, *Ilex verticillata*. Cultivars are available with red, orange, or yellow berries. Coniferous and broadleaf evergreens come into their own during late autumn, winter, and early spring. This group provides structure and substance when the garden is completely dormant. Cultivars of black spruce such as *Picea mariana* 'Nana' can form dense, evergreen, bluish green domes, while leatherleaf, *Chamaedaphne calyculata*, takes on bronze to plum hues during the cold winter months. A cultivar of bog rosemary, *Andromeda polifolia* 'Blue Ice' keeps its steel blue needlelike leaves year-round. As many of these native bog plants are not easily found in local nurseries, they may require collection of seeds or cuttings. Whatever your source of native plants, make sure that they are ethically sourced.

In addition to native plants, a myriad of exotic bog-loving plants are readily available in most nurseries. These herbaceous perennials are essential for bog gardens, but pay attention to their adaptability and vigor. Some species, such as *Iris sibirica* and *I. kaempferi*, are available in range of cultivars but are vigorous and best suited to larger bog gardens or along the margins of smaller gardens. The native blue flag iris, *I. versicolor* and *I. virginica*, may be used but are quite robust. Another herbaceous species suited to the borders of the bog garden is marsh marigold, *Caltha palustris*. Typically yellow, white forms are also available. Both light up the spring bog garden but can seed liberally at times if left to their own ways. Several primroses are ideal for bog gardens, including *P. japonica*, *P. alpicola*, *P. sikkimensis*, and *P. florindae*. These provide early to mid-summer blooms, while cardinal flower, *Lobelia cardinalis*, provide blazing red spires in late summer.

Bold foliage is a definite design feature for any garden including bog gardens. Plants such as the umbrella plant, *Darmeria peltata*, and shield rodgersia, *Astilboides tabularis*, are grown primarily for their dramatic leaves that can exceed a width of 50 centimetres. Some fern species also tolerate low-pH boggy conditions. Cinnamon fern, *Osmundastrum cinnamomeum*, has a vaselike growth habit. This deciduous fern produces pubescent, architectural fiddleheads in early spring, unfurling into green lacy fronds exceeding 1 metre in length. As autumn approaches, the fronds turn a rich cinnamon orange. This species can often be seen in full sun to partial shade areas in its native habitat. Bog gardens are generally too wet for most true grasses but some of the grasslike sedges, *Carex* species, rushes, *Juncus* species, and sweet flags, *Acorus* species, can provide a similar effect with evergreen and variegated foliage forms.

Bog gardens offer gardeners plants that border on the unusual if not bizarre. The skunk cabbages have early flowers composed of a modified leaf (spathe) and a clublike spike (spadix). The western skunk cabbage, *Lysichiton americanus*, with its yellow spathe, and its Asian counterpart *Lysichiton camtschatcensis* with a white spathe, flower in early spring at about the same time. Occasionally these two species hybridize producing creamy yellow intermediates. On the east coast, the eastern skunk cabbage, *Symplocarpus foetidus*, flowers in very early spring or even late winter in some locales. It has an uncanny ability to produce heat in its inflorescence. This infrequently seen adaptation, called thermogenesis, appears to help its fly pollinators function during cooler weather and speeds up flower development. It is not unlikely to see their flowers literally melting through the last snows of winter. Following flowering, all skunk cabbage species produce large, bold, tropical foliage.

Perhaps the most identifiable bog plants, and the group that garner the most attention, are the carnivorous plants. Even the coldest bog gardens support at least a few species of carnivorous plants. The sundews and butterworts are small insectivorous plants worthy of a place in any bog garden. The round-leaved sundew, *Drosera rotundifolia*, and spoonleaf sundew, *Drosera intermedia*, are the hardiest and are native to northeastern North America. They form small radially arranged red leaves with sticky hairs that look like dew. Of the many butterworts, only one speies is reliably hardy to zone 3. The common butterwort, *Pinguicula vulgaris*, produces a basal rosette of lime green foliage

with a slick, greasy feel. Small purple flowers comparable to violets are held high above the plant in June and July.

The most iconic carnivorous plants are the pitcher-plants. Most of the many genera of pitcher-plants are tropical. The only reliably hardy genus is *Sarracenia*. The natural range of *Sarracenia* is eastern North America. One of the hardiest and perhaps the one with the most extensive range is the northern pitcher-plant, *Sarracenia purpurea*. This species radiates its modified leaves (pitchers) from the base in an outward circular array. The pitchers are generally green in the summer, with purple venation, and turn a rich dark purple as the weather cools. Tall, waxy, nodding purple flowers rise above the plant in summer. Several natural variants exhibit colour variations on their pitchers. It is the hardiest of the *Sarracenia* species and will survive cold gardens in zone 3. Many species of the southern *Sarracenia* exhibit some cold hardiness and are worth trying in bog gardens situated in zones 5 and 6.

Sarracenia are easily hybridized with no apparent genetic barriers. Many have been hybridized with *S. purpurea* to produce a myriad of hybrids exhibiting colourful, surreal foliage, exotic flowers, and increased hardiness.

Constructing a bog garden is essentially creating a low-pH, wetland habitat. It expands and enhances the range of plants one can grow when gardening with acidic soils and centres on specific plant-soil requirements. Think of this type of garden as a feature area with a star-studded cast of unique plants that will earn lasting attention.

A bog garden featuring *Caltha*, *Iris*, and *Lysichiton*.

A bog garden with *Sarracenia* cultivars.

An example of a landscape created on acidic soil.

Aconitum henryi

ACONITUM
Monkshood

Over 100 species of *Aconitum* are found throughout the northern hemisphere, but mostly in the Himalayan region. Only a few are common in cultivation: those primarily of European descent. Common monkshood, *A. tuberosus*, produces a tuberous root from which stems grow 100 to 120 centimetres in height. The palmate leaves are dark shiny green and deeply dissected. The helmet-shaped flowers grow in a narrow raceme during mid-summer. The flowers are typically deep blue, but other colours include 'Album' (white) and 'Carneum' (dull pink). Virtually identical in appearance is the hybrid *A.* X *cammarum*, available in three primary cultivars: 'Bicolor' (blue and white), 'Stainless Steel' (light blue), and 'Pink Sensation' (light pink). Another monkshood hybrid, 'Spark's Variety', is deep purple blue, blooms later in early autumn, and may reach nearly 2 metres tall.

Wolfsbane, *A. lycoctonum*, native from northern Europe through to Mongolia, has larger leaves than common monkshood and is more compact, reaching 85 centimetres tall. Its individual flowers are narrower than those of common monkshood. The most popular cultivar on the market is 'Ivorine', with creamy white flowers. Similar but taller is the southern European yellow wolfsbane,

A. lamarkii, which can reach 2 metres and has pale yellow-green flowers.

The showy petals of monkshood are modified sepals; its true petals are small and insignificant. Monkshood grows in sun to partial shade, preferring humus-rich, evenly moist sites. While not fussy about the soil pH, they do not tolerate drought. Species may be grown from seed but named cultivars are propagated by division. All attract bees. Monkshood is generally pest- and disease-free and resistant to deer and rabbits. This is primarily because plants are highly toxic. Always wear rubber gloves when handling them. The above are all hardy to zone 3, but as they dislike excess summer heat, they are not recommended south of zone 7.

Design tips: These tall plants are best used in the back of a border or in a wildflower garden.

ACTAEA
Baneberry

The five species of *Actaea* found in the northern hemisphere are grown more for their decorative fruit than their unassuming small clusters of white bottlebrush-like flowers, which are produced in mid- to late spring. Flowers become red, white, or black poisonous berries, which appear in late summer. Plants form a bushy clump reaching

Actaea rubra

60 to 80 centimetres tall and have divided foliage reminiscent of that of a coarse-leaved astilbe. Two species of baneberry are native in North America. The red baneberry, *A. rubra*, has glossy red berries, or white on the variety *neglecta*, and is found throughout most of North America except the southeast. The other baneberry, doll's-eyes, *A. pachypoda*, whose white berries have a black "pupil" and are attached to the plant by thick red stems, is native to the eastern half of North America. From Europe comes *A. spicata*, which produces black berries, and *A. erythrocarpa*, with red. From China, Korea, and eastern Russia comes *A. asiatica*, which has black berries at the ends of contrasting thick red stems.

The bugbanes, *Cimicifuga* species, are now reclassified as *Actaea*, but for the purpose of this book, they are described later under their original name.

Baneberry are woodland plants and prefer acidic soil that is organically rich and evenly moist. In cooler coastal regions, they can be grown in full sun, but in warmer inland regions, they prefer dappled shade. Propagation is by seed or division. They are not bothered by pests or diseases. All are rated hardy to zone 3, but as they dislike excess summer heat and humidity, they are not recommended south of zone 7.

Design tips: Baneberry may be used in a mid-border but are also ideal for woodland and wildflower gardens. Combine with hosta, astilbe, and ferns.

ANEMONE
Anemone, windflower

The genus *Anemone* has some 120 species found in temperate regions worldwide. With such a large group, it is not surprising that there is great diversity in size and flowering season. The spring-bloomers are primarily European woodland plants. In the wild, they bloom before or just as the trees above them unfurl their leaves. By mid-summer, under the deep shade of the forest, they go dormant. In the garden, they follow a similar pattern and are referred to as spring ephemerals. They require careful situating as they can leave gaps in the garden later in the season. Ideally, they may be placed with ferns and hosta whose larger leaves hide their dying foliage and fill in the gaps.

The best of the spring-bloomers for acidic soil conditions is *Anemone nemorosa*, or wood anemone. It produces narrow rhizomes and, in time, can form large colonies. Each sprout produces a pair of divided leaves and a single saucer-shaped flower with six to eight "petals" (botanically modified sepals) on stems 20 to 30 centimetres long. White is the colour of the wild form, but selections in cultivation include 'Robinsoniana' (wisteria blue), 'Allenii' (lavender blue), 'Wisley Pink', 'Royal Blue', 'Blue Eyes' (white with blue centre, double), and 'Vestal' (white, double). Similar in appearance is *A. ranunculoides*, whose flowers are smaller and buttercup yellow. Both bloom from mid- to late spring.

Two fall-flowering anemone species are ideal for acidic soil: *A. hupehensis*, the Japanese anemone, and the closely related *A. tomentosa*, the grapeleaf anemone. Both are native to central and northern China; the former is also being naturalized in Japan. These two species form spreading clumps of long-stemmed basal leaves which are trifoliate; the latter are distinguished by having leaves with densely pubescent whitened undersides. Both produce pink flowers, 5 to 8 centimetres wide, on branching stems 90 to 120 centimetres tall, from mid-summer through autumn, helping to extend the flowering season. The Japanese anemone is available in several cultivars: 'September Charm' (pale pink), 'Hadspen Abundance' (medium pink with pale pink edges), and 'Prinz Heinrich' (semi-double pink). The grapeleaf anemone is primarily known by the cultivar 'Robustissima'. Hybrids also exist between the two species. Popular cultivars include 'Queen Charlotte' (semi-double pale pink), 'Serenade' (semi-double pink), 'Honorine Jobert' (white), 'Party Dress' (double pink), 'Pamina' (semi-double deep pink), and 'Whirlwind' (semi-double white). More recently, several semi-dwarf compact cultivars called the Pretty Lady™

Anemone nemorosa 'Royal Blue'

series, which reach only 30 to 50 centimetres in height, have been released: 'Pretty Lady Susan' (raspberry pink), 'Pretty Lady Emily' (semi-double medium pink), and 'Pretty Lady Diana' (deep pink).

The above anemone prefer a humus-rich, well-drained but evenly moist soil in full sun or partial shade. Propagation is primarily by division. Pests and diseases are uncommon, but the fall-flowering types may suffer from mildew diseases in some years. All of the above are hardy through zone 4.

Design tips: Use wood anemone to naturalize under trees and shrubs and combine with other similar plants such as *Trillium*, bunchberry, and early primroses. The fall-bloomers are more often used in borders. Try them alongside black-eyed Susan and autumn-flowering sedums.

Anemonopsis macrophylla

ANEMONOPSIS MACROPHYLLA
False anemone

This monotypic genus is endemic to the Japanese island of Honshu, where it grows in shady woodlands. Plants form a clump with large, divided leaves. Flower stems reach 75 centimetres in height, producing a loose cluster of nodding pale lavender flowers from July to September. Each bowl-shaped flower is 2 centimetres wide, with a cluster of petals in the centre. In the garden, it prefers rich soil and even moisture in partial to full shade. Extreme dryness or excessive sunshine can burn the foliage. Propagation is by stratified seed or division. It is hardy to zone 4.

Design tips: This uncommon but highly desirable perennial is ideal for the woodland garden and is valued for its small lotuslike flowers.

ARALIA
Spikenard

Most of the Asian and North American 68 *Aralia* species are woody plants, but a small number are herbaceous perennials.

Aralia cordata 'Sun King'

In fact, three species are native to eastern North America: smooth sarsaparilla, *A. nudicaulis*; bristly sarsaparilla, *A. hispida*; and American spikenard, *A. racemosa*. They have insignificant yellow-green flowers but produce black berries and have attractive compound leaves. For a border, consider the bold Japanese spikenard, *A. cordata*, which grows to 2 metres tall. Their leaves, up to 90 centimetres long, are compound with heart-shaped leaflets. The minute yellow-green flowers are produced in long bottle-brush-like panicles from July to September and develop into black berries in autumn. The eye-catching cultivar 'Sun King', a recent release, has spectacular golden yellow foliage.

ARISAEMA
Jack-in-the-pulpit, cobra lily

Most of the approximately 180 species of *Arisaema* are native to China, with only two species native to North America. As a group, *Arisaema* arise from a tuber. The divided leaves are vaguely hand-shaped. The flower is perhaps the most exotic of any hardy plant with the exception of orchids. *Arisaema* flowers (technically an inflorescence, as the entire "flower" is composed of many closely packed tiny flowers) have two main parts: the spathe (pulpit) and spadix (jack). The pitcher-shaped spathe often has an overlying hood. The spadix is the clublike "stalk" inside the flower that holds the sex organs. In some species, the spathe produces a long threadlike tail; in others, the spadix has the tail. Perhaps more bizarre: *Arisaema* can change sexes. Young plants are often males, while older, more mature, plants may be female or hermaphroditic. They can change sexes at any point in their lives; however, the "flowers" of either sex essentially look the same. Female flowers form closely packed red or orange berries which form a giant raspberry-like fruit in autumn.

The native Jack-in-the-pulpit, *A. triphyllum*, reaches 60 centimetres in height and produces white-striped, green to dark purple-black flowers in late spring. Each leaf has three leaflets. Similar in appearance and blooming at the same time is the Asian species *A. amurense*, with greenish flowers and leaves with three to five leaflets. Green Jack-in-the-pulpit, *A. dracontium*, the other native North American species, can reach up to 90 centimetres in height and has a horseshoe-shaped arrangement of leaflets

Aralia prefer evenly moist, organically rich soil. It grows in sun to partial shade, but 'Sun King' needs full sun to maintain its yellow foliage. The minute flowers are readily visited by bees. Insects and larger herbivores are generally not a problem but leaf spot may sometimes be troublesome. Propagation is by seed or division. These uncommon and underutilized plants are hardy to zone 3.

Design tips: All the *Aralia* above are woodland plants suitable for shady gardens. With its large size, Japanese spikenard is suitable for the back of the perennial border or for a woodland or wildflower setting. With its shrublike habit, it may even be planted as a stand-alone plant.

Arisaema sikkokianum

tall and has leaves with three to five leaflets which may have silvery patches in the middle of each leaflet. The flowers are dark wine with an erect white-striped hood. The brilliant white spadix is knob-shaped.

Among the summer-bloomers are the giant *A. consanquineum* and *A. jacquemontii*, both of which may reach 120 centimetres tall. The leaves of the former species have many narrow leaflets arranged like an umbrella, and its purple-and-white-striped flowers are produced below the leaves. The cultivar 'Poseidon' has silver-striped leaflets. The latter species also has an umbrella-like leaf, but its leaflets are fewer and broader. Its green white-striped flowers are held above the leaves. Perhaps the most delicate of the late bloomers is the 45-centimetre-tall *A. candidissimum*, with trifoliate leaves and light pink flowers with white stripes.

Arisaema prefer organically rich, evenly moist but well-drained acidic soil. In the wild, they often grow in partial shade, but if the soil contains enough moisture, they perform well in full sun. As some species, such as *A. jacquemontii* and *A. consangineum*, are slow to appear in spring, often not sprouting until well into June, carefully mark the area where they are planted. Pests and diseases are generally not a problem. Propagation is by seed or tuber offsets. Hardiness varies from zone 3 for *A. triphyllum*, zone 4 for *A. dracontium*, zone 6 for *A. candidissimum*, and zone 5 for the other species mentioned.

Design tips: *Arisaema* are commonly used in woodland gardens but may be in a border setting. Their bold foliage blends well with hosta, *Podophyllum*, and *Darmera* or contrasts with ferns and astilbes.

per leaf. In this species, the spadix has a long tail-like extension that extends from the spathe like a whip. The 60-centimetre-tall *Arisaema ringens* has a pair of glossy trifoliate leaves which may reach 60 centimetres wide, imparting a tropical effect. The flowers are dark wine with white stripes, appearing much like a cobra's head. Perhaps the most attractive of the early bloomers is *A. sikokianum*, reaching up to 60 centimetres

ARUNCUS
Goat's-beard

Only three species of *Aruncus* exist; just one, if you listen to some botanists. From a gardening point of view, most consider that there are two types: the tall goat's-beard, *A. dioicus*, and the dwarf goat's-beard, *A. aethusifolius*. The tall goat's-beard, native across much of the northern hemisphere, is an imposing, bold plant with large coarse, fernlike leaves. The flowers, produced on stems up to 2 metres tall, are produced in large creamy plumes in late spring to early summer. Plants are dioecious: they have separate male and female plants. The male plants have more attractive "fluffy" flowers than the females. The cultivar 'Kneiffii' has finer, more divided foliage and does not reach as tall, at 100 to 120 centimetres. In the wild, dwarf goat's-beard is native to Korea. From a distance, it may be mistaken for an astilbe. It has more filigree foliage than the tall goat's-beard and smaller, narrower plumes of flowers. The males produce the showier flowers. Hybrids between the two are intermediate between both parents. Named hybrid cultivars include 'Misty Lace', 'Guinea Fowl', 'Chantilly Lace', and 'Horatio'.

Goat's-beard are water-lovers; they quickly suffer if the soil is too dry and of poor quality. They need organically rich, moist soil that is preferably acidic. Full sun is ideal in cooler coastal regions but, inland, partial shade is recommended. These plants have an attractive fall colour, turning warm gold on the tall goat's-beard and a blend of yellow, orange, and red on the dwarf. Pests are uncommon but fungal spotting may be present in some regions, discolouring the leaves. Propagation is by division, or less commonly by seed. Both are rated hardy to zone 4, but as they dislike high

Aruncus hybrid

temperatures, they are not suitable south of zone 7.

Design tips: Tall goat's-beard is a plant for the back of a border and, with its shrublike habit, may be grown as a stand-alone plant. Dwarf goat's-beard is better suited to the front of a border or in a large rock-garden setting. Both types are useful in woodland or rain gardens or along the edges of water features.

ASARUM
Wild ginger

Seventeen species of *Asarum* are distributed across the northern hemisphere. As a group, they are ground cover in nature, with surface-creeping rhizomes and paired, often glossy, heart-shaped leaves. As the solitary flowers are produced at ground level, beneath the leaves, they are rarely visible. They are unique: maroon with three pointed sepals, blooming from mid-spring to early summer. The European wild ginger, *A. europaeum*, has 8-centimetre-diameter glossy, leathery, dark leaves that are evergreen. From eastern North America is *A. canadense*; its leaves, up to 15 centimetres wide, are downy, matte green, distinctly veined, and deciduous. From the Pacific Northwest is *A. caudatum*, which is much like *A. canadense* but its leaves are evergreen. From China come *A. maximum* and *A. splendens*. The former is often called the panda-faced wild ginger, as its 5-centimetre-diameter flowers are nearly black with white bases, reminiscent of a panda's face. Its evergreen glossy leaves are green with lighter veins and, often, pale mottling. 'Ling Ling' is a popular cultivar. *Asarum splendens* has the most decorative foliage: its dark green leaves are strongly mottled with patches of silver. 'Quicksilver' has the most eye-catching foliage, appearing similar to that of *Cyclamen*. The foliage is evergreen in mild areas. The flowers are mottled maroon and grey green.

From southeastern US comes *Hexastylis*, at one time considered *Asarum*. Plants look like *Asarum*, as they are evergreen with heart-shaped leaves, but their flowers are jug-shaped, greenish brown, and insignificant. Of the 11 species, the most popular are *H. shuttleworthii*, *H. arifolia*, and *H. virginica*. All have dark green leaves variously mottled with silver and resemble cyclamen.

Wild ginger prefer evenly moist, organically rich, acidic soil in partial to full shade. Propagation is most commonly by

Asarum maximum

division but is also possible by seed. Few diseases bother them and the most serious pests are slugs and snails, which may eat the newly emerging foliage. *Asarum canadense* and *A. europeaum* are hardy to zone 4 but dislike excess summer heat; they are not recommended south of zone 7. *Asarum caudatum* and *A. splendens* are hardy to zone 6 and *A. maximum*, zone 7; these tolerate more summer heat. *Hexastylis* is best in zone 6 and south, but if properly mulched in winter they may survive in zone 5.

Design tips: Wild ginger are well suited as ground-cover plants for shady sites. They may be used along the edges of woodland or rain gardens. Combine them with other woodlanders such as ferns, hosta, hepatica, and mayapple. They may even be used in a peat garden, combined with dwarf ericaceous shrubs, Chinese autumn-flowering gentians, and shrubby milkwort.

Asclepias incarnata 'Soulmate'

ASCLEPIAS
Milkweed

Of the approximately 140 species of milkweeds, all are exclusive to the Americas. The genus name honours Asklepios, the Greek god of medicine. The common name is a reference to the milky sap of most species. Many are weedy but a few are showy. Gardeners recognize the milkweeds as being the host plant for monarch butterflies. As many species of milkweed grow in agricultural areas, plants have been removed to make room for crops. The resulting reduction in the wild population of milkweeds has impacted the monarch population, with a dramatic decrease in their numbers. If you have a wildflower garden, help the monarchs by planting common milkweed, *A. syriaca*, a coarse 2-metre-tall native species. Monarchs lay eggs on the plants and their caterpillars then feed on the same plants. Common milkweed is too invasive to use in a typical garden as it spreads rapidly by underground rhizomes. At any rate, common milkweed is not as showy as the more popular milkweeds, the butterfly weed, *A. tuberosa*, and the swamp milkweed, *A. incarnata*.

Butterfly weed, *A. tuberosa*, is native primarily to eastern and central US. This plant forms a clump with unbranched stems reaching 75 centimetres in height. The orange star-shaped flowers are held in terminal flat-topped clusters from early to mid-summer. 'Gay Butterflies' has a mix of yellow, orange, or scarlet flowers; 'Hello Yellow', yellow. Swamp milkweed, *A. incarnata*, has small vanilla-scented flowers in terminal clusters atop 100- to 150-centimetre-tall stems. 'Cinderella' has rose pink flowers, 'Soulmate' has two-tone pink and white blossoms, and 'Ice Ballet' is pure white. The flowers of both species develop large spindle-shaped seed pods that split to reveal silky seeds. They are slow to establish and, because they have a taproot, dislike being transplanted, so start with young plants. As they are late to sprout in spring, carefully mark the area where they are planted.

Butterfly weed needs full sun and well-drained soil, especially in winter, as it is prone to rot if the soil is too wet. It is drought-tolerant once established and tolerates poor, rocky soil. Swamp milkweed, as the name suggests, prefers moist to wet soil. Neither butterfly weed nor swamp milkweed is particular about soil pH; they tolerate low pH. Insect pests and diseases are rare on both, and larger herbivores generally ignore them. Propagation is primarily by seed. As expected, they are magnets for butterflies but also attract bees and hummingbirds. Both act as host plants for monarch butterflies. They are rated hardy through zone 3.

Design tips: Butterfly weed is suitable for a mid-border, a cottage garden, and especially a wildflower setting. Swamp milkweed is better placed toward the back of a border but is also ideal for wildflower settings, wet depressions, or rain gardens.

ASTILBE
False goat's-beard

Astilbe are among the most popular garden plants. Of the 18 species, most are native to Asia. As a group, astilbe form clumps of basal, divided leaves that appear fernlike. Leaf colour is variable from light to dark green, chartreuse to red-tinted; some have dark red spring leaves. Plant height varies from 30 to over 120 centimetres. All produce feathery plumes of minute flowers from mid-summer to early autumn, depending on the cultivar. Flower colour ranges from white through shades of pink and red to lilac and lavender.

Only a few of the more than 100 astilbe hybrids are described here. The smallest, at only 10 centimetres in height, is *A. glaberrima*, which has small pale pink plumes. *A. simplicifolia* is about 30 centimetres tall: 'Sprite' (pale pink), 'Hennie Graafland' (rose pink), 'Key West' (deep pink), 'Pink Lightning' (light pink), and 'Moulin Rouge' (red) are popular. *Astilbe* X *crispa* 'Perkeo' has plasticlike stiff, dark green, glossy foliage, reaches 25 centimetres in height, and has pink flowers. The Younique™, Partiezz™, Vision, and Music series reach about 50 centimetres in height. With the bonus of attractive foliage

Astilbe X *arendsii* 'Amethyst'

are Partiezz™ 'Karaoke Party' and 'Amber Moon', both with chartreuse foliage, and Partiezz™ 'Surprise Party' with yellow and green foliage.

Most of the remaining hybrids are between 60 and 100 centimetres in height. Of note are 'Erika' and 'Fanal', which have dark red spring foliage and red-tinted summer foliage. 'Color Flash Lime' has chartreuse foliage and pink flowers, while 'Color Flash' itself is chartreuse in spring but becomes flushed with purple later in the season. 'Ostrich Plume' (pink) and 'Prof. van der Wielen' (white) are *A. thunbergii* cultivars with unique drooping plumes. Both reach 90 centimetres. The tallest and latest-blooming astilbe, *A. chinensis*, reach 90 to 120 centimetres with narrow, stiffly upright plumes in late summer to mid-fall. 'Purple Lance', 'Purple Candles', and var. *taquetii* 'Superba' are popular. Dwarf, 25-centimetre-tall *A. chinensis* cultivars include 'Pumila' (deep pink) and 'Finale' (light pink).

All astilbe prefer organically rich, moist, acidic soil and do not tolerate poor, droughty sites. In coastal regions, they tolerate full sun, but in warmer inland sites partial shade is best. They attract butterflies and bees and are essentially care-free, with few pests or diseases. Propagation is by division. All are rated hardy to zone 3.

Design tips: Ideal for a border, astilbe are also planted in woodland gardens and along the edges of water features. Most dwarf forms are suitable for rock gardens. To highlight their foliage, combine them with hosta, iris, or daylily. Those with red spring growth are particularly attractive if planted so that their foliage is backlit.

ASTILBOIDES TABULARIS
Shieldleaf rodgersia

At one time this plant was included with the *Rodgersia*, but today it is classified as *Astilboides tabularis*. This uncommon and underutilized perennial originates from China, where it grows along streams and open damp woodlands. The plant forms a large clump of basal leaves. Each bright green leaf is shieldlike and can measure 90 centimetres wide. Although it is grown primarily for its bold leaves, in mid-summer the plant produces dense plumes of tiny white flowers on arching stems up to 120 centimetres tall.

This plant requires a sheltered site, as the leaves may become tattered if they are subjected to too much wind. Partial shade is ideal but it tolerates full sun as long as the soil is evenly moist. The leaves quickly brown if the soil is too dry. Diseases are rare but slugs may be a problem and it may be browsed by larger herbivores. Propagation is by seed or, more commonly, division. It is hardy to zone 5, but, as it dislikes high

Astilboides tabularis

summer temperatures and humidity, it is not recommended south of zone 7.

Design tips: *Astilboides* is an ideal plant for use near water features or in open woodland or rain gardens. Its large leaves lend a tropical effect to any garden.

ASTRANTIA
Masterwort

The small number of *Astrantia* species are all natives of Europe. Most common in gardens is *A. major*, along with hybrids between it, *A. maxima* and *A. carniolica*. These plants are clumpers with long-stemmed, palmately lobed glossy leaves. The flower stems, which reach 70 to 90 centimetres tall, are held stiffly upright, topped with a loose cluster of starlike flowers in shades of silvery white, pink, or wine red. Blooms are produced from May through August. What appears to be a single flower is, in fact, a hemispherical umbel of tiny flowers surrounded by many pointed bracts, which form a collar below the true flowers. Masterwort makes a long-lasting cut flower and may be used in a dried-flower arrangements. Choice white selections include 'Star of Heaven', 'Star of Billion', 'Buckland', and 'Shaggy'. Among the pink shades are 'Lola', 'Roma', 'Pink Pride', and 'Primadonna'. The deepest wine red are 'Hadspen Blood', 'Ruby Wedding', and 'Lars'. With a wine-and-white two-tone effect are 'Star of Beauty' and 'Star of Fire'. For all-season interest, try variegated-leaf cultivars such as 'Sunningdale Variegated' with pale pink flowers or 'Vanilla Gorilla', whose flowers are deeper pink.

Astrantia prefer organically rich, moist, heavy soil and are quick to suffer if the soil

Astrantia 'Roma'

in which they are grown is too dry. If the soil is moist, full sun is perfect; otherwise, grow them in partial shade. If they are dead-headed after flowering, they may produce secondary flush later in the season. As it is a prolific producer of seeds and resulting seedlings, dead-heading helps keep this at bay. Insect and disease problems are rare, and these plants are generally ignored by larger herbivores. Propagation is by seed, but more often by division. The species and cultivars noted are rated hardy to zone 4.

Design tips: *Astrantia* species as well as the hybrids are stars in the summer perennial border. They are also suitable for wildflower and woodland gardens, combining well with other taller perennials such as *Ligularia*, monkshood, *Cimicifuga*, and willow gentian.

BAPTISIA
Blue false indigo

All 25 species of *Baptisia* are native to North America. The genus name comes from the Greek word *bapto*, which means to dye,

Baptisia 'Cherries Jubilee'

referring to blue clothes dye developed from its root. The species most grown as a garden ornamental is *B. australis*, native from Texas to the Great Lakes, east to the Atlantic coast. This tall shrublike plant reaches 90 to 120 centimetres in height. Its large trifoliate leaves are similar to those of clover. From late spring to early summer, plants produce 15 to 30 long, lupinelike spikes of blue flowers, which later develop into black swollen pods. Harvested stems with ripe pods may be used in dried-flower arrangements.

New *Baptisia* have been bred for their 90-centimetre-high branching habit and wide range of colours. These hybrids result from crossing the above species with southern US species such as *B. alba* and *B. tinctoria*. These hybrids, part of the Decadence™ series, include 'Blueberry Sundae' (lavender blue), 'Cherries Jubilee' (maroon and yellow bicolour), 'Dutch Chocolate' (maroon purple), 'Lemon Meringue', 'Vanilla Cream', 'Pink Truffles', and 'Sparkling Sapphires' (indigo blue). 'Carolina Moonlight' is a yellow-flowered hybrid developed from crossing *B. alba* with *B. sphaerocarpa*.

False indigo, best grown in full sun, tolerates poor, dry, acidic soil. It can form an extensive root system, making it nearly impossible to transplant once it has been established. It is not bothered by pests or disease, and it attracts bees. Propagation is by seed. Blue false indigo is hardy to zone 3, while the hybrids are rated for zone 4.

Design tips: *Baptisia* is a suitable replacement for lupines, which, while beautiful, can be invasive. It makes a perfect plant for the back of a border or in a wildflower garden.

BEESIA
Ginger-leaf false bugbane

Beesia calthifolia and *B. deltophylla*, both natives of China, are uncommon, but becoming less so. Although the two species are visually similar, *B. calthifolia* has about 50 small teeth on each side of its glossy, evergreen, heart-shaped leaves, whereas *B. deltophylla* has about 15. Both species have contrasting pale veins on their leaves and a mounding habit. In winter, the leaves often take on a purplish tint. In late spring to early summer, they produce wiry 30-centimetre-tall spikes with scattered tiny white starry flowers.

Beesia require evenly moist, humus-rich, acidic soil. They do not tolerate drought. Dappled shade is ideal but full shade is tolerated; full sun should be avoided. They are bothered by few pests or diseases. Propagation may be by seed, but division is more common. They are hardy to zone 6, but, if mulched in winter, they are worth trying in zone 5.

Design tips: Combine *Beesia* with other woodland plants, including *Asarum*, *Arisaema*, summer-blooming *Corydalis*, and small ferns.

Beesia deltophylla

BERGENIA
Giant rockfoil, pigsqueak

Of the 10 species of *Bergenia*, all are native to Asia. The genus was named in honour of the German botanist and physician Karl August von Bergen (1853–1933). Five main species, along with many hybrids, are grown by North American gardeners. Most are evergreen with rosettes of leathery rounded to heart-shaped leaves that often turn purple. The exception is *B. ciliata*, which is deciduous. All bloom in spring, within a few weeks of the snow melting, generally from April to May. The flowers are produced in a loose cluster on leafless 30- to 60-centimetre-tall stems. Typically, the flowers are shades of pink but may be white, dark reddish pink, or purple.

The largest-leaved and tallest-flowered is *B. crassifolia*, which forms large clumps with magenta-pink flowers atop 60-centimetre-tall stems. *Bergenia purpurascens*, which has the best purple-red winter colour, has purple flowers on 30- to 45-centimetre-tall stems. *Bergenia cordifolia* is similar but has pink flowers. The smallest is *B. stracheyi*, which reaches about 15 centimetres tall. Its flowers open white and age to light pink. Although it is deciduous, *B. ciliata* has the unique feature of having slightly pubescent leaves with wavy-edged margins. Its pale pink flowers open before leaves are produced and while the flower stems are quite short. However, stems continue to elongate as more flowers open, eventually reaching 30 centimetres. The many hybrids of *Bergenia* include 'Silver Light' (white), 'Bressingham White' (white aging to light pink), 'Baby Doll' (light pink), 'Appleblossom' (light pink), 'Winter Glow' (reddish pink), and 'Bressingham Ruby'

Bergenia ciliata

(reddish pink). The newest selections are the Dragonfly™ series, with smaller, more compact foliage and more abundant flowers: 'Pink Dragonfly', Dragonfly™ 'Angel Kiss', and Dragonfly™ 'Sakura'.

Bergenia are best grown in moist but well-drained, organically rich, slightly acidic soil. They tolerate short periods of drought but the foliage suffers if the drought is prolonged. In cooler coastal regions, they may be grown in full sun but generally are best in partial to full shade. They have no serious insect pests or diseases and deer usually ignore them. Propagation may be by seed, or more commonly by division. The evergreen types are hardy to zone 3, some to even 2, but as *B. ciliata* is rated for zone 5, it is only useful in milder regions.

Design tips: Those evergreen types whose leaves turn purple in winter are wonderful additions to a winter garden. *Bergenia* are generally grown near the front of a border, in woodland gardens, or along the edges of water features. Smaller selections may be used in rock gardens. To complement their rather bold foliage, combine them with ferns, grasses, and iris.

BRUNNERA MACROPHYLLA
Siberian bugloss

The genus *Brunnera* contains just three species, all native to northwestern Asia. Only one species is grown as an ornamental in North America, *B. macrophylla*. The genus was named in honour of the Swiss botanist Samuel Brunner (1790–1844), who discovered the plant. *Brunnera* is a clumping plant with relatively large, heart-shaped basal leaves. In mid- to late spring, it produces loose sprays of forget-me-not-like flowers, typically blue or occasionally white, atop 30- to 40-centimetre-tall stems. This plant is grown primarily for its foliage, with most selections having leaves variously marked with white or silver.

Of the many cultivars on the market, 'Variegata' has leaves with wide white margins; 'Hadspen Cream' is similar but its margins are cream rather than white; 'Langtrees' has silver spots along the leaf edges; and 'Emerald Mist'

Brunnera macrophylla 'Jack Frost'

has more extensive silver spotting. 'Jack Frost' was the first of the extensively silver-foliaged selections. More recent silver-leaved types include 'Sea Heart', which has silvery foliage with distinct green veins. 'Looking Glass' is now the winner for pure silver foliage, while the striking 'King's Ransom' is silvery green with creamy yellow margins. 'Mr. Morse' resembles 'Jack Frost' but has white flowers. 'Diane's Gold' has yellow to chartreuse foliage, while 'Gold Strike' has leaves irregularly mottled in yellow.

Brunnera prefer organically rich, evenly moist, acidic soil. Their leaves are quick to burn along their edges if grown in soil that is too dry. Partial to dappled shade is ideal. It is generally care-free but slugs can sometimes be bothersome. Propagation is by division. It is rated hardy to zone 3.

Design tips: *Brunnera* may be grown as an accent at the front of a border or a woodland garden but it also lends itself as a ground cover. Good companion plants are baneberry, astilbe, and ferns.

Caltha palustris 'Flore Pleno'

CALTHA PALUSTRIS
Marsh marigold

All 10 species of *Caltha* are confined to the northern hemisphere. The generic name *Caltha* is derived from the Greek word *kalathos*, meaning goblet, in reference to the shape of the flower. Although typically it is a wetland plant, if provided with evenly moist soil it can tolerate more typical garden situations. The most common species is marsh marigold, *C. palustris*, a species found across the northern hemisphere. Marsh marigold forms a mound with mostly basal, smooth, shiny, rounded leaves. The flowers, produced in April and May, are in loose clusters on stems up to 45 centimetres tall. Individual flowers are about 5 centimetres wide with five to nine waxy, deep yellow, petal-like sepals. Of two named selections, 'Alba' has white flowers and dark green foliage, while 'Flore Pleno' has fully double yellow flowers that look like golden pompoms.

Marsh marigold may be grown in full sun or partial shade. The soil should be organically rich and always moist. Propagation is by seed or division. Diseases are rare and, as the plant is mildly toxic, it is not bothered by pests. It is hardy to zone 2.

Design tips: Marsh marigold is a quintessential plant for any bog garden. It can also be planted near water features or low spots in a garden where the soil remains evenly moist throughout the growing season.

CAULOPHYLLUM THALICTROIDES
Blue cohosh

There are only three species of *Caulophyllum*, two from North America and one from East

Caulophyllum thalictroides

Chelone lyonii 'Hot Lips'

Asia. Blue cohosh, *C. thalictroides*, is native to the eastern half of North America. Each stem has one of two triple-compound leaves that are distinctly smoky blue in spring but later become blue green with a matte finish. From mid- to late spring, flower stems arise to 90 centimetres and are topped with a loose cluster of brownish to yellowish green 1.5-centimetre-diameter starlike flowers. These later become attractive but poisonous blue berrylike seeds.

Blue cohosh prefers evenly moist, organically rich, acidic soil in full sun to partial shade. It does not tolerate droughty conditions. Propagation is by seed, but plants are slow to mature. Few pests or diseases bother them. It is rated hardy to zone 3.

Design tips: Blue cohosh is a classic woodland plant and combines well with other woodlanders such as mayapple, bellwort, and trilliums.

CHELONE
Turtlehead

Of only four species of *Chelone*, all are native to eastern North America. In the wild, they often grow in moist locations but can adapt to more typical garden growing conditions. The genus name comes from the Greek word *chelone*, meaning tortoise, in reference to the turtlehead shape of the flowers. All turtleheads form clumps with stiff, unbranched, and upright 90- to 120-centimetre-tall stems. The leaves are lance-shaped and opposite, while the stems are square in cross-section. From late summer to early fall, snapdragon-like, two-lipped flowers up to 3 centimetres long are produced in dense terminal spikes.

Pink turtlehead, *C. lyonii* and *C. obliqua*, are most commonly grown. These two species are similar and, in fact, some horticulturists consider *C. obliqua* to be a hybrid derived from *C. lyonii*. Named selections include 'Hot Lips', whose foliage is bronzy green early in the season; 'Tiny Tortuga', a compact plant reaching just 40 centimetres tall; and 'Alba', with white rather than the typical pink flowers. White turtlehead, *C. glabra*, is not commonly seen in gardens as it requires quite wet conditions to do well. However, unlike the other turtleheads, it does have fragrant flowers.

Turtleheads may be grown in full sun to partial shade and require organically rich, evenly moist, acidic soil. Generally, they do not require staking unless they are grown in too much shade. They attract bees, and the blossoms make admirable cut flowers. Propagation is by seed, cuttings, or division. Pests and disease are generally not a problem, although under dry conditions or if too sheltered, mildew may occur. All are rated hardy to zone 3.

Design tips: Not often seen, *Chelone* should be more widely grown; it is well suited to a late summer and fall border, combining well with taller ornamental grasses, obedience plant, and rayflower. Under proper soil conditions, they are suitable for a mid- to back border and are ideal for using around water and in rain gardens.

CIMICIFUGA
Bugbane, black cohosh

The eight bugbane species are native to the northern hemisphere. They are now reclassified as *Actaea*, better known as baneberries, but are described here under their original name. The most popular garden bugbane, *Actaea (Cimicifuga) simplex*, from eastern Asia, is a bold plant with large, coarse, astilbe-like foliage and flower stems that tower to 2 or more metres. The flowers, which bloom in early autumn, are produced in narrow, arching, bottlebrush-like wands. They are white or pale pink and highly fragrant. The cultivar 'White Pearl' appears much like the wild species. Additional cultivars are all grown for their bronze to purple foliage. 'Atropurpurea', which has purple-tinted foliage, was the first of these cultivars. 'Brunette' has darker purple leaves, while 'Hillside Black Beauty' has unusual, nearly black foliage. 'Black Negligee' has purple foliage that is more finely divided. All of these have white flowers. 'Pink Spike', also known as 'Pink Spire', has purple foliage and light pink flowers.

Cimicifuga simplex

Black cohosh, *A. (C.) racemosa*, has an overall habit similar to that of *A. simplex*, but blooms earlier, in mid- to late summer. This North American native is distributed in the eastern half of the US north to southern Quebec and Ontario. The cultivar 'Chocoholic' is a purple-leaved version.

Bugbane, which may be grown in sun to partial shade, prefer rich, moist but well-drained, acidic soil. Despite its height, bugbane is wind-tolerant and rarely needs staking. Propagation is primarily by division. As these plants are toxic, they are not bothered by pests or diseases. All are rated hardy to zone 3.

Design tips: Bugbane is a beauty for the back of a border and *A. simplex* is especially valued for its late flowers and graceful arching stems. Bugbanes combine well with *Ligularia*, monkshood, and willow gentian.

Clintonia borealis

CLINTONIA
Corn lily, bluebeard lily

Of the five species of *Clintonia*, four are from North America and a single species is from eastern Asia. The genus was named after DeWitt Clinton, an American 18th-century botanist and politician. All species have two to five basal, ovate to elliptical, smooth leaves similar to those of lily-of-the-valley. A flower stem, up to 25 centimetres tall, arises from between the leaves. The stem is topped with a solitary or umbel of white, pink, or greenish yellow, 1- to 2-centimetre-diameter lilylike flowers in mid- to late spring. These later become blue to black poisonous berries. Plants often form large colonies, as they spread by rhizomes. Corn-lily or yellow clintonia, *C. borealis*, is native to eastern Canada and the northeastern US, south into the Appalachians; it has greenish yellow flowers. White clintonia, *C. umbellulata*, is generally restricted to the Appalachians and has a tight rounded cluster of white flowers. The Asian species, *C. udensis*, rare in cultivation, is similar. From the Pacific Northwest is queen's-cup, *C. uniflora*, which has solitary white flowers and Andrew's clintonia, *C. andrewsiana*, which has clusters of reddish pink flowers.

Clintonia require humus-rich, evenly moist, acidic soil. In cooler regions, it tolerates full sun but it generally prefers dappled shade. Although few pests and diseases bother them, they may be eaten by deer. Propagation is primarily by division, as seeds are slow to mature. Yellow clintonia is hardy to zone 2; queen's-cup, zone 3; and white clintonia, zone 4. As they cannot tolerate high heat and humidity, they are not recommended for areas south of zone 7. An exception is Andrew's clintonia, which is hardy only to zone 7.

Design tips: As a subject for a woodland garden, clintonia combines well with other woodlanders, such as bunchberry, bellwort, trillium, and hepatica. It may also be used as a ground cover in shady areas.

CODONOPSIS
Asian bellflower

Of about 40 species of *Codonopsis*, all are native to Asia, especially China. Several are grown primarily as herbal medicines and only a few are considered worthwhile garden plants. The most popular, *C. clematidea*, has lax stems to 70 centimetres tall that need to scramble

Codonopsis clematidea

through neighbours to stay upright. In mid-summer, the stems end in pendant pale blue bells whose insides are intricately marked in yellow and purple. *Codonopsis ovata* and *C. bulleyana* are similar but much shorter, at 40 centimetres tall. All arise from a thick taproot and emit a skunklike odour when bruised.

Codonopsis require deep, acidic soil high in organic matter. Full sun is preferred in cooler areas, but in other areas partial shade is acceptable. They disappear in winter and may be late in appearing in spring, so carefully mark where they are being grown. They are essentially pest- and disease-free and their odoriferous foliage keeps browsers away. The above are all hardy to zone 4.

Design tips: *Codonopsis* may be used in a rock-garden setting or combined with woodland plants such as primroses, astilbe, and ferns.

CONVALLARIA MAJALIS
Lily-of-the-valley

The only species of *Convallaria*, *C. majalis*, is a native of Europe. Each sprout has two or three smooth, elliptical leaves up to 20 centimetres long. A leafless stem, which grows between the leaves to a height of 20 centimetres, is topped with a one-sided spike of small, highly fragrant bell-shaped white flowers from April to May. Flowers become small scarlet berries in late summer. The variety 'Rosea' has pale pink flowers. 'Albostriata' has striking, showy white-veined leaves.

This is a popular ground-cover plant for partial to full shade as plants spread rapidly by underground rhizomes. In fact, in the right location, lily-of-the-valley can become

Convallaria majalis

invasive, so use with caution. It does need cooler conditions and moist, acidic soil to perform well, but once established it can tolerate some drought. Pests and disease are uncommon; this toxic plant is not eaten by larger herbivores. Propagation is by division. It is hardy to zone 2.

Design tips: Since most lawn grasses dislike acidic soil, plant *Convallaria* in acidic, shady areas where lawns do not thrive.

CORYDALIS
Fumitory

Although about 470 species of *Corydalis* exist, only a small number are commonly grown as garden ornamentals. The name comes from

Corydalis solida

the Greek *korydalis*, meaning crested lark, a reference to its unique flowers. The flowers of all *Corydalis* are narrow with long spurs and produced in spikes. The foliage is brittle, slightly succulent, and distinctively fernlike. Perhaps the most popular are the early spring-blooming tuberous-rooted selections of *C. solida*, which are available in white and many shades of pink and purple. 'George

reaches 60 centimetres tall. It has blue-tinted foliage and clusters of yellow flowers which have a central brown spot. It too is ephemeral and disappears in summer.

The most popular *Corydalis* are those with blue flowers: *C. flexuosa, C. curviflora,* and *C. elata.* The first two may go summer-dormant if the climate is too hot and dry, reappearing in the fall, while the latter generally stays green. 'Purple Leaf' and 'Golden Panda' are striking, with purple-tinted foliage and yellow foliage respectively and contrasting bright blue flowers. 'Berry Exciting' has yellow foliage and purple flowers. The above all reach from 30 to 45 centimetres tall.

Golden fumitory, formerly known as *C. lutea,* is now *Pseudofumaria lutea.* It is an ever-bloomer if kept reasonably moist, flowering from mid-spring to frost. It forms mounds up to 40 centimetres tall with bright yellow flowers. It is short-lived but happily self-seeds and may become a pest, but it is easily pulled where it is not wanted.

During the spring and summer, *Corydalis* prefer evenly moist, organically rich, acidic soil. The evergreen types require well-drained conditions in winter or are prone to rotting. In cooler regions, full sun is tolerated, but generally they grow best in partial shade. Propagation is by seed or division. They are bothered by few pests or disease. Most of the above species are rated hardy to zone 4, except the blue-flowered species, which are zone 5.

Design tips: These ephemeral species are ideal for planting under high-canopy shrubs and combine well with other ephemerals such as *Trillium, Uvularia,* and *Dicentra cucullaria.* Those that do not go dormant in the summer are suited to a woodland garden.

Baker' is noteworthy for its brilliant scarlet flowers. This species is ephemeral, with plants going dormant by late spring. *Corydalis cava* is a similar species. *Corydalis buschii* is another tuberous species with bright mauve-pink flowers, blooming from mid- to late spring. These tuberous-rooted species all reach about 20 centimetres tall.

The giant of the genus is *C. nobilis,* which

DARMERA PELTATA
Umbrella plant

Only one species of *Darmera*, *D. peltata*, exists. The genus name honours Karl Darmer, a 19th-century German horticulturist. The plant is native to western North America, where it grows along streams or damp open woodlands. It is a clumping to slightly running plant, with solitary leaves arising from a thick, creeping rhizome. It is an unusual plant in that the flowers are produced before the leaves. In mid- to late spring, thick, hairy but leafless stalks arise 100 to 150 centimetres tall, topped with a globular cluster of pink flowers. Just as the flowers fade, the leaves appear. Each bold leaf, up to 45 centimetres wide, is umbrella-like with lobed margins. The leaves are held atop hairy stalks up to 150 centimetres tall. Overall, the plant looks like a smaller version of *Gunnera*, a popular huge-leaved plant grown in the Pacific Northwest.

Darmera requires full sun to partial shade and humus-rich soil. It loves moisture and can grow in shallow water. The blossoms are suitable as cut flowers. Propagation is by seed, or more commonly by division. Although insects and diseases are not a problem, it may be browsed by larger herbivores. It is hardy to zone 5, but as it cannot tolerate high temperatures, it is not recommended south of zone 7.

Design tips: *Darmera* complements rayflowers, *Rodgersia*, and Japanese iris, which have similar moisture requirements. It is ideal for streamsides, water features, and wet depressions. With its large exotic leaves, it also gives a tropical effect in northern gardens.

DICENTRA
Bleeding-heart

With its unmistakable flowers, bleeding-heart is a garden mainstay. Of the eight species of *Dicentra*, seven are native to North America and one to Japan. The standard bleeding-heart, *Dicentra spectabilis*, has now been reclassified into its own genus, *Lamprocapnos*. For many gardeners, this is one of the most elegant garden perennials; the species name says it all … spectacular! This eastern Asian native created quite a stir in Europe when it was first discovered, since, at the time, no other garden plants had such bizarre yet beautiful flowers. It forms a large, branching, bushy plant up to 90 centimetres tall with large, compound, matte, grey-green foliage. The flowers are held on one-sided, arching racemes from the upper leaf axils. Individual bright pink flowers are distinctively heart-shaped with a narrow flaring petal on either side. It blooms from mid- to late spring. There are three named cultivars: 'Alba', with white flowers; 'Valentine', red flowers; and 'Goldheart', golden yellow foliage and pink flowers.

Darmera peltata

Lamprocapnos spectabilis

Native in rich woodlands of eastern North America is Dutchman's breeches, *D. cucullaria*. This ephemeral has grey-green, fernlike foliage and arching 20- to 30-centimetre-tall stems with white double-spurred flowers from early to mid-spring. By late spring, the plants have disappeared for the season. The pink-flowered North American native *Dicentra* are often referred to as dwarf bleeding-hearts. Their fernlike leaves are also basal and matte grey green. Their flowers, which arise from the ground on arching, leafless stems, are also heart-shaped, although not as distinct as those of the standard bleeding-heart. The two main species, *D. eximia* and *D. formosa*, are similar, with light pink flowers produced from mid-spring through summer, especially in cooler regions. 'Bacchanal' is perhaps the most popular cultivar of *D. formosa*, with grey-green foliage and wine red flowers. 'Aurora' is a white-flowered cultivar. Of the several hybrid dwarf bleeding-hearts on the market, 'Luxuriant', a cross between *D. eximia* and *D. formosa*, is perhaps the most popular, with blue-green foliage and clear pink flowers. Others include 'Langtrees' (pale pink), 'Adrian Bloom' (reddish pink, blue-green foliage), 'Bountiful' (pinkish purple, green foliage), and 'Stuart Boothman' (mottled pink, green foliage).

'Candy Hearts' is a small hybrid, up to 25 centimetres high, with blue-grey foliage and flowers that are darker pink than those of 'Luxuriant'. The white-flowered version is called 'Ivory Hearts'. 'King of Hearts' is smaller again, at 15 to 20 centimetres tall, with dark pinkish red flowers. 'Burning Hearts' has the darkest red flowers of any dwarf bleeding-heart and blue-grey foliage.

Bleeding-heart are primarily woodland plants and prefer lightly shaded, evenly moist, and moderately rich soil. They are not fussy about the soil pH; they grow well under acidic conditions. They have brittle roots and rhizomes, but it seems that any piece of rhizome with an active growing point regenerates into a new plant. If soil moisture is maintained, they tolerate full sun, but they thrive best in partial shade. They also tolerate deep shade but the flowering will be reduced. As all have fragile stems and leaves, avoid windy sites. Overall, bleeding-heart are care-free. Propagation is by division. They are rated hardy to zone 3.

Design tips: The standard bleeding-heart is best placed toward the back of a border but it goes dormant by mid-summer and leaves a gap in the garden. Dwarf bleeding-heart are suitable ground-cover plants for shady sites and ideal for woodland gardens. The 'Heart' hybrids are low clumpers and good for a woodland or shady rock garden.

DICTAMNUS ALBUS
Gasplant

The genus *Dictamnus* has a single species, *D. albus*, native to the open woodlands of southern Eurasia. The plant is bushy with glossy pinnate leaves resembling those of an ash tree. Flower stems, which arise to 90 centimetres tall, are topped with a spike of white to light purple-pink blossoms in late spring or early summer. The flowers are elegant, as the petals often have contrasting darker veins and stamens that project out from the flower. The entire plant is covered in sticky glands which exude volatile oils and

Dictamnus albus

a lemony fragrance. People with sensitive skin should not touch the plant, as it can cause dermatitis. On windless, hot days, it is reputed that a match lit above the plant can ignite the oils with a flash of fire, hence the common name gasplant. After the flowers have faded, plants produce star-shaped seed pods which can be used in dried-flower arrangements. As the seed capsules mature, they split and the black, shiny seeds are forcibly ejected.

Gasplant prefers full sun and well-drained soil that stays reasonably moist. It tolerates some drought once it matures. It is not at all particular about the soil pH and grows well under acidic conditions. It is slow to establish but is a long-lived plant that improves with age. As it produces an extensive root system, it is difficult to transplant once mature. As a result, it is propagated mostly by seed. It is a care-free plant, with its flowers appreciated by butterflies. While hardy to zone 3, it performs best in areas with cool nights.

Design tips: Gasplant is ideally sized for a mid-border. As companion plants, consider early-blooming daylily and Siberian iris.

DIGITALIS
Foxglove

The 20 or so species of *Digitalis* are primarily natives of Europe. Although the majority are perennial, the most popular in North America is the biennial species *Digitalis purpurea*, the common foxglove. This plant is now naturalized throughout much of the continent. Typical of most biennial plants, common foxglove forms a leafy rosette of evergreen leaves the first season. In the second

Digitalis X *mertonensis*

season, foxglove produces a leafy spike up to 2 metres tall. From late spring to early summer, purple or white tubular, nodding flowers are generally produced along one side of the stem. Plants maintain themselves in the garden by dropping copious seeds. The many named cultivars include 'Foxy' and 'Excelsior', along with the Dalmatian and Camelot series. The latter produces flowers all around the stem rather than just one-sided. The most strikingly coloured cultivar, 'Pam's Choice', is white with a contrasting maroon-purple throat.

Of the perennial species, perhaps the most common is the large yellow foxglove, *D. grandiflora*, similar to the common foxglove in habit but its early summer flowers are pale yellow on 60- to 90-centimetre-long stems. A hybrid between the large yellow and common foxglove is *D. X mertonensis*, a short-lived perennial with flowers in peach to coral pink tones. The Polkadot series, also of hybrid origin, is in tones of coral, peach, and apricot.

The other garden-worthy species have small tubular flowers in comparison to those of the preceding. Of these, perhaps the most impressive and unusual is *D. parviflora*, the small-flowered foxglove. It has narrow, shiny leaves and slender but dense candlelike spikes of rusty brown flowers on 60-centimetre-long stems. It is a true perennial. Similar, but biennial with larger flowers, is the rusty foxglove, *D. ferruginea*. Its flowers are the colour of Dijon mustard but the flower lip is white. The small yellow foxglove, *D. lutea*, looks similar but has more scattered pale yellow flowers on its spikes. These last two may reach 90 centimetres in height.

Foxglove may be grown in full sun to partial shade. All prefer organically rich, acidic, and evenly moist soil. They need good drainage in winter or their crowns rot. Insect pests include aphids and slugs; possible diseases, powdery mildew and rust. Plants are toxic to mammals, including people. The spikes make an excellent cut flower and the blossoms are a magnet for bees and hummingbirds. Propagation is by seed. The above species are all hardy to zone 4.

Design tips: Foxgloves are a classic cottage-garden plant but are also suited to wildflower gardens or the back of a border.

DISPORUM
Fairy-bells

At one time, there were 26 species of *Disporum*, mostly Asian, but the six species native in North America have now been moved to their own genus, *Prosartes*. Overall, these are clumping plants, reaching 30 to 90 centimetres tall with oval-shaped, ribbed leaves and small, nodding, lilylike flowers which are greenish white, yellow, or pink. Mid- to late spring is the typical blooming season. The most popular ornamental *Disporum* are *D. sessile*, especially 'Variegatum', whose leaves are thinly striped in white, and the many forms of *D. cantoniense*, which typically has pink flowers. 'Night Heron' has yellow-green flowers and nearly black spring leaves. 'Aureovariegata' and 'Gold Temple' have yellow-green leaves irregularly edged in green, while 'Moonlight' is white with wide, irregular green edges and pink highlights. 'Green Giant' has green leaves and white flowers on plants up to 100 centimetres tall, while 'Indian Purple' has dark purple flowers. *Disporum smilacinum*

Prosartes hookeri

is a dwarf 30- to 40-centimetre-tall species with many named Japanese selections, grown for their decorative foliage. Other *Disporum* available are *D. lutescens* and *D. flavens*. All true *Disporum* flowers develop into blue-black berries. From North America, the most popular *Prosartes* species are *D. hookeri*, *P. lanuginosa*, and *P. trachycarpa*, all with uniform green foliage, greenish white flowers, and orange to red berries.

All fairy-bells prefer acidic, organically rich, evenly moist soil. Dry conditions may cause them to go summer-dormant. These woodland plants prefer dappled to full shade. While insect pests are rare, slugs and snails can be troublesome, and they may be browsed by herbivores. Propagation is mostly by division. *Prosartes* are hardy to zone 3, while *D. sessile* is hardy to zone 4. Most of the other *Disporum* are hardy to zone 5, with the exception of *D. smilacinum*, which is the tenderest, zone 7.

Design tips: All the fairy-bells befit a woodland garden, combining well with other plants with similar growing requirements such as *Trillium*, *Clintonia*, and *Podophyllum*.

EPIMEDIUM
Barrenwort

The 65 or so species of *Epimedium* are found from the Mediterranean region to Japan, with the most found in China. Most are garden-worthy and many hybrids and selections have been made among the species. As a group, they are tufted, mounding or spreading in habit, the latter useful as ground covers. This group of plants are as valuable for their foliage as for their flowers. Generally, their leaves are trifoliate with heart- or arrowhead-shaped leaflets. Some are deciduous with spring foliage and fall colour; others are evergreen with spiny-edged leaves reminiscent of holly. Depending on the species or hybrid, it may range in height from 10 to 75 centimetres. The flowers are produced in loose panicles in mid- to late spring. Individual flowers have four petaloid sepals and an overall starlike shape. Several have nectar spurs that extend beyond the flowers, lending an exotic appearance. Floral colours may be white, pink, purple, red, orange, or yellow; they are often bicoloured.

Several barrenworts are particularly

Epimedium lishinchenii

common. Popular is *E. X rubrum*, with bronzy spring foliage 30 to 40 centimetres tall and red flowers. Equally popular is *E. X versicolor* 'Suphureum', with yellow flowers and bronzy spring leaves on plants reaching 50 centimetres tall. The species *E. grandiflorum*, which reaches 20 to 40 centimetres, has many named selections, with flowers in shades of reddish to pinkish purple or white and often puple-tinted spring foliage. *Epimedium youngianum* also has several named selections which reach 10 to 30 centimetres tall, with flowers ranging from white to rosy pink or lavender. The largest is *E. pubigerum* 'Orangekonigin', which reaches 75 centimetres and has orange flowers. One of the most garden-worthy evergreen types is *E. wushanense*, with bronzy spring leaves that turn shiny green with spiny hollylike foliage. The flowers are soft yellow on stems up to 40 centimetres tall. In recent years, many new barrenworts have been released on the market. All are worth trying.

Barrenworts are essentially forest-floor plants and, as such, prefer dappled shade and moist, organically rich soil. Only a small number of the more robust species, such as *E. X rubrum* and *E. X versicolor* 'Sulphureum', tolerate dry soil and shade. As spring growth arises early, frost pockets should be avoided. It is mostly care-free with the only major disease being Tobacco Rattle virus, which causes irregular yellow mottling on the leaves; infected plants should be destroyed, as the virus can spread to other ornamental plants. Propagation is by division. Most of the above are hardy to zone 5, or 4 if mulched well in the fall; the evergreen types, zone 6.

Design tips: Barrenwort is ideal for growing under trees, along the north side of buildings, or in a shady rock garden. Combine with hosta and ferns and position them near the front of a border where their decorative foliage can be best appreciated.

ERYTHRONIUM
Trout lily

The 20 or so species of *Erythronium* are found across the northern hemisphere, mostly in western North America. Trout lilies are bulbs, each plant producing a pair of elliptical, often brown-mottled basal leaves and leafless stems that produce one to several nodding, reflexed, lilylike flowers in white, yellow, or pink shades. Generally, they are ephemeral woodland plants that bloom from early to late spring, then promptly go dormant for the summer.

From western North America come *E. tuolumnense* (yellow flowers), *E. californicum*, *E. oreganum*, *E. helenae*, *E. howellii* (these latter four have white flowers with yellow centres), *E. hendersonii*, and *E. revolutum* (these last two, pink flowers). Of the hybrids among these species, the most popular are 'Pagoda' (yellow) and 'White Beauty'. As a rule, these all have variously brown-mottled foliage. Also from western North America, but an alpine species, is *E. grandiflorum*.

Erythronium 'White Beauty'

Unusual in having uniform green foliage, it is a challenging species to grow outside of its natural habitat.

From eastern North America come *E. americanum* (yellow) and *E. albidum* (white), both of which also have brown-mottled foliage, but with solitary flowers on stems only 15 centimetres tall. From Japan, Korea, and the Russian Far East is *E. japonicum*, another mottled-leaf, solitary bloomer with deep purple-pink flowers that are intricately marked deeper purple on their insides.

From Europe comes *E. dens-canis*, with striking mottled leaves. It too is short with solitary flowers, but in deep pink. It is also one of the earliest-blooming species. On the border of Europe and Asia comes *E. caucasicum*, similar to *E. dens-canis* but with white flowers. Finally, from Siberia comes *E. sibericum*, another pink-flowered species, but its leaves are often plain grey green.

Erythronium prefer partial to full shade and organically rich soil that stays reasonably moist, even during the dormant summer period. Diseases are rare and the main pests are slugs and snails. Propagation is by seed or division of large clumps of bulbs. Bulbs are sold and planted in the autumn in a similar fashion to tulips and daffodils. The western North American species are hardy to zone 5, while the others are rated hardy through zone 3.

Design tips: *Erythronium* are suited to a woodland garden. Smaller trout lilies may be used in shady rock gardens. As trout lilies disappear in summer, try interplanting them with primroses, dwarf bleeding-heart, or smaller hosta.

EUTROCHIUM
Joe-pye weed

Until recently, the eight species of North American joe-pye weed were included in the genus *Eupatorium* but, today, the purple-flowered members of *Eupatorium* have been moved to their own genus, *Eutrochium*. Only the white-flowered members, commonly called boneset, are still botanically considered to be in the genus *Eupatorium*. The genus name *Eutrochium* comes from the Greek *eu*, meaning well, in reference to the wet habitat, and *troche*, meaning wheel-like, referring to the whorled leaves. The common name joe-pye was originally named after a First Nations healer named Jopi, who used this plant as an herbal remedy. As a group, the tall, bold joe-pye weed are useful for the back of a border.

Spotted joe-pye weed, *E. maculatum*, is native throughout much of North America, growing along streamsides and lake margins. It reaches a height of 2 metres, with whorls of three to five lance-shaped, rugose leaves. Stems are topped with flat-topped panicles of fluffy purple-pink flowers in mid- to late summer. 'Gateway' is a more compact selection, reaching 150 centimetres tall. Similar to spotted joe-pye weed is the sweet joe-pye weed, *E. purpureum*, whose vanilla-scented flowers have a more conical outline. 'Atropurpureum' has nearly black stems. For smaller gardens, try the cultivar 'Little Joe', which reaches 120 centimetres, or 'Baby Joe', which reaches just 75 centimetres. The latter is recommended as it has super-sized flower heads in relation to the plant. The sole European species of *Eutrochium*, *E. cannabinum*, commonly called hemp-

Eupatorium cannabinum

agrimony, can reach 150 centimetres tall; it has narrower whorled leaves and looser clusters of flowers. From China comes *E. fortunei* 'Pink Frost', which has white-variegated leaves and pink flowers on 90-centimetre-tall plants. Among the true *Eupatorium*, the most popular is *E. rugulosum* 'Chocolate', whose leaves are purple-tinted. It can reach 120 centimetres in height, with flat-topped clusters of white flowers.

Joe-pye weed love moisture and quickly wilt if the soil is too dry. They prefer full sun and organically rich soil. All joe-pye weed attract hummingbirds, butterflies, and bees. The most serious problem is leaf scorch, which occurs if the plants are grown in soil that is too dry. Propagation is by seed or division. All are hardy to zone 4.

Design tips: These bold plants suit the back of a border but the dwarf types may be used in a middle border. They are ideal for planting near water features and rain gardens. Companion plants include rayflower, Japanese iris, and *Darmera*.

GENTIANA
Gentian

The genus *Gentiana* is cosmopolitan, with over 400 species, most of which are found in the Himalayas of China. The genus name is a tribute to Gentius, an Illyrian king who may have been the discoverer of tonic properties in gentians. As a group, they are prized for their intensely blue flowers. Entire books have been dedicated to the growing of gentians. However, only a small number are commonly grown, either as woodland or rock-garden subjects. Some prefer acidic soil,

others alkaline. Perhaps the most impressive of the acid-lovers is the willow gentian, *G. asclepiadea*. This European woodlander produces a fountainlike clump of unbranched stems that reach 90 centimetres tall. The leaves are dark green and lance-shaped. The 3.5- to 5-centimetre-long, intense deep blue, trumpetlike flowers are produced in the upper leaf axils during late summer. Because this plant produces a deep taproot, it should not be disturbed once it is planted. It can be slow to establish but is long-lived and improves with age. The selection 'Alba' has white flowers, while 'Pink Cascade' and 'Pink Swallow' have pink blossoms.

Of lower stature is the crested gentian, *G. septemfida*, native to the Caucasus region. This plant forms a low clump with sprawling 15- to 30-centimetre-tall stems. From mid- to late summer, the stems end in clusters of blue trumpets. *Gentiana scabra* is similar. The selection 'Zuki-rindo' has purple-pink flowers. 'True Blue' is a hybrid gentian that reaches 45 centimetres tall with blue flowers in late summer. One outstanding gentian is the trumpet gentian, *G. acaulis*, which has 5-centimetre-tall, electric navy blue flowers in mid- to late spring. This plant forms a low mat of evergreen leaves.

Popular in Europe but not as often seen in North America are the Chinese autumn-flowering gentians. These form low mats with small, linear leaves and trailing stems. In the fall, the stems tips terminate in relatively large, funnel-shaped azure blue flowers whose outer corolla tube is striped in dark purple. *Gentiana sino-ornata* is the most popular choice, but also look for *G. ornata*, *G. ternifolia*, *G. farreri*, *G. veitchiorum*, and hybrids among them.

The above gentians require evenly moist, organically rich, acidic soil. Most are sun-lovers, with the exception of willow gentian, which tolerates some shade. All attract bees and are mostly pest- and disease-free. Propagation is by seed or division. The above are all rated hardy to zone 3.

Design tips: Place willow gentian in a woodland garden or border. Crested gentian may be used in the front of a border, a woodland garden, or a large rockery, while trumpet and fall-flowering gentians are mostly used in rock-garden settings. The low types may also be used in a peat garden, combined with dwarf ericaceous shrubs.

GERANIUM
Cranesbill

The genus *Geranium* is among one of the larger plant genera, with over 400 species worldwide. The genus name comes from the Greek word *geranos*, meaning crane, in reference to the fruit, which are reminiscent of the head and beak of that bird. Although there are several weedy species, many are highly ornamental. Add to this the innumerable hybrids, and this presents a very important group of garden perennials.

Of the many species that exceed 60 centimetres, among the most popular is meadow cranesbill, *G. pratense*. A clumping plant with stems that grow to 90 centimetres tall, its saucer-shaped flowers are produced in open clusters from late spring to early summer. The colour of the wild plants is purple blue but white and double-flowered types exist. 'Splish Splash' has white flowers flecked and splashed with purple. Several

have purple-tinted foliage; perhaps the best of these is 'Oakey Dokey'. Other similar species and hybrids include *G.* X *magnificum*, *G. himalayense*, and the hybrids 'Brookside' and 'Johnson's Blue'. 'Rozanne' is a 50-centimetre-tall mounding hybrid, with blue flowers with a pale central eye and a blooming season from late spring through fall.

One of the tallest is *G. psilostemon*, which can reach 120 centimetres. It is shrublike with an abundance of magenta, black-eyed flowers from mid- to late summer. 'Dragon Heart' is similar but reaches only 60 centimetres tall. 'Ann Folkard' is also similar but has contrasting chartreuse foliage.

Among the pink-flowered geranium are *G. endresii* and *G.* X *oxonianum* selections. These bloom all summer if planted in an area that does not receive too much sun and are kept reasonably moist. *Geranium endresii* reaches a height of 40 centimetres with a spreading habit. The similar *G.* X *oxonianum* 'Wargrave Pink' can reach 60 centimetres. The selection 'Claridge Druce' is also 60 centimetres tall but has pale pink flowers, while 'Katherine Adele' is pale pink with maroon-blotched foliage.

Maroon-purple flowers make the mourning widow cranesbill, *G. phaeum*, a standout. This species is reasonably tall, reaching 80 centimetres. The flowers are smaller than those of most geranium, with petals that reflex back. It too blooms all summer. A white-flowered selection, 'Album', also exists, but perhaps the best choice for North American gardens is 'Samobor', which has striking purple-black blotched leaves.

Gentiana sino-ornata

Geranium dalmaticum

Among the cranesbills that remain less than 30 centimetres, the most popular, and indeed another heritage species, is the big-root cranesbill, *G. macrorrhizum*. This species reaches 30 centimetres tall but spreads 90 or more centimetres, making it a suitable ground cover for sun or shade. The relatively small pink flowers are produced in late spring to early summer. The soft, slightly sticky foliage is pungent and takes on shades of yellow, orange, and red in the autumn. The leaves of 'Variegatum' are thinly margined in white. The smallest of the ground-cover species is *G. dalmaticum*. It reaches only 10 to 15 centimetres tall and creeps among rocks in a rock-garden setting. It blooms in early summer, with light pink flowers and glossy foliage. The hybrid between the former two is *G. X cantabrigiense*, an ideal ground cover for sun to partial shade, with glossy, fragrant foliage. 'Cambridge', 'Westray', 'Karmina', and 'Crystal Rose' have flowers in varying shades of pink, while 'Biokova' has white blossoms with a hint of pink.

One of the most popular cranesbills for the front of a border is bloody cranesbill, *G. sanguineum*, a mounding plant 20 to 30 centimetres tall with many bright pink flowers from late spring to frost. 'Elke' has two-tone flowers, neon pink with white edges, while 'Striatum' has soft pink flowers. 'Album' has white flowers.

Geranium cinereum has a similar habit to that of *G. sanguineum* and has several named selections: 'Ballerina', pale pink with darker veins and nearly black centres; 'Splendens', deep magenta; and 'Purple Pillow', dark reddish purple. *Geranium wallichianum*

'Buxton's Blue' is a low spreader whose purple-blue flowers have white centres. The hybrid 'Rosetta' is similar but has pink flowers with white centres.

Cranesbills are not fond of dry soil and perform best if the soil is organically rich. All grow in full sun to partial shade, but *G. phaeum* is noteworthy for its shade tolerance. The *G. pratense* types can become rangy by mid-summer and often benefit from being cut back. Many of the above self-seed with abandon, especially *G. phaeum*. Overall, they are care-free. Propagation is by seed or division. Most of the above are hardy to zones 3 to 4, with the exception of 'Rozanne', *G. cinereum*, and *G. wallichianum*, which are rated for zones 5 to 6.

Design tips: The taller *G. psilostemon*, *G. pratense*, and similar hybrids are best used in a perennial border or wildflower garden. The ground cover *G. X cantabrigense* and *G. macrorrhizum* are ideal under high-canopy trees, while the smaller mounding types are perfect for the front of a border or in a rock garden.

GEUM
Avens

The genus *Geum* is nearly cosmopolitan, with about 50 species, but gardeners grow only a limited number of these species. As a group, they are evergreen, with hairy basal leaves and thick rhizomes. Each leaf is pinnately compound with a single large deeply lobed terminal leaflet. A popular older selection is *Geum* 'Borisii', a hybrid developed from the European species *G. coccineum*. From mid-spring to early summer, loose flower clusters

Geum coccineum

arise on wiry stems up to 45 centimetres tall. The 3.5-centimetre-diameter flowers are orange with a dense central clump of yellow stamens. Two other popular avens are selections of *G. chiloense*, a species native to southern Chile: 'Mrs. J. Bradshaw', with double scarlet flowers, and 'Mrs. Strathedon', with double yellow flowers, on stems reaching 60 centimetres tall. If promptly dead-headed, they can be coaxed to bloom all season. Recently, a series of new hybrids has been developed, called the Cocktails™ series: 'Mai Tai', 'Tequila Sunrise', and 'Banana Daiquiri'. These offer a wider colour range.

Native to eastern North America is water avens, *G. rivale*. It has unassuming, nodding flowers that are apricot to purple pink. This species has been hybridized to the previous species to create several lovely hybrids which are a little shorter than the *G. chiloense* hybrids, reaching about 45 centimetres tall. These often have delicate, nodding flowers like those of *G. rivale* but with larger, showier flowers of the *G. chiloense* or *G. coccineum* parent. These hybrids include 'Totally Tangarine' (orange), 'Lemon Drop' (pale yellow), 'Pink Frills' (soft pink), 'Flames of Passion' (scarlet), and 'Leonard's Variety' (coral pink). If you are looking for a dwarf avens to grow in a rock-garden setting, try *G. montanum*, a European species from the Alps. It has relatively large yellow flowers in June on 15-centimetre-tall stems held above a tuft of evergreen leaves.

These avens all prefer evenly moist, organically rich soil and grow in full sun or partial shade. However, excess winter wetness can lead to rhizome rotting. As they are not fond of high summer temperatures, they are not recommended south of zone 7. Plants benefit from being divided every three to four years. Propagation is by seed or division. These care-free plants are rated hardy to zone 4.

Design tips: Avens are ideal plants for the front of a border, a woodland setting, or rain garden or near water features.

Gillenia trifoliata

GILLENIA TRIFOLIATA
Bowman's root

The sole species of *Gillenia*, *G. trifoliata*, is a woodland plant native to eastern North America, from Ontario to Georgia. The plant is also known under the Latin name *Porteranthus*. A clumping plant with upright 60- to 120-centimetre-tall stems, its spring shoots are an attractive wine red. The leaves are trifoliate and deeply serrated. The white starlike flowers have narrow, often twisted petals and are produced in loose terminal clusters from late spring to early summer. The burgundy wine calyx contrasts beautifully with the white petals. Its foliage turns orange to red in autumn, providing another attractive aspect to this underutilized plant. 'Pink Profusion' is a pale pink-flowered selection.

Bowman's root prefers organically rich, acidic, evenly moist soil. Dappled shade is ideal. It is not bothered by pests or diseases.

Propagation is by seed or division. It is rated hardy to zone 4.

Design tips: As a natural woodland plant, bowman's root is ideal for shady gardens, woodland settings, and wildflower gardens. It combines well with hosta, astilbe, *Prosartes*, and various ferns.

GLAUCIDIUM PALMATUM
Japanese wood poppy

The single species in this genus, *Glaucidium palmatum*, is endemic to northern Japan, growing in open subalpine woodlands. These plants are clumpers, with a shrublike appearance. Several unbranched stems arise 45 to 60 centimetres tall. Each stem has a pair of bright green maplelike leaves and a single 15-centimetre-diameter mauve or white flower that looks like a cross between a peony and a poppy. The blooming season is

Glaucidium palmatum

from mid- to late spring. This connoisseur's plant may be expensive, if you can track it down. However, it is well worth the investment, as it is long-lived and, like a fine wine, improves with age. It is considered by the Royal Horticultural Society to be one of the top 200 plants in the world.

Glaucidium prefer partial shade and acidic, humus-rich, moist but well-drained soil. It does not tolerate dry soil or hot temperatures; gardeners in cooler coastal regions have the best success. Pests and diseases are not generally a problem and their flowers attract bees. Propagation is primarily by seed, but larger plants may be divided. However, they have a large root system and resent being transplanted. As a result, they may sulk for years after being divided. It is hardy to zone 4 if properly mulched in winter but does not perform well south of zone 7.

Design tips: *Glaucidium* is best grown in a woodland garden or a partly shaded border. For an aesthetically pleasing effect, combine it with the equally rare and desirable Japanese waxbells and Himalayan blue poppy.

HELONIAS BULLATA
Swamp pink

A single species among the genus *Helonias*, *H. bullata* is native to bogs mostly among the New Jersey barrens but extends south to Georgia. It is an endangered species in the wild and, as such, a protected species, but it is sometimes offered in the nursery trade. Plants produce a basal rosette of evergreen, narrow lance-shaped leaves arising from a thick rhizome. The leaves turn purplish in autumn and through the winter. In early spring,

Helonias bullata

flower stems arise 30 to 60 centimetres tall, topped with a dense 3- to 10-centimetre-long, cone-shaped cluster of fragrant pink flowers which have contrasting blue anthers.

Swamp pinks are best grown in bog gardens, where the soil remains evenly moist. The growing media is ideally a mix of sand and peat, with the pH below 6. It performs best in dappled or partial shade; avoid hot afternoon sun. Propagation is by seed. It is hardy through zone 5.

Design tips: With their requirement for consistent moisture, swamp pinks are best grown in a bog garden with other acid-loving bog species such as pitcher-plants, cranberry, and blue flag iris. It may also be grown in woodland gardens if the proper soil moisture can be maintained.

HELONIOPSIS ORIENTALIS
Oriental swamp pink

The six species of *Heloniopsis* are all rare in

Heloniopsis orientalis

cultivation. The most likely to be encountered is *H. orientalis*, which is native to Korea, Japan, and the Sakhalin Peninsula of Russia. Plants produce a basal rosette of evergreen, lance-shaped leaves. In early spring, 10- to 20-centimetre-tall leafless stems arise, topped by a nodding cluster of lavender-pink, starlike flowers with distinctive blue stamens. New leaves develop after the flowers have faded.

Heloniopsis require acidic, organically rich, well-drained but evenly moist soil. It tolerates full sun if kept moist, but in warmer areas, partial shade is suggested. Pests and diseases are rare. Propagation is by seed, or more commonly by division. It is hardy to zone 5b if mulched in winter.

Design tips: *Heloniopsis* is ideal for a partly shaded rock garden, along the edges of water features, or beneath taller rhododendrons. Ideal companion plants are *Asarum*, *Arisaema*, *Trillium*, and *Hepatica*.

HEMEROCALLIS
Daylily

It is the rare garden that does not have at least one daylily, one of the most popular perennials. The 19 daylily species are all native to eastern Asia, yet from these have arisen thousands of hybrids, with more being added each year. As a group, they produce large clumps with grasslike leaves and naked flower stems that end in several relatively large, lilylike flowers that last a single day, hence the common name "daylily." Although the flowers are short-lived, they are produced sequentially over several weeks. Depending on the species or hybrid, you can have daylily blooming from late spring through autumn. The flower colour range among the species is restricted to yellow or orange but modern hybrids are available in creamy white through every imaginable shade of yellow, orange, pink, red, to nearly pure purple. Many are bi- or even tricoloured. Petal edges may be frilled or the petals may be long and narrow. Some have double flowers or variegated leaves. The majority of modern hybrids are tetraploid, resulting in thicker petals than those of the wild types. The overall flower stem heights vary from 90 to 120 centimetres on the taller standard types to about 30 centimetres on the dwarf types such as the 'D'Oro' and 'Returns' hybrids. Daylilies are an indispensable group of plants.

For these long-lived plants, cultivation is easy; they seem to thrive just about anywhere except soggy sites. They are drought-tolerant, reasonably shade-tolerant, and salt-tolerant; they tolerate acidic or alkaline soil; and they are extremely hardy. However, they perform best with regular watering and full sun. Pests and diseases are uncommon, but newly

Hemerocallis hybrid

Hibiscus Summerific® 'Cherry Choco Latte'

Hosta border

emerging foliage may be eaten by slugs, deer, or moose. Propagation is by division or seed. They are hardy to zone 2.

Design tips: The standard types are suited to a mid-border, with the dwarf types better suited to the front border. All are ideal for coastal gardens and can be used as ground covers on slopes.

HIBISCUS
Hardy hibiscus, rose mallow

Hibiscus are popular flowering shrubs in tropical countries. Although most hibiscus are woody plants, a few herbaceous species are available; the most popular is *Hibiscus moscheutos*, native to south and eastern US and southernmost Ontario. Several additional similarly hardy herbaceous species include *H. coccineus*, *H. laevis*, *H. militaris*, and *H. palustris*. The modern hardy garden hibiscus probably has genes from some if not all of the above species; commercially, all are sold as *H. moscheutos*.

As a garden ornamental, this plant can become quite large, forming a bushy clump over 2 metres tall. The huge flowers, up to 20 centimetres in diameter, are produced from August to October, making it a valuable plant for the late summer to early fall garden. Typical of all hibiscus, the flowers last a single day. Plants are slow to start in the spring but grow rapidly. 'Southern Belle' has flowers in white and shades of red and pink. Other tall cultivars include 'Cherry Brandy', 'Plum Fantasy', 'Fantasia', 'Peppermint Schnapps', and 'Lord Baltimore'. If space is limited, try the dwarf, 1-metre-tall Luna series, available in white, pink, and red.

Garden hibiscus require full sun and organically rich, slightly acidic, evenly moist soil. The wild species usually grow in swamps and marshes and, as a result, do not tolerate drought. Watch for insects and disease, as hibiscus can be bothered by rust, leaf spots, aphids, and especially Japanese beetle. Deer, moose, and hares are not a problem. Propagation is by division. It is hardy to zone 5.

Design tips: Hibiscus is suitable for the back of a border and, with its love of moisture, near water features. For contrast, plant it near taller *Miscanthus* grasses.

HOSTA
Hosta

Hosta are among the most popular perennials grown in North America. This genus is not large; it has only 23 species, two found in China and the rest in Japan and Korea. However, the number and variation available today from such humble beginnings is mind-boggling. Does the world need another hosta? Apparently so, as new ones are released every year and their popularity does not seem to be waning. With so many hundreds, if not thousands, of selections on the market, it is impossible to describe them except as a group. On the whole, these plants are grown primarily for their foliage. Their leaves may be shades of green, yellow, or blue. Leaves may be variegated in white or yellow along their margins, in their centres, or as mottles and streaks scattered throughout. Some have attractive wine-coloured petioles. Their bell- to trumpet-shaped flowers are usually nodding and produced on one-sided spikes. These are mostly lavender to violet but can be variously marked on the inside with darker purple; some are pure white. The blooming season ranges from mid-summer through autumn depending on the species or hybrid. They are generally scentless but the species *H. plantaginea* and the hybrid 'Fragrant Bouquet' have pure white, highly fragrant flowers.

The size variation is tremendous. The American Hosta Society divides them into six size classes: dwarf, miniature, small, medium, large, and giant. Among the smallest is 'Collector's Choice', whose green leaves are only 2 to 3 centimetres long. At the other extreme is 'Empress Wu', whose leaves may be longer than 45 centimetres with flower stems approaching 150 centimetres tall. In the garden setting, hosta may be used from the front to the back of a border. They are perhaps most popular in shady woodland gardens or others areas of shade where other perennials simply cannot perform. In the wild, they grow along partly shaded streams, so in the garden, regular watering is required. They perform best in organically rich, evenly moist soil. They are not fussy about soil pH. They tolerate full sun to relatively deep shade, but light requirements vary with leaf colour. As a rule, those with yellow foliage or yellow variegation need the most sun; in fact, if it too shaded, the yellow colour turns chartreuse. White variegated leaves like partial shade. Blue foliage tolerates the most shade; in warmer zones, it needs shade or foliage bleaching is inevitable. Plain green-leaved types seem to be able withstand full sun to full shade.

Although they are extremely popular, hosta are snail and slug magnets. Those with thick blue foliage are the most resistant, while the thin-leaved types can be shredded by snails and slugs. Hosta are also attacked by the disease Hosta Virus X, which may be spread by aphids or infected pruning shears. The symptoms appear as light or dark green discoloration and/or spotting, brown streaking, or unusual leaf puckering. Infected plants loose vigour and are condemned to a long, lingering death. The virus can spread rapidly to other hosta, so suspected infected plants should be destroyed. Hosta are hors d'oeuvres for hares, rabbit, deer, and moose. Despite these problems, growing hosta can be addictive; you cannot have just one! Propagation is by division. These hardy perennials are rated hardy through zone 2.

Design tips: Hosta have innumerable uses in a garden. All may be massed as ground covers, although the mid-sized cultivars are perhaps best for this. Streamsides, woodland gardens, borders—anything goes. Use the miniature types in rock gardens or alpine troughs; consider planting spring bulbs

Impatiens omeiana

among them. Combine them with ferns, *Ligularia*, Solomon's-seal, *Rodgersia*, or *Darmera* for a dramatic foliar effect.

IMPATIENS OMEIANA
Hardy impatiens

Most gardeners are familiar with the annual bedding *Impatiens* but there is one hardy perennial species, discovered in 1983 on Mount Omei in the Sichuan Province of China. There, it grows in the shade of fir trees and rhododendrons, a testament to its preference for acidic soil. Like firs and rhododendrons, it prefers organically rich soil that stays reasonably moist. Plants form large clumps with stems up to 45 to 60 centimetres tall. The decorative leaves are lance-shaped, green with a central yellow stripe, arising from red-tinted stems. In late summer to early fall, it produces yellow, snapdragon-like flowers. Provide it with evenly moist, organically rich soil in partial to full shade. In cooler climates, hardy impatiens can tolerate full sun. It does not tolerate drought. Propagation is by division. It is hardy to zone 6.

Design tips: This impatiens is a lovely subject for the woodland garden; combine with other Asian species such as ferns, *Arisaema*, *Astilbe*, and *Glaucidium*.

INCARVILLEA
Hardy gloxinia

The genus *Incarvillea* has just 16 species, all native to central and eastern Asia. The genus name honours Pierre d'Incarville (1706–57), a French missionary in China. Only one species is commonly available, *I. delavayi*,

Incarvillea mairei

or hardy gloxinia. This plant is often sold as a dormant root in local nurseries and box stores. The plant produces a rosette of dark green, fernlike leaves up to 30 centimetres in length. The leafless flower stems, which arise to 60 centimetres tall, are topped with a cluster of large pink, trumpetlike flowers in late spring to early summer. The cultivar 'Alba' has white flowers.

Although it is not easy to find, the dwarf garden gloxinia, *I. mairei*, is equally desirable. It is essentially a scaled-down version of the hardy gloxinia, with oversized flowers atop 30- to 40-centimetre-long stems. It is well worth trying to track down.

Both garden gloxinia noted are best in full sun but they do tolerate partial shade. They need an organically rich but sandy soil that is well drained, especially in winter. As they are not fond of heat and humidity, they often perform poorly south of zone 7. They are both care-free plants, with few problems.

They attract bumblebees. Propagation is by seed. Garden gloxinia is hardy to zone 6 but may be grown in zone 5 if provided with a thick winter mulch. The dwarf garden gloxinia is much hardier, tough enough to survive zone 3.

Design tips: Garden gloxinia is suitable near the front of a border or in an open woodland setting. Dwarf garden gloxinia is perhaps better used in a rock garden.

IRIS

Siberian iris, Japanese iris, beardless iris

This group of iris is distinguished by falls which lack any hairs at their base. Broadly, they fall into two major groups: the Siberians, *I. siberica* selections, and the Japanese, *I ensata* selections. Both have long, narrow, sword-shaped leaves and plants that form large grasslike clumps. The flowers of Siberian iris are smaller than those of Japanese iris and bloom a few weeks earlier than the latter. The typical blooming season of Siberian iris is late spring to early summer, while the Japanese iris are mostly early to mid-summer. Many named selections among both groups are available in a wide range of colours. Both commonly reach 90 to 120 centimetres tall. All are lovely as cut flowers. *Iris ensata* 'Variegata' has particularly attractive white-margined foliage. Also noteworthy are the Sino-siberian iris: the blue-flowered *I. delavayi*, *I. clarkei*, and *I. bulleyana*; the yellow *I. forrestii* and *I. wilsonii*; and the deep purple *I. chrysographes*. All Sino-siberians have flowers smaller than those of the typical Siberians, more narrow foliage, and shorter stature but bloom concurrently. *Iris*

Iris pseudacorus 'Variegatus'

chrysographes 'Black Form' or 'Black Gold' have special merit in that they are close to black.

Also included in the beardless iris are the native northern blue flag iris, *I. versicolor*; the southern blue flag, *I. virginica*; and the slender blue flag, *I. prismatica*, as well as the introduced yellow flag, *I. pseudacorus*. All are commonly found near or in shallow water but may be grown in regular garden soil if kept reasonably moist. The variegated version of yellow flag has yellow spring foliage and makes a bold statement in the garden. For a rock or coastal garden, try the North American native *I. hookeri*, sometimes sold as Arctic iris, *I. setosa* var. *arctica*. This species is found where it can be kissed by the sea. It reaches 30 centimetres tall and has porcelain blue flowers. Similar in appearance but twice as tall is *I. setosa*. All the above bloom from late spring to early summer.

All of the beardless iris prefer full sun and require organically rich soil that does not dry out. Japanese, yellow flag, and blue flag iris may even be grown submerged in shallow water. These iris are not as affected by botrytis and iris borer, which can devastate bearded iris. Herbivores generally ignore these iris. Propagation is by division or, for species, seeds. The Siberians, yellow flag, northern blue flag, and *I. setosa* are hardy to zone 2, while the Japanese and other blue flags are rated for zone 4.

Design tips: All of the above iris are ideal for a border or rain gardens or for planting near water features. For a contrasting foliage effect, try combining them with astilbe, hosta, ferns, and primroses. In wet locations, use the above iris as a substitute for ornamental grasses.

Iris cristata

IRIS CRISTATA
Dwarf crested iris

Iris cristata is an unusual iris in that it prefers shaded locations. In the wild, this eastern US native is found in organically rich soil in woodlands, bluffs, and ravines. Plants spread by narrow rhizomes, forming large colonies. The wide, swordlike leaves are naturally pale green and reach 15 to 20 centimetres in length. In mid- to late spring, they produce nearly stemless pale blue, pale violet, or white flowers which are 5 to 7 centimetres in diameter. Named cultivars include 'Navy Blue Gem', 'Eco Bluebird', 'Powder Blue Giant', and 'Tennessee White'.

This iris is ideal for dappled shade under high-canopy hardwood trees; however, it also tolerates full sun. The organically rich soil should be acidic and well drained. Once established, crested iris tolerate some drought. Pests and diseases are rare and, typical of most iris, they are not bothered by larger herbivores. Propagation is by division or seed. Dwarf crested iris is hardy from zones 3 to 9.

Design tips: This iris is ideal for the front of a border, rock gardens, and woodland gardens. Under ideal conditions, it can be used as a ground cover. Try combining it with other spring ephemerals such as trilliums, Virginia bluebell, and bellworts.

KIRENGESHOMA
Yellow waxbells

Both species of *Kirengeshoma* are native to eastern Asia. The genus name comes from the Japanese name for the plant: *ki* means yellow; *renge*, lotus blossom; and *shoma*, hat, all referencing the plant's blossoms. The species most commonly encountered is yellow waxbells, *K. palmata*. This woodland plant is valued as much for its leaves as its unusual

Kirengeshoma palmata

late-blooming flowers. It is not regularly found in local nurseries but may be offered in specialty nurseries. A bushy plant with many unbranched stems reaching 120 centimetres, its paired leaves are coarsely toothed and maplelike, reaching up to 20 centimetres wide. From mid-summer to early fall, plants produce terminal clusters of nodding bell-like, 5-centimetre-long yellow flowers that have thick, waxy petals. The flowers are reminiscent of a badminton shuttlecock. It is an invaluable plant for extending the blooming season. Korean waxbells, *K. koreana*, is only subtly different and also worth growing.

This plant prefers partial shade but tolerates full sun if the soil is evenly moist. The soil should be organically rich, well drained, and acidic. It does not tolerate dry soil. Diseases are not a problem nor is it bothered by pests, with the possible exception of slugs and snails. Propagation is by seed, or more commonly by division. It is hardy to zone 5.

Design tips: Yellow waxbells is an ideal plant for woodland gardens or shady borders; despite its height, place it close to the front of a border so that its leaves and exotic flowers can be best appreciated.

LAMIUM
Dead-nettle

Although close to 30 species of *Lamium* exist throughout Eurasia and North Africa, the majority are weedy. In fact, several of these weedy species are found throughout disturbed areas in North America, namely henbit, *L. amplexicaule*, and purple dead-nettle, *L. purpureum*. Two ornamental species—yellow archangel, *L. galeobdolon*, formerly known

Lamium maculatum 'Pewter Silver'

as *Lamiastrum galeobdolon*, and spotted deadnettle, *L. maculatum*—are grown primarily for their decorative foliage. Yellow archangel has paired, heart-shaped leaves that are spotted and streaked with silver markings. In mid- to late spring, plants produce a spike of yellow, helmet-shaped flowers on 30-centimetre-long stems. As this plant is aggressive, and even invasive, use it with caution. The cultivar 'Hermann's Pride' is more refined, with narrower, smaller leaves, bolder silver spotting, and a more clumping habit.

Spotted deadnettle is, overall, less invasive but still seeds around. It forms a low clump up to 20 centimetres tall, producing dense spikes of white, pink, to purple-red flowers mostly in mid- to late spring, with scattered flowers throughout the rest of the summer. The many cultivars of spotted deadnettle are selected for their attractive foliage. Those whose leaves have a silver central stripe include 'Chequers' (purple flowers) and 'Shell Pink' (light pink flowers). 'White Nancy' (white flowers), 'Pink Pewter' (light pink flowers), 'Orchid Frost' (rose pink flowers),

'Beacon Silver' (deep pink flowers), 'Red Nancy' (purple-red flowers), and 'Purple Dragon' (magenta flowers) have pure silver leaves. For yellow foliage, try 'Aureum' (pure yellow) or 'Lemon Frost' (yellow with a central silver stripe); both have bright pink flowers. Perhaps the most striking in colour are 'Golden Anniversary' and 'Anne Greenaway', both of which have tricoloured leaves of yellow, green, and silver with magenta-pink flowers.

Lamium prefer organically rich, moist but well-drained, acidic soil. Yellow archangel is reasonably drought-tolerant once established, but spotted deadnettle needs regular moisture. Both are ideal for shade to partial shade. In cooler coastal regions, they may be grown in full sun, but in hotter, inland areas, the leaves may scorch under sunny conditions. Spotted deadnettle in particular suffers if the winters are too wet. Pests and diseases are rare. The pungent foliage makes them unpalatable to larger herbivores. Propagation is by seed, cuttings, or division. They are rated hardy to zone 3.

Design tips: Use yellow archangel as a ground cover in sun or shade. It is also popular in hanging baskets, where it is treated as an annual. Spotted deadnettle may also be used as a ground cover, but it is not as dense as yellow archangel. It is more commonly used along the front of a border or in a rock garden.

LIGULARIA
Rayflower
Most of the nearly 150 species of *Ligularia* are found in Asia. Despite their diversity, only a few are grown as garden ornamentals. As a

Ligularia dentata 'Othello'

group, these bold plants with large leaves fall into two groups: those with narrow spires of small yellow daisylike flowers and those with larger flat-topped clusters of orange-yellow flowers. The former includes *L. przewalskii* and *L. stenocephala*, and cultivars among them; the latter are cultivars of *L. dentata*. The blooming season is throughout the summer.

Among the first of the spire types to be introduced was *L. stenocephala* 'The Rocket', which has large, serrated, heart-shaped leaves with long flower spikes on stems up to 2 metres tall. 'Little Rocket' is a half-sized version, reaching 90 centimetres tall, while 'Bottle Rocket' is smaller again, reaching 80 centimetres tall. The species *L. przewalskii* resembles 'The Rocket' but has deeply serrated leaves, especially the cultivar 'Dragon Wings'. The smaller 'Dragon's Breath' reaches 75 centimetres tall. If you can find them, the species *L. siberica*, *L. wilsoniana*, and *L. fischeri* are also desirable spire types.

Ligularia dentata has large, rounded leaves held at the ends of long stems. Their golden orange flowers, on flat-topped clusters, are up to 9 centimetres wide and held on stems up to 100 centimetres long. The cultivar 'Desdemona' has slightly purple-tinted leaves. 'Othello' has deeper purple leaves, while 'Britt-Marie Crawford' and 'Midnight Lady' have dark purple foliage. 'Osiris Fantaisie' and 'Osiris Café Noir' both have cut foliage with a dwarf 65-centimetre-tall habit. The former has purple-tinted foliage, the latter is darker purple.

Rayflowers perform best in moist, organically rich, acidic soil in full sun to partial shade. They are one of the quickest perennials to wilt if the soil becomes too dry. Its flowers are suitable for cut flowers and are excellent nectar and/or pollen sources for bees and butterflies. Although diseases are rare, slugs and snails can severely damage their foliage. Large herbivores generally ignore them. Propagation may be by seed or, more often, division. They are rated hardy to zone 3.

Design tips: The large size of most *Ligularia* makes them ideal for the back of a border. They are also suited to woodland and rain gardens or around water features. Combine them with other bold plants such as rodgersia or Solomon's-seal.

LILIUM
Oriental lily

For hundreds of years, lilies have captured the admiration of gardeners and that is not likely to change. Thousands of hybrids have been developed from the over 100 lily species that occur throughout the Northern Hemisphere. As a whole, they are bulbs from which arise

Lilium 'Black Beauty'

unbranched stems topped with several six-petalled flowers. The blooming season ranges from June to October; flower colours include every colour except blue. With such diversity, it is not surprising that lilies have been divided into different groups. Officially, there are nine divisions: Asiatic hybrids, Martagon hybrids (the Turk's-caps), Candidum hybrids, American hybrids, Longiflorum hybrids (Easter lily), Trumpet hybrids, Oriental hybrids, "other hybrids," and the species. Within the divisions, the flowers may be upward-facing, outward facing, or reflexed.

While most lilies prefer soil of near neutral pH, the Oriental species and hybrids prefer soil pH of 5.5 to 6.5, allowing them to be included among the acid-loving plants of this book. The main species within this group are *L. auratum* from Japan and *L. speciosum* from Japan, Thailand, and China. Many of the modern-day Oriental lily hybrids are derived from these two species. The species and hybrids generally grow 100 to 150 centimetres tall with fragrant flowers in shades of pink, yellow, and white. Their flowers are either outward-facing or recurved like a Turk's-cap. They bloom later than most lilies, from mid- to late summer with some extending into autumn. They prefer full sun and rich fertile soil that has excellent drainage. Propagation is primarily through division or bulb scales. Deer and rabbits may browse your lily plants. Oriental lilies are among the most resistant lilies to lily leaf beetles. All are hardy to zone 5.

Design tips: Lily bulbs are easily positioned among other acid-loving perennials, where their tall straight stems provides punctuation marks among the border.

Lobelia cardinalis

LOBELIA
Lobelia, cardinal flower

More than 400 species of *Lobelia* are found worldwide. The genus name honours Matthias de l'Obel (1528–1616), a French physician and botanist. Two main species of perennial lobelia are popular as garden ornamentals. Perhaps the more popular of the two is cardinal flower, *L. cardinalis*, a species native from New Brunswick to Ontario and south through the eastern US. This plant has upright unbranched stems up to 120 centimetres in height, topped with a spike of bright red flowers. It is generally short-lived but often self-seeds. Cultivars such as 'Fried Green Tomatoes' are longer lived than the wild species. 'Black Truffle' and 'Queen Victoria' have dark purple foliage. The great blue lobelia, *L. siphilitica*, has a habit similar to that of cardinal flower but is longer lived and reaches a height of 90 centimetres with spikes of blue flowers, or white in the cultivar 'Alba'. The hybrid between great blue lobelia and cardinal flower is called *L.* X *speciosa*; its cultivars come in shades of red, purple, and blue, often with bronze-tinted foliage.

Perennial lobelia all require consistently moist soil in sun or partial shade and do not tolerate drought. They attract hummingbirds and butterflies. Diseases are not generally a concern, but slugs can be troublesome and large herbivores may occasionally browse the plants, which are poisonous if ingested by humans. Propagation is most often by seed, but large clumps of great blue lobelia may be divided. The species listed above are rated hardy to zone 4; but the hybrid is more suitable for zone 5 or higher.

Design tips: Great blue lobelia may be used in perennial borders or wildflower gardens or along water features. With its love for water, cardinal flower is an ideal subject for a bog garden.

LYSICHITON
Skunk cabbage

There are only two species of *Lysichiton*. From western North America comes *L. americanus*.

This species blooms from March to May with a foetid yellow spathe flower 10 to 20 centimetres long. After flowering, the plant develops large cabbagelike leaves that can reach nearly 1 metre tall. From northeastern Asia comes *L. camtschatcensis*, which is similar to *L. americanus* but with a white spathe flower. Both require wet, boggy conditions. In the wild, they often grow under semi-aquatic shrubs, so they receive spring sun but summer shade. Propagation is by seed or division. American skunk cabbage is hardy to zone 4; the Asian species, zone 5.

Design tips: Skunk cabbage are bold foliage plants for bog gardens or wet depressions.

Lysichiton americanus

Lysimachia clethroides

LYSIMACHIA
Loosestrife

Nearly 200 species of *Lysimachia* are found across the northern hemisphere. The genus name honours King Lysimachus (661–281 BC), Macedonian king of Thrace. This group of plants should not be confused with the unrelated purple loosestrife, *Lythrum salicaria*, which is invasive in wetlands across North America. Most of the ornamental *Lysimachia* are garden thugs and quickly overpower more delicate neighbours; however, they can make quite a splash of colour in a border if space allows. The garden loosestrifes vary from low ground covers to tall back-of-the-border clumpers. Yellow is the predominant flower colour but some have white flowers; a few loosestrifes are grown for their ornamental foliage.

The European garden loosestrife, *L. punctata*, is a clumping plant with many unbranched stems reaching 100 centimetres in height. The stems are topped with a leafy spike of 2.5-centimetre-wide, cup-shaped yellow flowers in June and July. Soft lance-shaped leaves are produced in whorls of three or four. 'Alexander' has white variegated leaves, tinted pink in spring; 'Golden Alexander' has yellow-edged leaves. Both are compact, reaching 60 centimetres in height, and less vigorous than the wild species.

Perhaps the most elegant species of *Lysimachia* is the gooseneck loosestrife, *L. clethroides*, another vigorous spreader. Reaching

90 centimetres tall, the unbranched stems of this eastern Asia native end in a dense tapered spike of white star-shaped flowers during July and August. These spikes, which form a distinctive arch above the foliage, attract butterflies. It makes a suitable cut flower.

Fringed loosestrife, *L. ciliata*, native to eastern North America, is also a thug and an abundant self-seeder with stems reaching 90 centimetres tall. From June to July, it produces solitary or paired yellow flowers among the axils of the upper leaves. 'Firecracker' has burgundy-purple leaves in spring, which become purple-tinted in summer. The spring stems are often used in floral arrangements.

Creeping Jenny, *L. nummularia*, is a ground cover that grows well in sun or shade with trailing stems that root as they clamber over the soil surface. Throughout the summer, solitary, yellow, nearly stemless flowers are produced from the leaf axils. 'Aurea', a cultivar with yellow foliage, is popular for use in hanging baskets.

Loosestrife require full sun to partial shade. The clumpers benefit from being divided every three to four years to keep them in check. They all prefer moist to wet soil and are suitable for damp depressions. Pests and disease are rare, although garden loosestrife may occasionally be attacked by moth caterpillars. Loosestrife are hardy through zone 4 or even into zone 3, if mulched in winter.

Design tips: With their robust habit, *Lysimachia* are effective in wildflower gardens. Creeping Jenny, a viable lawn substitute, tolerates limited foot traffic. All are suitable for wet depressions.

Maianthemum racemosum

MAIANTHEMUM
False lily-of-the-valley, false Solomon's-seal
Of the nearly 40 species of *Maianthemum* found across the northern hemisphere, three are native in North America, of which two may be grown as garden ornamentals on acidic soil. From eastern North America is the false lily-of-the-valley or Canada mayflower, *M. canadense*. This species is common in a variety of woodland habitats. Plants spread by threadlike rhizomes to form large colonies. Non-flowering stems produce a single ribbed, heart-shaped leaf, while flowering stems, 10 to 20 centimetres tall, have two or three leaves and a narrow spike of tiny, starlike, fragrant white flowers. It blooms in mid-spring.

Flowers become red berries in summer.

Once belonging to the genus *Smilacina*, false Solomon's-seal, *M. racemosum*, is one of the largest members of the genus, reaching 90 centimetres tall. It is native across much of North America. It has unbranched stems and oval to lance-shaped, ribbed leaves. In late spring, it produces terminal clusters of tiny white starlike flowers which later become small red berries. Superficially, the plant looks much like the true Solomon's-seal, Polygonum.

Both of these *Maianthemum* are woodlanders which grow in humus-rich, acidic, well-drained soil. If the soil is too dry, they become summer-dormant, but if they are kept moist, they remain green for much of the season. Although they grow mostly in dappled to full shade, they tolerate full sun in cooler regions. Pests and diseases are rare. Propagation is by division. Both are hardy to zone 2.

Design tips: Both of these species are ideal subjects for a woodland or wildflower garden. Canada mayflower may be grown as a ground cover beneath rhododendrons and other acid-loving shrubs. False Solomon's-seal is perhaps better combined with other woodlanders such as fairy-bells, trillium, mayapple, and bellwort.

MECONOPSIS
Himalayan blue poppy

Considered by many gardeners as the Holy Grail of garden plants, Himalayan blue poppies are an instant favourite wherever they are seen. Gardeners in Atlantic Canada, coastal Maine, and the coastal Pacific Northwest are among the few areas in North America that have any chance of growing this challenging plant. Himalayan blue poppies need cool summers and suffer when temperatures rise above 25°C, especially when combined with high humidity. Of about 40 species of *Meconopsis*, *M. baileyi* (aka *M. betonicifolia*) is the best one to try; it is also the longest-lived. Most *Meconopsis* are biennials or monocarpic. Even *M. baileyi* can be monocarpic; the trick is not to allow it to bloom the first time it tries! This can be heart-breaking, but if you cut off any flowers in the first year it tries to bloom, it becomes perennial. Himalayan blue poppies come in various shades of blue. 'Lingholm' is one of the best. 'Hensol Violet' is white and

Meconopsis grandis

Oxalis oregana

purple. Himalayan blue poppies bloom from late spring to early summer, producing flower stems that grow 80 to 150 centimetres tall. Individual flowers are up to 8 centimetres wide.

Himalayan blue poppies perform best in areas with cool summers. As a result, they are ideal for the coastal Pacific Northwest or Atlantic Canada. They need consistently moist, acidic, organically rich soil. In the coolest regions, it performs well in full sun but, generally, dappled shade is best. Pest and diseases are rare and hares, deer, and moose ignore them. Propagation is by seed. Himalayan blue poppies are hardy to zone 3.

Design tips: Himalayan blue poppy is an ideal subject for a woodland garden, combining well with primroses, astilbes, and ferns. It may also be combined in a peat garden with late-flowering gentians, heaths, and heathers.

OXALIS OREGANA
Wood-sorrel

This species, native to the redwood and Douglas fir forests of western North America, has two forms: one evergreen, the other deciduous. The former is much more refined and far less vigorous than the latter, which may become invasive in the right situation, but, unfortunately, it is not as hardy. Both produce trifoliate leaves with heart-shaped leaflets. The leaves may have a silvery or lighter green blotch in the centre of each leaflet. The leaves arise on short 5- to 10-centimetre-high stalks directly from the narrow rhizomes. Small starlike white to pink flowers are produced throughout much of the summer. The selection 'Klamath Ruby' has leaves with purple undersides.

This oxalis prefers dappled shade but tolerates deep shade. Organically rich, acidic soil is ideal. Once established, it tolerates some drought. Overall, it is care-free. Propagation is by division. The deciduous form is hardy to zone 4; the evergreen is suitable only in zone 7 or warmer.

Design tips: Try combining this oxalis with Japanese painted fern, golden hakone grass, and other spring ephemerals. It is also ideal as an underplanting beneath rhododendrons and various hazels.

PERSICARIA
Fleeceflower, bistort

Like several other plant genera, this group of plants has recently gone through name changes. In earlier literature, most of the following were included in *Polygonum*, but this genus is now split into several new genera and many of the garden-worthy species have been moved to the genus *Persicaria*.

As a group, the ornamental species produce narrow spikes of tiny flowers, usually white through various shades of pink. Several have attractive foliage. However, as most are robust plants, they are not suitable for smaller gardens. The height range is variable, depending on the species. Dwarf fleeceflower, *P. affine*, is among the lower, with matted, narrow leathery leaves that take on burgundy tones in autumn. Throughout the summer, it produces red to pink spikes on stems up to 20 centimetres tall. At only 10 centimetres is the similar creeping

Persicaria polymorpha

fleeceflower, *P. vaccinifolium*. Pink bistort, *P. bistorta* 'Superba', forms a spreading mound with narrow triangular leaves and many spikes of soft pink flowers on 75-centimetre-tall stems. A rapid spreader, it can swamp timid neighbours. Its flowers are suitable as a cut flower.

Mountain fleeceflower, *P. amplexicaulis*, has a bushy habit and forms spreading mounds 45 to 95 centimetres tall. It has heart-shaped foliage and numerous narrow spikes from mid-summer through autumn. Popular cultivars include 'Orange Field' (salmon rose, 95 centimetres tall), 'Taurus' (crimson red, 75 centimetres), and 'Pink Elephant' (pink, 45 centimetres). White or giant fleeceflower, *P. polymorpha*, appears shrublike and forms a large clump up to 120 centimetres high. It has relatively large narrow leaves and numerous fluffy spikes of off-white flowers from late July to early September. Despite its size, it is less prone to spreading than many *Persicaria*. Grown for its fantastic foliage is tovara, *P. virginiana* 'Painter's Palette'. It is also a neat shrublike plant and can reach 120 or more centimetres. Although it produces narrow deep pink spikes in September and October, its foliage is its selling feature; its large, rounded leaves are irregularly splashed and spotted with white, along with a central pink V-shaped blotch. It is late to appear in spring, so carefully mark the spot where was planted.

Fleeceflower may be grown in sun or partial shade. Most of the ornamental varieties prefer evenly moist, organically rich soil. They are not generally bothered by any diseases or pests. Pink bistort, white fleeceflower, and dwarf fleeceflower are hardy through zone 3; mountain and creeping fleeceflower to zone 4; while tovara is the least hardy, useful in zone 5 or milder.

Design tips: Pink bistort may be used as a large ground cover but dwarf fleeceflower is less aggressive and perhaps better suited for this purpose. Creeping fleeceflower may also be used as a ground cover but is not as robust; it is perhaps better in a rock garden. Mountain fleeceflower may be used in a border. Large and shrublike giant fleeceflower and tovara may be stand-alone plants or planted in the back of a border.

Phlox stolonifera

PHLOX
Woodland phlox

The genus *Phlox* is exclusive to North America, with some 67 species. There are two main woodland phlox. Creeping phlox, *Phlox stolonifera*, produces leafy, creeping stems and rosettes. It is native throughout much of the Appalachians. In late spring, plants produce loose clusters of fragrant, lavender flowers on 20- to 30-centimetre-high stems. As the name suggests, 'Sherwood Purple' is a darker purple selection. Wild blue phlox, *Phlox divaricata*, is similar but larger, with

stems that reach 30 to 45 centimetres tall. It is also native to the eastern US but is more widespread than creeping phlox. Popular cultivars include 'Clouds of Perfume', 'Blue Moon', and 'May Breeze', the latter pale ice blue.

These woodland phlox prefer partial shade and organically rich soil that stays evenly moist but, once established, tolerate some drought. These phlox attract butterflies and hummingbirds. Woodland phlox are susceptible to powdery mildew; adequate spacing and good air circulation help alleviate this problem. The main insect pest is spittlebugs, which may cause the leaves to become curled. Deer, moose, and hares generally ignore them. Propagation is by division or cuttings. Wild blue phlox is hardy to zone 3; creeping phlox is rated for zone 5 or milder.

Design tips: Use woodland phlox in a wildflower garden; they combine well with similar eastern woodlanders such as cornlily, *Trillium*, *Anemone*, and bunchberry.

PHYSOSTEGIA VIRGINIANA
Obedient plant

The 12 species of *Physostegia* are all native to North America. The most popular as a garden ornamental is *P. virginiana*, a native wildflower throughout much of the US. This narrow upright plant produces many unbranched stems that may reach 120 centimetres in length. The sharply toothed, narrow leaves are paired and relatively shiny. From late summer through autumn, plants produce 30- to 45-centimetre-long spikes of pink to pale lilac, narrow, snapdragon-

Physostegia virginiana

like flowers. It is particularly valued for its late blooms which help extend a garden's season of interest. It is a favourite plant for hummingbirds and bees and suitable as cut flowers. Named selections include 'Bouquet Rose' (bright pink, 120 centimetres), 'Red Beauty' (lilac pink, 90 centimetres), 'Miss Manners' (white, 90 centimetres), and 'Summer Snow' (white, 90 centimetres). More recently, there have been some compact selections which reach only 50 centimetres, such as 'Crystal Peak White' and 'Vivid'. For attractive foliage and flowers, try 'Variegata', which has white-edged leaves and lavender-pink flowers and reaches 90 centimetres tall.

Obedient plant prefers evenly moist, acidic soil that is not too organically rich; otherwise, the plants may flop. Full sun is best, but plants perform well in partial shade. Overall, it is a care-free plant. Propagation is by seed or division. It is hardy through zone 3.

Design tips: Obedient plant is ideal for a mid- to back border but is also suitable for wildflower, cottage, or rain gardens.

PINELLIA CORDATA
Miniature green dragon

This unusual *Arisaema* relative is native to China. Although other species of *Pinellia* can be invasive, *P. cordata* is well behaved. It forms clumps with arrow-shaped leaves up to 15 centimetres high. The dark green leaves are veined in silvery white and have purple-tinted undersides. Hooded green flowers have a protruding rattail-like extension, making them particularly bizarre when blooming in late summer. Provide it with humus-rich, evenly moist acidic soil in partial to full

Pinellia cordata

shade. Plants produce little bulbils which facilitate propagation. It is hardy to zone 5.

Design tips: With their small size, *Pinellia* suit a shady rock garden or toward the front of a woodland garden where their distinct flowers and attractive foliage can be best appreciated.

PLATYCODON GRANDIFLORUS
Balloon flower

The genus *Platycodon* has a single species: *P. grandiflorus*, a bellflower relative native to eastern Asia. The genus name comes from the Greek *platys*, meaning broad, and *codon*, meaning bell. The plant forms a clump with several unbranched stems arising from a thick taproot. The wild form can reach 80 or more centimetres, but many of the named selections are smaller in stature. The flowers are produced in loose clusters at the ends of the stems in mid- to late summer. The flower buds are large and look balloon-like immediately before they burst open to reveal the 5- to 8-centimetre-wide, outward-facing,

Platycodon grandiflorus 'Nana'

Podophyllum delavayi

bell-shaped flowers. The original wild colour is purple blue, but modern selections may be pink, mauve, white, or white with blue veins. Recommended selections include the 'Fuji' series, which are blue, pink, or white and reach 60 centimetres tall, and the dwarf 25-centimetre-tall 'Astra' series in the same colour range. The smallest is 'Sentimental Blue', which is only 20 centimetres tall. Double-flowered selections include 'Double Blue', which reaches 60 centimetres tall, and the dwarf version 'Astra Double Blue' at 25 centimetres.

Balloon flowers prefer full sun but tolerate partial shade. They need even moisture and like an organically rich soil yet they dislike excess winter wetness. As they are taprooted, they dislike being transplanted: set them as young plants and leave them to improve each year. Balloon flowers are late to emerge in the spring, so mark the spot carefully lest you accidentally think that it died during the winter. The blossoms are suitable cut flowers. Pests and diseases are uncommon but snails and slugs may be problematic. Propagation is by seed. Balloon flower is hardy to zone 3.

Design tips: The taller forms of balloon flower are ideal for a mid-border but the dwarfs may be used both along the front of a border or in rock gardens.

PODOPHYLLUM
Mayapple

Of the nine species of *Podophyllum*, one is native to North America and the rest to Asia. The name comes from the Latin *podos*, meaning foot, and *phyllon*, meaning leaf, in reference to the footlike leaf shape of the American mayapple, *P. peltatum*. The American mayapple, native in southern Ontario, Quebec, and points farther south in the US, is an attractive plant with parasol-like leaves. Each 30- to 45-centimetre-tall stem has either a single leaf or a pair of leaves. In mid- to late spring, plants produce a nodding white flower held under the paired leaves. This later develops into a yellow applelike fruit. The problem with this species is that it can run quickly, swamping its neighbours, and may go summer-dormant, leaving a bare patch in the garden.

Far more desirable are the Asian species. The most popular is the Himalayan mayapple, *P. hexandrum*. The best forms have leaves that emerge olive green with plenty of brown mottling. A clumper, it stays tidy in the garden and does not go summer-dormant. Its leaves are also single or paired on each 50-centimetre-tall stem. In mid- to late spring, it produces a single white to pink flower that sits atop the paired leaves. This later becomes a red, teardrop-shaped, tomato-like fruit. Expensive but choice are selections of *P. delavayi*, *P. versipelle*, and *P. pleianthum*. These have leaves in uncommon shapes: umbrellas or starfish or even squares! They may be plain green or brown spotted. The selection 'Spotty Dotty' is particularly attractive. These clumpers have either single or paired leaves on 30- to 50-centimetre-tall stems. Their flowers are red, in nodding clusters beneath the paired leaves, and later develop green fruit. Like Japanese wood poppy, Glaucidium, these expensive plants are a worthwhile investment, as they are long-lived and improve with age.

Mayapple prefer partial shade and evenly

moist, organically rich soil. They are not bothered by diseases and the most likely pest is slugs feeding on the fresh spring growth. Propagation is by seed, or, more commonly, by division. American mayapple is hardy to zone 4, Himalayan to zone 5, and the remaining Chinese species to zone 6. However, if provided a good winter mulch, the Chinese species should survive in zone 5.

Design tips: Mayapple are ideal under deciduous trees where they get more sun in the spring when actively growing and blooming, but more even shade in mid-summer. In a border, use the Chinese species near the front where their decorative leaves can be best appreciated. American mayapple is best used in a woodland or wildflower setting. Combine any of the mayapples with ferns, trillium, and astilbe for contrasting leaf forms.

Polygonatum X hybridum

POLYGONATUM
Solomon's-seal

Around 60 species of *Polygonatum* are found throughout the northern hemisphere, but most commonly in Asia. The genus name comes from the Greek *poly*, meaning many, and *gonu*, meaning knee joint, in reference to the jointed plant rhizomes. As a group, their flowers are modest; they are grown more for their foliage, which is bright green, distinctively ribbed, and located on either side of arching stems. Primarily in North America two species and the hybrid between them are grown. Solomon's-seal, *P. multiflorum*, a European native, is nearly identical to, and often confused with, hybrid Solomon's-seal, *P. X hybridum*. Both *P. multiflorum* and *P. X hybridum* can reach 125 centimetres tall

and produce 2-centimetre-long, bell-shaped, nodding white flowers with green tips in 2s or 3s from the upper leaf axils. They bloom from mid- to late spring and have a light fragrance. The common Solomon's-seal later produces blue-black berries, while the hybrid is sterile, never producing fruit—this characteristic differentiates the two. Both have variegated versions but they are difficult to obtain.

Originally from Asia, the fragrant Solomon's-seal, *P. odoratum*, is a smaller stature plant, reaching about 60 centimetres tall. Its flowers are almost invariably in pairs and are highly fragrant. It also develops blue-black berries later in the season. The most popular is the variegated selection 'Variegatum'.

Solomon's-seal prefer organically rich,

evenly moist soil in full sun to dense shade. All spread by rhizomes and form large colonies. Fragrant Solomon's-seal is generally slower growing than the other two. All parts of the plant are toxic if consumed by humans. Propagation is mostly by division. Pests and disease are not a problem, but they can be relished by deer and moose. The common and hybrid Solomon's-seal are hardy to zone 2; the fragrant is hardy to zone 3.

Design tips: Common and hybrid Solomon's-seal are useful for the back of a border, while the fragrant is better suited to a mid-border. With their moisture requirements, all are also appropriate for rain gardens and their vigorous habit suits their wildflower settings. They contrast well with ferns, hosta, and astilbe.

PRIMULA
Primrose

Because there are over 500 species of *Primula*, and innumerable hybrids, the following description does not do them justice. For simplicity, they have been divided into early bloomers (early to mid-spring) and late bloomers (late spring to early summer). Among the early bloomers, the most popular are the English primroses, *Primula* X *polyanthus*, hybrids between *P. vulgaris* and *P. veris*. These have been highly bred over the centuries and now include every conceivable colour, with both single and double forms. Some selections have solitary flowers but most produce flowers in small clusters. Closely related and blooming concurrently are the Julian primroses, *P.* X *pruhonicensis*. These have masses of solitary flowers in rich magenta, red, and pink shades. The popular species *P. veris*, cowslip, and *P. elatior*, oxlip, are readily available.

The other popular group of early bloomers are the drumstick primroses, *P. denticulata*. Although the previous groups are European in origin, the drumsticks are from the Himalayas of Kashmir. The wild form has lilac flowers but modern selections come in a range of colours from white through shades of purple and pink to nearly red, all with a contrasting yellow eye. The flowers are produced in perfect spheres on stems reaching 30 centimetres tall.

The late bloomers are all native to eastern Asia. One of the largest groups of later-flowering primroses are the Candelabra or Japanese primroses. These produce a basal rosette of leaves from which rise unbranched, naked stems reaching 45 to 60 centimetres tall. The flowers are produced in several whorls, each above the other. Flower colours include white, shades of pink to nearly red, purple shades, yellow and orange, all with striking yellow eyes. This group contains several species and hybrids: *P. pulverulenta*, *P. japonica*, *P. beesiana*, *P. bulleyana*, and *P. chungensis*, among others. Requiring similar conditions and blooming a little later are *P. florindae*, which can reach 60 to 90 centimetres tall. Its yellow, orange, or red flowers are produced in nodding clusters.

The other group of later-flowering primroses are low-growing clumpers with rounded, maplelike foliage. They reach 20 to 30 centimetres tall and have flowers in shades of pink. These include *P. heucherifolia*, *P. cortusoides*, and *P. sieboldii*. Another species which may not bloom until as late as mid-summer is *P. capitata*. Its flowers are deep purple and produced in a dense, rounded cluster, similar to those of the drumstick primrose. The undersides of their spoon-shaped leaves are covered in a white powder. *P. vialii* produces a rocketlike flower spike on stems up to 45 centimetres tall. The lavender-pink flowers emerge from a contrasting red calyx. It is among the last primrose to bloom, often well into mid-summer.

English and drumstick primroses prefer partial shade and organically rich, evenly moist soil. The later-blooming primroses prefer full sun and acidic, organically rich soil that stays moist; they suffer even in slight drought. Drumsticks and candelabra primroses make admirable cut flowers. All primroses are visited by bees and butterflies. Diseases are not generally a problem but pests include slugs, snails, and root weevils.

Primula japonica

Propagation may be by seed or, more commonly, by division. All the above are hardy to zone 3.

Design tips: Early-blooming primroses are ideal for the front of a border or in rock gardens. English, drumstick, and candelabra primroses are also appropriate in woodland gardens or near water features. Candelabra primroses are also suitable for rain gardens.

PULMONARIA
Lungwort

There are about a dozen species of *Pulmonaria*, primarily native to Europe. The Latin name is derived from the Latin *pulmo*, which means lung, in reference to the spotted leaves that look like a human lung. In the garden, the most common are *P. officinalis* and *P. saccharata*, both of which have white spotted leaves and nodding clusters of flowers, from early to late spring, which change from pink to blue as they age. They form spreading evergreen clumps up to 30 centimetres tall. The difference between the two species is subtle and many of the named selections are hybrids between them. Some have permanently blue flowers, such as 'Purple Haze' (purple blue) and 'Roy Davidson' (pale blue), while others have pink flowers, such as 'Bubble Gum' and 'Dora Bielefeld'. Pure white selections include 'Sissinghurt White' and 'Opal'. However, the main recent breeding emphasis has been on developing plants with all-silver foliage. Perhaps the most popular of these are 'Majeste' and 'Excalibur', which have nearly pure silver foliage. Others with silver coloration include 'Moonshine', 'Silver

Shimmers', 'Silver Bouquet', and 'High Contrast'. Perhaps the most visually striking selection is 'Raspberry Ice'; it has grey-green leaves spotted and edged in white and raspberry pink flowers.

Of similar size and habit is *P. angustifolia*. This species has plain green deciduous leaves and brilliant blue flowers. 'Azurea' and 'Blue Ensign' are common selections. A little larger in size, reaching 45 centimetres tall, is *P. rubra*. This species also has plain green leaves but they are evergreen; their flowers are a deep coral pink. It blooms so early that it may be in flower as the snow melts around it. 'Redstart' is the most popular selection. For decorative foliage, try 'David Ward', whose leaves are edged in white. Less commonly seen but worthwhile to find is *P. longifolia* ssp. *cevennensis* or *P. longifolia* 'Bertram Anderson'. Both have heavily spotted, narrow, deciduous leaves and bright blue flowers. It blooms a little later than the other lungwort species. This species spreads by underground runners but it is not invasive.

Lungwort prefer organically rich, moisture-retentive but well-drained soil. They suffer greatly if they become too dry. If the soil is reasonably moist, they tolerate full sun; otherwise, partial shade is best. They even tolerate reasonably heavy shade. Lungwort are an important early pollen and nectar source for bees. Pests are not a problem but mildew can be in some areas. Propagation is by division. Most lungwort are hardy to zone 3, but *P. rubra* is a little tenderer, rated for zone 4.

Design tips: Lungwort are indispensable subjects for an early spring border. They may also be used in woodland and rain gardens. After flowering, cut the plants back and you'll

Pulmonaria 'Raspberry Ice'

Rodgersia podophylla

be rewarded with attractive foliage for the remainder of the season. Their decorative foliage contrasts well with hosta, ferns, and astilbe.

RODGERSIA
Rodgersia

The five species of *Rodgersia* are all native to the woodland regions of eastern Asia. The genus was named for US admiral John Rodgers, commander of the expedition which discovered *R. podophylla* in the 1850s. Today, four of the species are available on the market and are grown for both their bold foliage and large astilbe-like plumes of white or pale pink flowers produced in early summer. All produce thick rhizomes from which arise a clump of compound leaves up to 100 centimetres tall. The flowers arise on stems up to 150 centimetres tall. The most common is *R. podophylla*, which has palmately compound leaves with five to seven leaflets with jagged edges. There are two named selections: 'Braunlaub' has bronzed foliage and 'Rotlaub', whose newly emerging leaves are vivid red, becoming bronzed as they mature. Both can be shy bloomers and are grown primarily for their foliage. A quickly spreading species, it needs plenty of room. *Rodgersia aesculifolia* is similar but its leaves have serrated edges and it is a more reliable bloomer, with white or pale pink plumes. 'Irish Bronze' and 'Cherry Blush' have distinctly bronzed foliage.

Rodgersia pinnata resembles *R. aesculifolia* but its leaflets are pinnately compound rather than palmately compound and its flowers are usually pink. 'Elegans' and 'Superba' both have green leaves but darker pink plumes;

'Fireworks' has bronze-edged leaves; and 'Chocolate Wings' has deep bronze leaves. *Rodgersia sambucifolia* has similar pinnate leaves but typically white flowers.

All *Rodgersia* prefer partial shade and evenly moist, humus-rich soil. Intense sun can scorch the foliage. Their leaves are early to emerge in the spring and may be damaged by late frosts: avoid low-lying areas. The flowers attract bees and butterflies. Diseases are rare but slugs and snails may sometimes damage the newly emerging leaves. Larger herbivores ignore them. Propagation may be by seed, but is more commonly by division, particularly the named selections. They are reliably hardy in zone 5 but, if given a thick winter mulch, are worth trying in zone 4.

Design tips: Choose *Rodgersia* for waterside, woodland, or rain gardens. In a border, position them mid-range so that their foliage can be best appreciated. Combine them with other bold perennials such as *Ligularia*, *Astilboides*, and ostrich fern.

SANGUINARIA CANADENSIS
Bloodroot

The sole species of *Sanguinaria*, *S. canadensis*, is a woodland species found throughout eastern North America. A classic harbinger of spring, it is an early-blooming wildflower. Plants form large colonies as they spread by thick, red rhizomes, which ooze red sap when cut. Each shoot produces a single matte grey-green basal leaf that is rounded with five to nine narrow but deep lobes. When fully expanded, the leaves may arise 20 to 50 centimetres with individual leaves up to 20 centimetres wide. The flowers are solitary,

Sanguinaria canadensis 'Rosea'

Sanguisorba obtusa

up to 5 centimetres wide, arising on naked flower stems that are clasped by the emerging leaf. Each flower has eight to 12 white petals surrounding a cluster of yellow stamens. The flowers are short-lived. The flowers of the double-flowered cultivar 'Multiplex' last a little longer.

Bloodroot prefers evenly moist, organically rich, acidic soil. It tolerates drought later in the season but may go summer-dormant under such conditions. Partial to full shade is best. Propagation is by division or seed; seed propagation is slower. Few pests or diseases bother bloodroot. It is hardy through zone 3.

Design tips: Bloodroot is an ideal ground cover beneath high-canopy trees and shrubs. Suggested companion plants are *Arisaema*, *Clintonia*, *Uvularia*, and various ferns.

SANGUISORBA
Burnet

Of the 20 or so species of *Sanguisorba*, all are native to the northern hemisphere. The genus name comes from the Latin *sanguis*, blood, and *sorbere*, to soak up, from the reputed power of these plants to stop bleeding. It is not often seen in gardens but, with its attractive architectural elements, it will probably become more popular as plant breeders begin to realize the plant's potential. As a group, all form large mounds with many basal, pinnate leaves that give the plant a fernlike appearance. From mid- to late summer, upright stems arise 90 to 120 centimetres tall, topped with many bottlebrush-like flowers ranging from burgundy red to white, depending on the species.

Canada burnet, *S. canadensis*, native to northeast North America, usually grows near the sea or along larger rivers. This plant has lovely grey-green leaves and stiffly upright, white bottlebrush flowers 10 to 20 centimetres long. Japanese burnet, *S. obtusa*, is similar but its leaves are bright green and its flowers are arching and bright pink. Alaskan burnet, *S. menziesii*, is a look-alike but its maroon flowers contrast wonderfully with blue-tinted foliage. Great burnet, *S. officinalis*, has leaves similar to those of the preceding species but are rather small oval-shaped bottlebrushes. The regular species is pale pink and not as showy, but 'Tanna' and 'Red Thunder' are maroon and look like an airier version of the Alaskan burnet. For lovers of variegated foliage, try *S. minor* 'Little Angel', which forms a compact mound with white-edged leaves and small deep pink bottlebrushes on 60-centimetre-tall stems.

All the burnets are moisture-lovers and do not tolerate drought. They are best in full sun with organically rich soil, but tolerate some shade. The blossoms make a good cut flower. Overall, they are care-free plants. Propagation is by division. Canada burnet is rated hardy to zone 3; the remaining, zone 4.

Design tips: As burnet are rather robust, they should be used with caution in a border, but for a wildflower or rain garden or near water features, they are ideal subjects.

SARRACENIA
Pitcher-plant

The 11 species of *Sarracenia* hail from North America. The genus was named in honour of Michel Sarrazin, a French doctor who sent specimens of pitcher-plants to Europe. The most widely distributed species is the purple pitcher-plant, *S. purpurea*, found from Newfoundland to Alberta and south to Florida. The remaining species are primarily restricted to the southeastern US. Many, with the exception of *S. purpurea*, are endangered species due to habitat destruction. There are many hybrids. All produce a rosette of unusual and unique pitcherlike leaves that hold water. These leaves vary in length from 15 to 60 centimetres, depending on the species. The leaves may be green to red to purple, with various coloured spots and veins. Some, like *S. purpurea*, are evergreen; others go dormant in winter. All are carnivorous and take advantage of digesting insects that fall into the pitchers, but they survive well even if they do not have access to insects. The solitary flowers, which are as unusual as the leaves, are held above the foliage in late spring to early summer. They resemble an upside-down umbrella. They may be red, purple to pink, white, or yellow.

Among the best garden species are *S. purpurea, S. flava, S. rubra*, and *S. leucophylla*. Some noteworthy hybrids include 'Dixie Lace', 'Flies Demise', 'Ladies in Waiting', and 'Mardi Gras', but, in reality, all the species and hybrids are spectacular.

As *Sarracenia* require consistent high moisture, they are mostly restricted to culture in bog gardens or specialized containers without drainage holes. The best rooting media is pure peat moss, but a peat-sand mix is also effective. The pH must be below 5. Full sun is required to develop the best floral and foliage colours. Propagation is by division but most commercially sold plants have

Sarracenia purpurea

been propagated by tissue culture. *Sarracenia purpurea* is hardy to zone 3; the others are best in zones 5 to 6.

Design tips: Pitcher-plants are exotic-looking subjects for a bog garden. Generally, they are grown in the wettest part of a bog garden; in slightly drier areas, use *Primula japonica*, *Iris versicolor*, *Iris ensata*, Helonias, and ornamental *Carex* as companions.

SARUMA HENRYI
Upright wild ginger

The sole species of *Saruma*, *S. henryi*, is native to the forests and streamsides of China. A clumping plant with unbranched stems reaching 60 centimetres tall, its leaves are heart-shaped and covered in downy hairs which lend them a silvery appearance when they first emerge in spring. Showy, three-

Saruma henryi

petalled, yellow flowers up to 2.5 centimetres wide bloom from the leaf axils in late spring and sporadically throughout the rest of the summer. This plant is similar in foliage appearance to the wild gingers, Asarum. In fact, the genus name *Saruma* is an anagram of Asarum!

Saruma prefers full to dappled shade and well-drained but evenly moist, humus-rich soil that is at least slightly acidic. It tolerates some drought once it is established. It is overall a care-free plant, with few pests or diseases. Propagation is by seed or, more commonly, division. It is hardy to zone 5.

Design tips: *Saruma* blends well with other woodlanders such as ferns, hosta, *Trillium*, and Japanese forest grass.

STREPTOPUS
Twisted-stalk

Seven species of twisted-stalk exist worldwide, three in North America, the others are Eurasian. From a gardening perspective, two main species are grown: white twisted stalk, *S. amplexifolius*, and rose twisted-stalk, *S. lanceolatus* (formerly *S. roseus*). Both species are found across much of North America and have oval to lance-shaped ribbed leaves and solitary, nodding lilylike flowers from among the upper leaf axils in mid-spring to early summer. The former has white flowers, the latter pink; both produce orange-red berries later in the season. Typically, the white twisted-stalk reaches 90 to 120 centimetres tall; the rose twisted-stalk is shorter, at 30 to 60 centimetres.

Twisted-stalk prefer organically rich, moisture-retentive, acidic soil. Dappled

Streptopus lanceolatus

Symphyotrichum novi-belgii 'Brocade'

shade is ideal but full shade is tolerated. Propagation is by division. Few pests or diseases bother them. They are rated hardy to zone 2.

Design tips: Twisted-stalk are classic woodland plants and combine well with similar-needs plants such as bellwort, ferns, *Clintonia*, and fairybells.

SYMPHYOTRICHUM
Michaelmas daisy

The fall-blooming Michaelmas daisy, once classified and still often known as Aster, are now known botanically as *Symphyotrichum*. This genus has about 80 species, mostly native to North America. The tallest is the New England aster, *S. novae-angliae*, which forms a clump of stems 1 to 2 metres tall, topped with clusters of pink-purple daisies from late summer to mid-fall. 'September Ruby' (reddish pink), 'Alma Potschke' (pink), and 'Hella Lacy' (lavender blue) reach 120 centimetres. Dwarf cultivars, such as 'Purple Dome' and 'Vibrant Dome', reach about 50 centimetres and are appropriate for smaller gardens.

New York aster, *S. novi-belgii*, often grows by the sea. It ranges from 30 to 100 centimetres in height, is domed and bushy, and typically has lavender-blue flowers in late summer or early fall. Garden forms range in colour from white through pink to deep red and lavender blue to dark purple blue. Taller cultivars reaching 60 centimetres include 'Blue Lagoon', 'Diana' (pink), 'Porcelain' (pale blue), 'Crimson Brocade' (reddish violet), and 'Winston Churchill' (light purple pink). Around 45 centimetres in height are 'White

Swan', 'White Opal', and 'Royal Ruby'. The lowest, at 30 centimetres tall, are sometimes called *S. dumosum* in the trade but chances are they are simply dwarf forms of *S. novi-belgii*. They include 'Violet Carpet', 'Pink Beauty', 'Lady in Blue', 'Hein Richard' (magenta), 'Jenny' (magenta), 'Alert' (reddish purple), 'Professor Anton Kippenberg' (deep violet blue), and the Woods series (variable colours).

Hybrid Michaelmas daisies, including the Kickin® series, are available in a variety of standard aster colours. They form dense mounding plants up to 60 centimetres in height and smother themselves in blossoms. Another Michaelmas daisy worth trying is heath aster, *S. ericoides*. Although it may reach 100 centimetres tall, this species forms a dense mound, smothered in tiny daisies. Named cultivars include 'Earl King' (pale lavender), 'Pink Cloud' (pale pink), 'Snow Flurry' (white), and 'Lovely' (violet purple).

All of the above prefer full sun and well-drained, evenly moist soil. They are not at all fussy about soil pH and grow well under acidic conditions. All are suitable cut flowers and are magnets for bees and butterflies. The main disease is powdery mildew, if grown in a too-sheltered site. Spittlebugs can cause curled foliage, but otherwise these species are not bothered by insect pests. Herbivores usually ignore them. Propagation is by division. All are hardy to zone 4, with New York aster hardy to zone 3.

Design tips: Depending on their mature height, Michaelmas daisy may be used in the back, middle, or front of a border. They also suit a cottage or wildflower garden. New York aster is particularly well suited to seaside gardens.

THALICTRUM
Meadow-rue

Over 100 species of *Thalictrum* grow in the northern hemisphere, but as a garden plant they are not particularly well known—though several are well suited to a garden with acidic soil. *Thalictrum rochebruneanum*, known as lavender mist meadow-rue, is a tall 2-metre-high slender plant with lacy blue-tinted foliage reminiscent of columbine or maidenhair fern. From mid- to late summer, plants produce airy sprays of small, pendant, lavender flowers with a tuft of yellow stamens. Similar in appearance is *T. delavayi* 'Hewitt's

Thalictrum aquilegiifolium

Double', whose flowers are a deeper purple and fully double like miniature pompoms. A little more compact, to 120 centimetres in height, is *T. aquilegiifolium*, which has denser clusters of lavender mauve flowers. The selection 'Black Stockings' has striking black stems. Yellow meadow-rue, *Thalictrum flavum* 'Illuminator', has blue-tinted foliage and lemon yellow fluffy flower clusters.

If space is limited, try *T. kiusianum*, dwarf meadow-rue, which reaches only 15 centimetres tall. It has maidenhair-like foliage and open airy clusters of lilac flowers. Grown for its foliage rather than its flowers

is *T. ichangense* 'Evening Star'. It has maroon-purple foliage with a central silver "star" of whitened veins and it forms a clump up to 30 centimetres tall.

Meadow-rue prefer full sun to partial shade and organically rich soil that stays reasonably moist, but they have poor tolerance to salt or drought. Pests and diseases are not a probem. The flowers are suitable cut flowers, similar in appearance to baby's-breath. Propagation is by seed or division but divisions take several years to settle back in. With adequate winter mulch, most should survive to zone 4.

Design tips: Use the taller meadow-rue to naturalize moist open woodlands or wildflower meadows. Their height also makes them ideal specimens near water features or in rain gardens. The dwarf types are lovely plants for a moist, partly shaded rock garden or border edges.

TIARELLA
Foamflower

Of the five species of *Tiarella*, two are from North America and three from Asia. Creeping foamflower, *Tiarella cordifolia*, is native to eastern North America; the wild form has basal, evergreen, maplelike leaves and spikes of tiny white to pale pink, star-shaped flowers atop 25-centimetre-tall stems in late spring. Plants form large mats through the production of stolons. The leaves of the cultivar 'Running Tapestry' have dark, nearly black veins. *Tiarella wherryi*, a runnerless version of *T. cordifolia*, forms discrete clumps. It looks much like coralbells, *Heuchera*, and, in fact, have been hybridized with them to

Tiarella cordifolia

create X *Heucherella*. Like many *Heuchera*, most of the modern selections of foamflower are grown for their decorative leaves. Although the selections are not as numerous as in *Heuchera*, in recent years many new cultivars have been produced. Most of these have varying amounts of black veins and/or vary in the degree of divisions and leaf lobing. Selections include 'Sugar and Spice', 'Neon Lights', 'Iron Butterfly', 'Cascade Creeper', and 'Black Snowflake', the latter with nearly black leaves. 'Candy Stripper' has the deepest-cut foliage, while the leaves of 'Crow Feather' take on pink and red tones during the winter months. 'Pink Skyrocket' has green leaves but has been selected for its pink blossoms.

X *Heucherella* are also grown for their evergreen foliage. Their often pink flowers are similar to those of foamflowers but with the bolder foliage colours of *Heuchera*. 'Sunspot', 'Stoplight', 'Gold Zebra', and 'Mojito' have yellow to chartreuse leaves with red veins. With more orange-toned leaves are 'Sweet Tea', 'Honey Rose', 'Buttered Rum', and 'Brass Lantern'. 'Redstone Falls' has a striking blend of red, gold, orange, and bronze with distinctive dark veins on a plant that trails. 'Solar Eclipse' has nearly black leaves with a green margin.

Tiarella and X *Heucherella* both prefer partial shade and evenly moist, acidic soil. Although they tolerate full shade, under those conditions their foliar colours are less vibrant. Despite their need for moisture, they do not tolerate winter wetness; the soil must be well drained. Diseases are generally not a problem and the main pests are slugs and root weevils. Hares may nibble the leaves too. Propagation is by division. Both are hardy to zone 4 but are more reliably evergreen in zone 5 or warmer.

Design tips: Creeping foamflower may be used as a ground cover in shady areas. *Tiarella wherryi* and X *Heucherella* hybrids may be used along the edges of borders, in woodland gardens, and in shady rock gardens.

TRICYRTIS
Toad lily

All 16 species of *Tricyrtis* are native to eastern Asia. The genus name comes from the Greek *tri*, three, and *kyrtos*, humped, as the bases of the three outer petals are swollen. As a group, they are woodland plants with heart- to teardrop-shaped leaves positioned alternately along the unbranched stems. Small, usually spotted, lilylike flowers are produced among the upper leaf axils or at the ends of the stems. Most grow 60 to 90 centimetres tall.

With mid-summer blooms is *T. latifolia*. This species grows 60 centimetres tall and has straw yellow flowers spotted with brown. 'Yellow Sunrise' has paler, butter yellow flowers with cinnamon brown spots. *Tricyrtis hirta* is a later-flowering species, blooming from late summer to early fall. It grows to 90 centimetres tall and typically has white flowers heavily spotted with dark purple. 'Miyazaki' has pale pink flowers with darker pink spots. 'Albomarginata' is grown for its cream-edged leaves. *Tricyrtis formosana* is similar. 'Seiryu' is pale violet blue with darker purple spots; 'Dark Beauty' is heavily spotted in purple. This species' variegated selections include 'Gilt Edge', 'Samurai', and 'Autumn Glow'. 'Guilty Pleasure' has pure yellow foliage that may be appreciated without its mauve-pink flowers. Several fall-blooming

Tricyrtis formosana

Trillium luteum

hybrids are available: 'Empress', white with dark purple spots; 'Blue Wonder', whose blossoms are heavily spotted in purple blue; 'Togen', whose flowers are lavender mauve and unspotted; and 'Shirohotogisu', with pure white flowers. The leaves of 'Lightning Strike' are streaked with cream.

Reaching 45 centimetres and arching in habit is *T. macrantha*. It has nodding, bell-like yellow flowers with heavy red spotting in the throat, blooming from late summer to early fall. Similar in habit and height but with upward-facing, lilylike nearly pure yellow flowers are *T. perfoliata* and *T. flava*.

Toad lilies prefer shade to partial shade and soil that is evenly moist, organically rich, and acidic. They are not fond of drought. Diseases are not a probem but slugs can damage the newly unfurling leaves. Unfortunately, they may be browsed by deer and moose. Propagation is by division. *Tricyrtis latifolia* and *T. hirta* are both rated for zone 4; *T. formosana* and the hybrids, zone 5; and *T. macrantha*, *T. perfoliata*, and *T. flava*, zone 6.

Design tips: Plant toad lilies in a woodland garden or near the front of a border. With their love of moisture, they are also suitable for rain gardens.

TRILLIUM
Trillium, wakerobin

The nearly 40 species of *Trillium* are confined to North America and East Asia. All trillium form spreading clumps with thickened rhizomes and unbranched stems that are topped with a single trifoliate leaf and a solitary three-petalled flower. Heights vary from 15 to 45 centimetres, depending on the species. Bloom time is also variable, from early to late spring. Among the easiest to grow, and most widely available, are the white and red trillium. White trillium, *T. grandiflorum*, is perhaps the showiest of the species, with the largest flowers, up to 9 centimetres wide. The snow-white flowers often turn pink as they age. Very expensive but highly desirable double forms exist. Western trillium, *T. ovatum*, is similar but has slightly smaller flowers. Red wakerobin, *T. erectum*, has showy purple-red flowers. While painted trillium, *T. undulatum*, is one of the most beautiful, with its white flowers and central pink veins, it is also one of the most difficult to grow in cultivation. Snow trillium, *T. nivale*, is among the smallest, at 15 centimetres tall, and earliest flowering. It has white blossoms and grey-green leaves. Several trillium have nodding flowers. *Trillium flexipes* has white flowers; *T. cernuum*, greenish white; and *T. catesbaei*, soft pink. For decorative foliage, try the yellow toad trillium, *T. luteum*, or red toad trillium, *T. sessile*, and *T. cuneatum*. These have unassuming stemless flowers that sit atop the leaves, but the foliage is mottled and spotted silvery green. Their fragrant flowers are the last to bloom of the trilliums, well into late spring. Although there are many other garden-worthy trillium, they are generally only available in specialist nurseries. *T. rivale*, now *Pseudotrillium rivale*, has grey-green leaves with silvery veins and white flowers beautifully peppered with pink spots.

Trillium are best grown in partial shade with acidic, humus-rich, evenly moist soil. If the soil is too dry, they go summer-dormant. Diseases are rare, although fungal leaf spot is occasional, and the main pests are browsing herbivores, slugs, and snails. Propagation may be by seed, but these can take two years to germinate; propagation by division is more popular. Most of the above trillium are hardy to zone 4, but the mottled-leaved types are better for zone 5 or warmer.

Design tips: *Trillium* are woodland treasures that may be used in a shady border but are more commonly planted in woodland or wildflower settings. They combine beautifully with plants of similar habitats such as bellwort, lady's-slippers, and celandine poppy. Snow trillium is small enough to use in a shady rock garden.

TROLLIUS
Globeflower

The genus *Trollius* has about 30 species found in cooler regions of the northern hemisphere. It is closely related to buttercup but far more refined. The Latin name comes from the German *trol*, which means round, in reference to the flowers. All globeflowers form a clump of rounded, deeply cut leaves and stems topped with round, 5-centimetre-wide white, yellow, or orange flowers from mid-spring to early summer. Two main species, along with their hybrids, are commonly grown as border plants. *Trollius europaeus* 'Superbus' has semi-double yellow flowers atop 60-centimetre-tall stems. The tallest cultivar is *T. ledebourii*, with deep orange flowers held on 90-centimetre-tall stems. Named hybrids include 'Lemon Queen' (60 centimetres, lemon yellow), 'Orange Queen' (70 centimetres, light orange), 'Alabaster' (70 centimetres, butter yellow), 'Cheddar' (70 centimetres, soft cream), and 'New Moon' (60

centimetres, creamy yellow). Sometimes seen in local nurseries are the dwarf globeflowers *T. acaulis* and *T. pumilus*. Their flower stems reach 25 centimetres tall with large, single, yellow flowers in mid- to late spring.

Globeflower may be grown in full sun to intense shade, although it is shy flowering in the latter situation. All types prefer moist, organically rich soil. Even boggy soil is tolerated, but the slightest drought can seriously impact the plants. Bees visit the flowers. Because the plants are toxic if ingested, they are rarely bothered by any pests. Diseases are also rare, although powdery mildew may be a problem in some areas. Propagation is primarily by division, but species may be grown from seed. It is a very hardy plant, hardy to zone 3, but as it does not perform well with high summer heat and humidity, it is not recommended south of zone 6.

Design tips: Globeflower, often grown in a border, are classic cottage-garden subjects, but they are also ideal for rain gardens or planted along water features. The dwarf species may be used in a damp rock garden.

UVULARIA
Bellwort

The five species of *Uvularia* are all native to the eastern half of North America. Classic woodland plants, they grow in rich hardwood forests, often in shady ravines. Plants grow from 45 to 60 centimetres tall, with smooth, often waxy, elliptical leaves. Young stems are droopy in habit. The flowers are nodding, terminal or axillary, solitary or paired, yellow to greenish white, with six narrow tepals.

Trollius ledebourii

Uvularia perfoliata

The blooming season is mid- to late spring. Large-flowered bellwort, *Uvularia grandiflora*, is perhaps the most showy and robust with multiple stems and relatively large bright yellow flowers. The variety *pallida* has pale greenish white flowers. *Uvularia perfoliata* is similar but has pale straw yellow flowers. Both of the previous species have stemless leaves that clasp the stems. 'Jingle Bells' has white-edged foliage and nearly white flowers. Mountain bellwort, *U. puberula*, has sessile leaves and pale yellow-green flowers. Straw-lily, *U. sessilifolia*, is similar to mountain bellwort but the plant has a looser habit, with widely spaced stems. The leaves of the cultivar 'Albomarginata' are thinly edged in white.

Bellworts prefer evenly moist, organically rich soil but tolerate some drought. Partial shade is best. Pests and diseases are rare, but in early spring bellworts can be damaged by slugs. Propagation is primarily by division. The above species are all rated hardy to zone 4.

Design tips: Bellwort are ideal for shady woodland gardens but they may also be used in partly shaded borders or wildflower gardens. Combine them with other classic eastern hardwood forest wildflowers such as *Trillium*, *Anemone*, *Clintonia*, and various native ferns.

VANCOUVERIA HEXANDRA
American barrenwort

Vancouveria was named in honour of George Vancouver, a British explorer who spent much of his time exploring the Pacific Northwest. Not surprisingly, it is native to the Pacific Northwest, from southwest Washington to northwest California. Plants form clumps 25 to 50 centimetres high. The trifoliate leaves have leaflets shaped like a duck's foot. Foliage

Vancouveria hexandra

is evergreen in milder areas but deciduous in colder areas. In late spring to early summer, plants produce spikes of tiny six-petalled white flowers on wiry stems.

Vancouveria prefers partial to full shade and cool, humus-rich, acidic, reasonably moist soil. It is reasonably drought-tolerant once established. Pests and diseases are rare but it may be eaten by deer or moose. It is hardy to zone 6.

Design tips: *Vancouveria* is suited to a woodland garden and blends well with *Epimedium*, *Sanguinaria*, *Uvularia*, and other acid-loving woodlanders.

VINCA MINOR
Periwinkle, creeping myrtle

The most common hardy *Vinca* is lesser periwinkle, *Vinca minor*, a European native. Plants produce long trailing stems that root as they creep over the soil surface. In April, May, and into June, and periodically throughout the summer, solitary, periwinkle blue, 2.5-centimetre-diameter flowers are produced in the leaf axils. The leaves are shiny deep green and mound to a height of 15 centimetres. The cultivar 'Alba', has white flowers; 'Atropurpurea' has purple. 'Double Bowles' is a double-flowered blue cultivar. Several variegated forms are popular for containers or hanging baskets, where they are grown as annuals, but they may also be grown as a perennial in the garden. 'Argenteovariegata' has blue flowers and leaves irregularly edged in white; 'Alba Variegata' has white flowers with irregular yellow edges. The blue-flowered 'Ralph Shugert' and white-flowered 'Evelyn' both have evenly white-

Vinca minor 'Atropurpurea'

edged foliage. Perhaps the most striking is 'Illumination', with bright yellow leaves thinly edged in green. It has the typical blue flowers of the species.

Periwinkle may be grown in full sun to full shade. However, in sunny locations, winter sun may burn the foliage if snow cover is not consistent. It prefers evenly moist, acidic, humus-rich soil but, once established, tolerates considerable drought. Diseases and pests are not generally a problem. The main concern is the aggressiveness of the plant; in some regions, it can become invasive. The all-green cultivars are rated for zone 3; the variegated cultivars are best in zone 4 or higher.

Design tips: Periwinkle is ideal for stabilizing embankments or as a lawn substitute under large trees, especially in areas where lawns do not perform well.

VIOLA
Violet

The over 500 species of *Viola* are mostly native in the north temperate regions but a few are from tropical regions. From a gardening perspective, the most important *Viola* are pansies. Although these may sometimes survive for a second year, and self-seed to maintain themselves in the garden, they are not considered perennials. However, a few truly perennial violets are attractive additions to the garden. Perhaps the most common violet is the North American native woolly blue violet, *V. sororia*. This species forms a low mound up to 20 centimetres tall, with basal, heart-shaped leaves and leafless stems that are topped, in mid- to late spring, with solitary 2-centimetre-wide blossoms. There are two named selections: 'Albiflora', with white flowers, and 'Freckles', ice-blue with fine, darker blue spotting. Although this species does not run, it can self-seed with abandon. The North American native marsh blue violet, *V. cucullata*, usually grows in wet areas but can adapt to more typical garden settings. It too is a clumper.

The European sweet violet, *V. odorata*, produces creeping stolons, resulting in a more matlike habit. The many named cultivars are in various shades of blue or violet, but unique is 'Sulphurea', which has apricot flowers; 'Phyllis Dove' and 'Perle Rose' have pink blossoms.

Grown for its purple foliage is *V. conspersa* 'Purpurea'; it is also erroneously called *V. labradorica*. This selection can breed true from seed and has violet-blue flowers. It forms a low mound with slightly trailing stems, but, unlike *V. odorata*, these do not root. Downy

Viola cucullata

yellow violet, *V. pubescens*, is more upright with up to 30-centimetre-high stems, and the similar Canada violet, *V. canadensis*, has white flowers with a yellow eye. Looking more similar to the annual viola, but are short-lived perennials, are *V. cornuta* and *V. corsica*. Both have trailing stems and form low mats. They have relatively large flowers and bloom from mid-spring to early fall, if promptly dead-headed. Both are periwinkle blue but white and ice-blue selections exist.

The above violets tolerate full sun but are more commonly grown in partial or dappled shade. All prefer organically rich, evenly moist soil. Slugs may eat the blossoms but generally insects and diseases are not a problem; however, hares and rabbits like to browse them. Propagation is by seed or division. They are all hardy to zone 3.

Design tips: Violets are classic woodland plants and well suited to a wildflower setting or being grown as a ground cover in partly shaded areas. They combine well with other woodland plants such as hepatica, bunchberry, and trilliums.

YPSILANDRA THIBETICA
Ypsilandra

The single species of *Ypsilandra*, *Y. thibetica*, grows on mossy, shady cliffs in southwest China. This small perennial forms a basal rosette of straplike evergreen leaves up to 12 centimetres long. Vanilla-scented flowers, which are produced in late winter to mid-spring, are in a raceme up to 20 centimetres tall. Individual starlike flowers are nodding and white with contrasting dark blue stamens.

Ypsilandra prefers evenly moist, organically rich, acidic soil but tolerates regular garden soil if it does not dry out. Dappled shade is ideal. Propagation is by division. Few pests or diseases bother it. It is rated hardy to zone 6.

Design tips: *Ypsilandra*, suited to woodland gardens, should be planted near the front of a path so that its fragrance can be appreciated. It grows well alongside hepatica, bunchberry, and foamflower.

Ypsilandra thibetica

Acorus gramineus 'Ogon'

ORNAMENTAL GRASSES AND GRASSLIKE PLANTS

ACORUS
Sweet flag

There are only two species of *Acorus*: *A. calamus*, which is found across the northern hemisphere, and *A. gramineus*, from East Asia. The former has swordlike foliage up to 75 centimetres tall. The cultivar 'Variegatus' has leaves narrowly margined in white. The latter has narrower, grasslike foliage 20 to 30 centimetres tall. Its cultivar 'Ogon' has leaves edged in yellow. Neither species has particularly showy flowers. Both may be grown in consistently moist, organically rich soil and in standing water up to 15 centimetres deep. Propagation is by division. *Acorus calamus* is hardy to zone 4, while *A. gramineus* is hardy to zone 5b.

Design tips: Both species of *Acorus* are suitable for placement in bog gardens or along water features. They may even be grown as shallow-water plants. *Acorus gramineus* 'Ogon' may also be grown as an ornamental grass in areas where the soil remains evenly moist.

CAREX
Sedge

The genus *Carex* has nearly 2,000 species. *Carex* is Latin for cutter, referring to the sharp leaves and stem edges. Several are grown for their tufted, shiny green

Carex oshimensis 'Evergold'

foliage: *C. stricta*, 90 centimetres tall; *C. muskingumensis*, 50 centimetres; and *C. eburnea*, 30 centimetres. For decorative seed heads, consider *C. grayi*, 90 centimetres, with spiky clubbed flowers, and *C. pendula*, 150 centimetres, with broad leaf blades and nodding clusters of narrow seed heads. *C. elata* 'Bowles Golden', which has yellow foliage with blades up to 60 centimetres long in a fountainlike arrangement, thrives in wet soil and can be grown as a shallow marginal plant in pools.

From Japan come several sedges grown for their variegated broad-bladed foliage. *Carex morrowii* 'Ice Dance', with white-edged leaves, has a mounding habit up to 30 centimetres in height. 'Ice Ballet' has stronger white variegation, while 'Silver Sceptre' has broad white margins and looks nearly white from a distance. 'Aureo-variegata' leaves have cream-yellow margins. More dwarf, at 15 centimetres high, is *Carex conica* 'Snowline', which has white-edged leaves. Taller, reaching

45 centimetres, is *C. oshimensis*. A popular cultivar is 'Evergold', with cream-yellow leaves edged in green. The recent Evercolor® series include 'Everest', with white-edged leaves; 'Everoro', green leaves with a central yellow stripe; and 'Everillo', entirely yellow leaves.

Sedges may be grown in sun or shade but, in either situation, require acidic soil that stays consistently moist. Pests and diseases are not a problem. Propagation is by seed for species or division for cultivars. The Japanese species are rated for zone 5, the others primarily for zones 3 and 4.

Design tips: These sedges are suitable for the front of shady borders, in woodland gardens, and around water features. They combine well with other shade plants such as ferns, hosta, and astilbe. Most of the above sedges are evergreen.

FARGESIA
Umbrella bamboo
Of the relatively few hardy bamboo, many are notorious spreaders. *Fargesia*, a Chinese genus, is an exception. It is one of the rare hardy clump-forming bamboo. *Fargesia muriale* (zone 5) and *F. dracocephala* (zone 6) are the tallest, reaching 3 to 5 metres tall. *Fargesia nitida* (zone 5) and *F. rufa* (zone 6) both reach 2.5 metres tall. All look quite similar with yellow to green stems and narrow bright green foliage. Plant form is much like a fountain, narrow at the base but wide-spreading and arching at the top. In milder areas, it is evergreen, but at its northern limit or if exposed to winter winds, it may be nearly deciduous. Flowers are rare

Fargesia muriale

and not particularly showy. Grow them with evenly moist, rich, acidic loam in sun or partial shade. Position it in a sheltered site to reduce foliage winter burn. Propagation is by division.

Design tips: A row of *Fargesia* can provide a windbreak or screen. Individual plants grown among other acid-loving plants contribute a fountainlike accent in the landscape.

HAKONECHLOA MACRA
Japanese forest grass

Japanese forest grass, *Hakonechloa macra*, is endemic to Japan, where it grows in open woodlands and along rocky cliffs. As a result, it is one of the few grasses that tolerates shade. Plants form graceful mounds of ribbonlike arching leaves 30 to 45 centimetres long. A deciduous species, it completely disappears in winter. It is also late to emerge in spring. Flowers are produced in late summer but are narrow and inconspicuous. Of several cultivars, the most popular is 'Aureola', with yellow-edged leaves. 'Sunny Delight' is similar but with reverse variegation to 'Aureola'—its leaves are yellow with green edges. 'Albostriata' has white-edged leaves and, at 45 centimetres, is the tallest and most robust of the cultivars; 'Fubuki' is a dwarf version of 'Albostriata'. 'All Gold' is relatively small, reaching only 20 centimetres tall, with entirely golden to chartreuse leaves. 'Nicolas' is green in summer but turns a blend of yellow, orange, and red in autumn. The yellow-striped 'Naomi' takes on purple tones in autumn.

Hakone grass, a cool-season species that performs best in partial shade, tolerates full shade but the plants are thinner. Full sun is tolerated if the soil is consistently moist. It is not a grass for droughty conditions, nor does it tolerate too much winter wetness. As it is shallow-rooted and prone to heaving in winter, mulching is recommended. As a woodland plant, it thrives in humus-rich soil but is not fussy about the soil pH. Diseases and insect pests are not a problem, but hares and rabbits relish the new growths. Propagation is by division. It is hardy to zone 5.

Hakonechloa macra 'All Gold'

Design tips: Japanese forest grass can be an accent plant for the front of a border, in a rock garden, or in a woodland garden. It is the most desirable ornamental grass for shady and semi-shaded areas. Try combining it with ferns, hosta, *Asarum*, and *Arisaema*. It is also useful as an accent among dwarf ericaceous shrubs.

MISCANTHIS SINENSIS
Maiden grass

The maiden grasses are among the most important ornamental grasses grown in North American landscapes. Although many cultivars are available, all have arisen from the species *Miscanthus sinensis*, a native of eastern Asia. As a group, they are clumpers, reaching from 1 to 2.4 metres in height when in bloom. Although they are grown primarily for their foliage, a few cultivars are grown for their pink-tinted plumed seed heads. In fall, the foliage takes on hues of yellow and orange before turning beige in winter. Their leaves and flowers are stiff enough to provide winter interest.

Those grown for decorative seed heads, often called Japanese silver grass, include the silver-plumed 'Gracillimus' (2 metres tall), 'Silberfeder' (2 metres), and 'Yaku-jima' (120 centimetres). 'Malepartus' can also reach 2 metres tall and has large silver plumes, similar to those of a pampas grass. It is also the earliest bloomer of the maiden grasses and reliable in cooler areas where other maiden grasses may not flower. 'Rotsilber' reaches 150 centimetres tall with reddish pink flower plumes that later turn silvery. 'Purpurascens' reaches 150 centimetres tall and its fall foliage becomes a blend of purple, orange, and yellow.

Miscanthus sinensis 'Morning Light'

Molinia caerulea 'Variegata'

Ophiopogon planiscapus 'Nigrescens'

Several maiden grasses are grown for their variegated leaves, in addition to their flowers. One such group have transverse yellow bands across their wide blades. Most popular are 'Zebrinus' and 'Strictus', both commonly called zebra grass. In ideal conditions, they reach over 2 metres in height. 'Little Zebra' is a relatively dwarf cultivar reaching 120 centimetres tall, while 'Gold Bar' has wide yellow bands and can reach 150 centimetres. 'Flamingo' has blades with a central silvery stripe. Its plumes begin reddish pink and turn coppery later in the season. Those with leaves margined in white include 'Variegatus' at a height of 90 centimetres, 'Silberpfeil' at 120 centimetres, and 'Morning Light' at 180 centimetres.

Maiden grass is a warm-season grass that requires full sun and well-drained soil, but it is not fond of dry sites. It prefers acidic soil. It is slower to green in the spring than the cool-season grasses. It grows well in high heat and humidity and performs better in inland locations than along the cooler coasts. Pests and diseases are rare. Propagation is by division. It is rated hardy to zone 5.

Design tips: Maiden grass is used mostly in the back of a border or as stand-alone plantings featuring other ornamental grasses. For a visual feast, combine maiden grass with Michaelmas daisies, larger sedums, and purple and/or yellow coneflowers.

MOLINA CAERULEA
Moor grass

Molinia caerulea is a cool-season grass native to the damp grasslands of Eurasia. Several named cultivars are available, ranging in height from 75 centimetres to over 2 metres when in bloom. Overall, this is a clumping grass whose leaves create a fountain effect. Narrow bronze-purple flower spikes are produced in mid- to late summer. Although the flexible stems are wind-resistant, they promptly flop in winter, providing little winter interest in the garden. As a result, moor grass may be trimmed back in late fall. Plants are slow to establish. 'Moorhexe', a popular cultivar, has dark green leaves and flower stems that reach 75 centimetres tall. 'Variegata' has leaves edged in cream white; it also reaches 75 centimetres. The most impressive in terms of height is 'Skyracer', whose tall imposing spikes may exceed 2 metres.

Moor grass, a sun-lover, prefers consistently moist, organically rich, acidic soil. It tolerates wet soil. All cultivars turn golden in autumn and the flower spikes may be used as a cut flower. Propagation is primarily by division. Pest and diseases are rare. It is hardy through zone 4.

Design tips: With the variety of heights among the cultivars of moor grass, some may be used toward the front of a border, while others, like 'Skyracer', are bold additions to the back of a border. 'Skyracer' may also be used as a stand-alone ornamental grass. With its love for moist soil, moor grass is also suitable for using near water features.

OPHIOPOGON PLANISCAPUS
Mondo grass

Despite the common name, mondo grass is not a true grass. The narrow straplike foliage appears grasslike. Of over 60 species, North American gardeners grow primarily two: *O. planiscapus* and *O. japonicus*, both from Japan. They have tough evergreen matte green foliage and develop into 15- to 20-centimetre-high tufted clumps that, in time, may spread to form a ground cover. In late summer or early autumn, they produce spikes of small, nodding, bell-like pale pink flowers that develop into shiny black berries. The most popular cultivar of *O. planiscapus* is 'Nigrescens', commonly called black mondo grass, whose leaves are a unique matte purple black. Among *O. japonicus*, the cultivar 'Nana' is noteworthy for forming tight little clumps up to 10 centimetres tall.

Mondo grass needs full sun to partial shade and humus-rich, acidic, well-drained soil. It is reasonably tolerant to both drought and salt. Pests and diseases are rare and its tough foliage is resistant to most browsers. *Ophiopogon planiscapus* is hardy to zone 6; *O. japonicus*, only to zone 7.

Design tips: Mondo grass may be grown as a ground cover, but with their slow spreading they are also useful for rock gardens. Their salt tolerance makes them appropriate for seaside gardens. Black mondo grass provides a pleasing contrast when planted near silver- or yellow-foliaged plants.

PENNISETUM
Fountain grass

Many gardeners are familiar with the annual red-foliaged fountain grass seen in containers and ornamental plantings. Two species of fountain grass may be grown as perennials: *Pennisetum alopecuroides* and *P. orientale*, both warm-season grasses with a mounding habit up to 45 centimetres in height. In mid-summer, plants produce silvery to pink-tinted

Pennisetum alopecuroides 'Hameln'

bottlebrush-like flowers held on stems 75 to 90 centimetres tall. In autumn, the foliage turns yellow. Among *P. alopecuroides*, the cultivar 'Hameln' is the most popular, with silvery flowers at the ends of 90-centimetre-long stems. Other cultivars include 'Red Head', with grey-pink flowers; 'Moudry', with purple-tinted flowers; and 'Desert Plains', with red-tipped foliage. Dwarf cultivars which grow to a maximum of 40 centimetres tall include 'Little Bunny' and 'Burgundy Bunny', the latter with red-tinted leaves. The most popular *P. orientale* cultivar is 'Karley Rose', reputed to be the hardiest of the fountain grasses.

Fountain grass prefer full sun and sandy, acidic soil; avoid heavy wet clays. The seed heads make attractive cut flowers. Diseases are rare and the only pest is likely to be hares. Propagation is by division. Perennial fountain grass is rated hardy to zone 6.

Design tips: Fountain grass is most often used as an accent toward the front of a border.

PHYLLOSTACHYS
Running bamboo

Phyllostachys bamboo is included in this book with some reservations. For gardeners in cooler climates who want to grow bamboo, *Phyllostachys* is among the hardiest. However, as they are rampant spreaders, they are not suggested for small gardens. Most of the hardy species grow 4 to 7 metres tall. Most have blue-green stems, with the exception of *P. aureosulcata*, whose stems are yellow. Their foliage is longer and darker green than that of umbrella bamboo, *Fargesia*. Species hardy to zone 5 include *P. aureosulcata*, *P. atrovaginata*, *P. nuda*, and *P. bissetii*. The species *P. parvifolia* and *P. heteroclada* are hardy to zone 6. These bamboos prefer full sun and a well-drained, loamy, acidic soil. Position them in a sheltered site to reduce winter wind-burn. Propagation is by division.

Design tips: This bamboo provides a windbreak or privacy screen for large landscapes but avoid it in smaller gardens, where it could become invasive.

Phyllostachys aureosulcata

Athyrium 'Ghost'

ATHYRIUM
Lady fern

Although there are about 180 species of lady fern throughout the world, only a small number are grown as hardy garden ornamentals. The common lady fern, *Athyrium filix-femina*, is native across the entire northern hemisphere. From a stout crown, it forms a spreading clump of bright green fronds up to 90 centimetres tall. The deciduous fronds turn yellow in the fall before they shrivel. The many named selections differ in their size and frond shape. 'Frizelliae' has unique rounded pinnae and narrow fronds rarely exceeding 45 centimetres long. Its common name is "tatting fern." 'Dre's Dagger' and 'Victoriae' have short pointed pinnae that criss-cross each other. 'Lady in Red' has red frond stems that contrast beautifully with the light green fronds.

Japanese painted fern, *A. nipponicum* 'Pictum', is one of the most colourful ferns. It forms a mound up to 45 centimetres high with a combination of grey-green and silvery grey fronds, with a contrasting burgundy stem. 'Burgundy Lace', 'Pewter Lace', 'Silver Falls', 'Apple Court', and 'Wildwood Twist' are additional named cultivars which vary in their silver or burgundy highlights. 'Ghost' and 'Brandford Beauty', of hybrid origin, have silvery green fronds. Also from eastern China is eared lady fern, *A. otophorum*, which grows

60 centimetres tall with light apple green fronds and maroon stems.

The lady ferns are best grown in partial shade with evenly moist soil but tolerate deep shade and drier conditions than most ferns. Although they tolerate acidic soil, they are not restricted to it. Insect pests and diseases are not a problem, but hares sometimes eat the newly emerging fronds. Propagation is by division or spores. The common lady fern is hardy to zone 3; the Chinese types are rated for zone 4.

Design tips: Use lady ferns near the front in a shady border, under trees, as a foundation plant on the shady side of a house, or along water features. The Japanese lady fern are small enough to use in a shady rock garden.

BLECHNUM
Deer fern

Of the 200 or so species of *Blechnum*, most are tropical, but two are hardy for temperate gardens. Deer fern, *B. spicant*, is native to western North America and parts of Europe. This glossy evergreen species produces two types of fronds. Sterile fronds, located on the outside of the crown of fronds, have broader pinnae and are held more horizontal; the fertile inner fronds are erect, with narrow pinnae. Both may reach about 60 centimetres in length. From the other side of the world

Blechnum penna-marina

comes Antarctic hard-fern, *B. penna-marina*. This small evergreen fern reaches only 10 to 20 centimetres tall and has a mat-forming habit. It is native to southern Chile, Argentina, Australia, and New Zealand. New fronds emerge copper red but later become shiny dark green.

Blechnum prefer acidic, humus-rich, evenly moist, well-drained soil. Deer fern prefer partial to full shade, while Antarctic hard-fern prefer higher light levels to help develop the best spring colour. Pests and diseases are rare. Propagation is by division. Deer fern is hardy to zone 5; Antarctic hard-fern, zone 6.

Design tips: Deer fern may be used in shady borders or along foundations, mixing well with bleeding-heart, astilbe, and trilliums. Antarctic hard-fern may be grown as a ground cover in dappled shade or in a rock-garden setting. Combine with dwarf conifers or golden-foliaged heaths and heathers.

DRYOPTERIS
Wood fern

Of the about 250 different types of wood fern, several are native to eastern North America, such as mountain fern, *Dryopteris campyloptera*; spinulose wood fern, *D. carthusiana*; marginal shield fern, *D. marginalis*; and male fern, *D. filix-mas*. Any of these native species are worthwhile

Dryopteris erythrosora

additions to a shady garden. As a group, most of the wood ferns form vaselike clumps with triangular to lance-shaped fronds 60 to 150 centimetres tall, depending on the species. Some are evergreen; others are deciduous. A surprising number of wood ferns are commercially available. Male fern is one giant, with evergreen fronds reaching 120 centimetres. Named selections include 'Barnesii', 'Crispa', and 'Linearis'. 'Linearis Polydactyla' has threadlike pinnae, imparting a lacy effect. 'Parsley' is unique, with congested parsleylike fronds on compact 45-centimetre-tall plants. From Europe comes the golden-scaled male fern, *D. affinis*. 'The King' (aka 'Cristata') is a popular selection, with large shiny evergreen fronds up to 120 centimetres tall. At the other extreme is 'Crispa', which has compact 20- to 30-centimetre-tall fronds. Also from Europe is the broad buckler fern, *D. dilatata*, which has semi-evergreen fronds up to 60 centimetres tall. The most visually striking *Dryopteris* is the autumn fern, *D. erythrosora*. The fronds of this Japanese species emerge copper-coloured, later turning shiny bright green. It is another smaller species that reaches 60 centimetres tall. 'Brilliance' has particularly vibrant new growth. Autumn fern is late to emerge in spring, so be patient. With a wide range throughout the Himalayas and even extending to Hawaii and Mexico is Wallich's wood fern. This large robust fern's new fronds are covered in golden brown scales. Mature glossy deep green fronds also have scaly stems. Fronds may reach 120 centimetres long. The wood ferns noted above tolerate full shade but perform better with partial sun.

The soil for wood ferns should be organically rich, reasonably moist but not soggy. The North American and Asian species prefer acidic soil but the European types are not so fussy. They may be grown in full sun, if evenly moist, to full shade. Pests and diseases are not a problem. Propagation is by division or spores. Most are hardy to zone 3, with the exception of autumn fern, which is rated for zone 5, and Wallich's wood fern, which is rated for zone 6.

Design tips: Species which have a short profile may be used near the front of a shady border, while the taller may be placed farther back. They are ideal as a ground cover for high shade under deciduous trees or used in a woodland garden. Companion plants include Siberian bugloss, astilbe, and hosta.

MATTEUCCIA STRUTHIOPTERIS
Ostrich fern

The single species of ostrich fern, *Matteuccia struthiopteris*, is found throughout the northern hemisphere. The genus name honours Carlo Matteucci, an 18th-century Italian physicist. This is the classic edible fiddlehead fern, a spring delicacy in northern New England and Atlantic Canada. It is perhaps the tallest hardy fern, with sterile fronds approaching 2 metres when grown under ideal conditions. The fronds are bright green and feather-shaped, upright, and arise from a stout crown. The much shorter fertile fronds, reaching 30 to 45 centimetres tall, are very dark green, turning black in winter. This fern produces underground stolons, with new plants arising some distance from the parent; provide it with room to run.

Matteuccia struthiopteris

Osmundastrum cinnamomea

Ostrich fern are best grown in dappled shade but tolerate full sun if the soil is consistently moist. The soil should be organically rich and acidic. As with ferns in general, pests and diseases are rare. Propagation is mostly by removing the young plants that arise at the end of the underground stolons. This fern is rated hardy to zone 2.

Design tips: As ostrich fern can run quite significantly, it is probably best used in a woodland garden or as a ground cover beneath high-canopy deciduous trees. It combines particularly well with hosta, astilbe, and spring woodland wildflowers. The stiff, black, sterile fronds add interest to a winter garden.

OSMUNDA
Royal, interrupted, and cinnamon fern

Of about 10 species of *Osmunda*, three are native to eastern North America; royal fern commonly grows along streams, cinnamon fern in bogs and fens, and interrupted fern in damp woodland glades. However, these adaptable ferns make the move to gardens quite easily without the need for extremely wet soil. The cinnamon fern, *O. cinnamomea* (now *Osmundastrum cinnamomea*), and interrupted fern, *O. claytoniana*, are similar in appearance: both produce a vaselike arrangement of lance-shaped fronds about 90 to 120 centimetres high. The fronds of cinnamon fern are glossy green, while those of interrupted fern are more matte green. Both turn golden yellow in autumn. Cinnamon fern also produce central narrow fertile fronds that, while short-lived, turn a lovely cinnamon red as they release their spores. Interrupted fern fronds have mostly sterile pinnae, with a few fertile pinnae located between the sterile pinnae halfway along the length of their frond. Royal fern, *O. regalis*, is different: its arching fronds are more divided, triangular in outline, with oval-shaped leaflets. New fronds emerge coppery maroon but turn deep green. Their fertile pinnae are located at the ends of the fronds. Robust specimens may reach 160 centimetres tall.

Unlike most ferns, *Osmunda* ferns prefer full or at least partial sun. However, to survive in full sun, the soil must be consistently moist or browning will occur along the frond edges. The soil should also be organically rich and acidic for them to perform at their best. Pests and diseases are rare. Propagation is by division. All three are hardy through zone 3.

Design tips: All of these ferns are suitable toward the back of a border, in wildflower and woodland gardens, or along water features. They are also ideal for rain gardens. They blend well with hosta, astilbe, and Siberian bugloss.

PHEGOPTERIS
Beech fern

Three main species of beech fern are commonly grown as garden ornamentals.

Phegopteris connectilis

Long beech fern, *P. connectilis*, is found across the northern hemisphere, while the similar broad beech fern, *P. hexagonoptera*, is found in eastern North America. Both are running ferns with individual fronds arising from a narrow rhizome. Each frond is triangular in outline with the lowermost pair of pinnae angled backward. Japanese beech fern, *P. decursive-pinnata*, is a clumping fern with feather-shaped fronds.

Beech fern prefer humus-rich, moisture-retentive, acidic soil with good drainage. Dappled shade is ideal but both tolerate full sun if the soil stays consistently moist. Propagation is by spores or division. Pests and diseases are rare. Japanese beech fern is hardy to zone 4; long beech fern, to zone 3.

Design tips: Long and broad beech fern spread well and are suitable as a ground cover under trees and shrubs. Japanese beech fern is better suited to the front of a shady border, blending well with *Pulmonaria*, *Brunnera*, and small hosta.

POLYSTICHUM
Shield fern, holly fern

About 260 species of *Polystichum* are found throughout the world, with nearly half in China. As a group, the holly ferns are evergreen with glossy fronds. The plant habit is mounding and, depending on the species, have fronds 30 to 120 centimetres long. North America has three garden-worthy species. The eastern holly fern, *P. acrostichoides*, is native to shady glades and cliffs from Nova Scotia to Ontario and south to northern Florida and Texas, with fronds that reach up to 60 centimetres tall. Braun's holly fern,

P. braunii, is native from Newfoundland to Ontario, south to Minnesota, the Pacific Northwest, and parts of China; its fronds reach up to 90 centimetres tall. The western sword fern, *P. munitum*, native to the Pacific Northwest, has fronds reaching 120 or more centimetres tall. From Europe comes the soft shield fern, *P. setiferum*, with fronds up to 70 centimetres tall. Many selections are available in this fern, which typically has finely dissected fronds. 'Divisilobum' and 'Herrenhausen' have fronds even more finely cut than those of the species, while 'Plumosum' and 'Congestum' have mosslike fronds. From Japan comes Japanese tassel fern, *P. polyblepharum*; Japanese shield fern, *P. rigens*; and Makinoi's holly fern, *P. makinoi*, all with glossy fronds 30 to 60 centimetres tall.

Polystichum require soil that is organically rich and moist but well drained. Although they perform well under acidic soil conditions, they are not restricted to it. Dappled shade is ideal but they tolerate fairly deep shade and even full sun if the soil stays reasonably moist. Although they are evergreen, in colder zones the fronds may be tattered by the time spring arrives and require removal to allow the new fronds to expand. Pests and diseases are not a problem. Propagation is by division or spores. Hardiness depends on the species. Braun's and eastern holly fern are hardy to zone 3. Soft shield fern, Japanese tassel fern, and Makinoi's holly fern are rated for zone 5, while the western sword fern is the tenderest, rated for zone 6.

Design tips: Shield and holly ferns are ideal for dappled sunlight under high-canopy deciduous trees. Western sword fern, the most shade-tolerant, can be grown under

Polystichum acrostichoides

coniferous trees. In a woodland garden, try combining them with astilbe, lungwort, hosta, and wood poppy.

WOODWARDIA
Chain fern

Most *Woodwardia* ferns are tropical to subtropical. Eastern North America has two native species. Netted chain fern, *Woodwardia areolata*, is now botanically known as *Lorinseria areolata*. It is native to shady swamps and damp woodlands from the southern United States to southernmost Nova Scotia. This deciduous fern spreads rapidly by underground rhizomes. Each matte green frond, up to 60 centimetres long, arises individually. Virginia

chain ferns, once known as *Woodwardia virginica*, is now botanically called *Anchistea virginica*. Its fronds also arise individually from a creeping rhizome. Its fronds are much larger than those of netted chain fern, reaching 120 centimetres long, and darker green and slightly glossy. It also prefers wet to damp soils.

Both of the above chain fern prefer damp to wet, organically rich, acidic soil in shade to partial shade. Pests and diseases are rare. Propagation is by division or spores. Both are rated hardy to zone 3.

Design tips: Chain ferns are effective as ground-cover plants under trees and shrubs in wet to damp shady sites. As they are aggressive, they should not be planted near timid neighbours.

Woodwardia virginica

Acer palmatum 'Koto-no-ito'

ACER

Maples

Of around 130 species of maple, ranging from 2-metre-high shrubs to towering giants over 40 metres tall, most reside in Asia, with several found in Europe, North America, and North Africa. Most species are deciduous and many are renowned for their autumn foliage displays. Some species, like *A. griseum*, have colourful exfoliating bark, while others, like *A. pensylvanicum*, have highly ornamental striped bark. Species like *A. rubrum* have intensely coloured red flowers that are highly ornamental and arrive in early spring. Maples carry their seeds in divergent samaras. Samaras can be extremely showy during their early stages of development. Maples can occupy a wide range of garden niches depending on the size and cultivated variety. They tolerate a range of conditions and many prefer acidic, moisture-retentive soils. In fact, maples are among the first trees to experience chlorosis when they are exposed to alkaline soils.

Among the taller maples that prefer acidic soils are those species native to northeastern North America: sugar maple, *A. saccharum*; red maple, *A. rubrum*; and silver maple, *A. saccharinum*. All may reach 30 metres tall. Sugar maple leaves reach 15 centimetres wide; the other two species have slightly smaller leaves, often with distinctly whitened undersides. Sugar maples have spectacular fall colour in shades of yellow, orange, and red. Red maple has primarily red fall foliage, but selections may be orange or yellow. Silver maples are primarily yellow. *Acer* X *freemanii*, a hybrid between *A. rubrum* and *A. saccharinum*, is available in several named cultivars.

For smaller gardens, consider a maple species that rarely exceeds 9 metres. Primarily natives of east Asia, these include Japanese maple, *A. palmatum*; full moon maple, *A. shirasawanum*; trident maple, *A. buergerianum*; Pere David maple, *A. davidii*; and paperbark maple, *A. griseum*. The hundreds of cultivars of Japanese maple offer a variety of leaf shapes, foliar colour, and height, all with vibrant fall foliage. Full moon maple resembles Japanese maple in appearance but has wide, fanlike leaves which turn a blend of colours in the fall. 'Aureum' is a popular selection with brilliant yellow summer foliage. Trident maple has three-lobed leaves reminiscent of those of highbush cranberry, *Viburnum opulus*, which turn brilliant red in fall. Pere David maple has elliptical leaves similar to those of a beech or birch. Its claim to fame is its white-striped bark. Its fall colour is shades of yellow, orange, and red. Paperbark maple leaves consist of three leaflets. It has shiny, cinnamon-coloured exfoliating bark and orange to red fall colour.

From eastern North America is the snakebark maple, *A. pensylvanicum*, which has white-striped bark similar to that of *A. davidii*, but its foliage is three-lobed like that of the highbush cranberry. From the Pacific Northwest is vine maple, *A. circinatum*, North America's equivalent to Japanese maple. Its leaves are similar in shape to those of the full moon maple, with red to orange fall colour. 'Little Gem', a recommended dwarf, globular form, rarely exceeds 1 metre in height.

Most maples need full sun but snakebark, Japanese, and vine maples tolerate considerable shade. Although larger-sized maples tolerate open or unsheltered conditions, the smaller trees prefer shelter. Propagation is primarily by seed for species or grafting for named cultivars. The larger species noted, plus snakebark maple, are hardy to zone 3; the others are rated primarily for the milder side of zone 5.

Design tips: The larger maple species can be used as specimen plants providing dense shade and cover. Smaller maples are suitable companion plants for other acid-loving shrubs and herbaceous perennials. As large maples can be root, light, and moisture competitive, caution should be taken when siting them for planting. With their eye-catching bark, paperbark, Pere David, and snakebark maples add interest to the winter landscape. All maples have exceptional fall colour.

AESCULUS PARVIFLORA
Bottlebrush buckeye

This small suckering tree, related to the common horse chestnut, *Aesculus hippocastanum*, is native to the open woodlands of Alabama and Georgia.

Aesculus parviflora

Bottlebrush buckeye have palmately compound leaves with five leaflets that are dark green on the surface with slightly pubescent, whitish grey undersides. This species can reach a height and spread of 3 to 6 metres. This eye-catching plant is valued for its mid-summer blooms. The pinkish white flowers, with long stamens, are produced in elongate, cylindrical racemes, reminiscent of its common name, a bottlebrush. Flowers are followed by large, light brown, smooth capsules that contain glossy brown seeds. Seed set in the north is not prolific due to the shorter growing season. This species prefers moist, organically rich, acidic soils. They tolerate some shade but are best grown in full light conditions. Plants are hardy to zone 4. Bottlebrush buckeye can be propagated from seed or suckers.

Design tips: Bottlebrush buckeye grows well in open bright sites and can be used for massing or as a specimen plant. In any garden scenario, bottlebrush buckeye offers attractive foliage, but as a feature plant, it comes into its full glory in mid-summer with its array of flowers. Its late-season yellow foliage makes it suitable to be sited as a background plant with autumn-flowering perennials and shrubs or showy late-season fruit selections.

ASIMINA TRILOBA
Common pawpaw

A tree of the southern Appalachians and Carolinian forest, the pawpaw ranges from Florida and Texas northward to southern Ontario. The pawpaw forms a small tree 4.5 to 6 metres tall that has a tropical appearance. Its attractive leaves are smooth and dark green with paler undersides, growing up to 30 centimetres wide. Small, six-petalled, reddish purple flowers appear in mid-May slightly before the leaves emerge. Flowers are followed by large edible, greenish yellow fruit that are covered in a waxy blush. The common pawpaw prefers relatively rich, slightly acidic, moist soils and grows at a medium rate. Plants are hardy to zones 5b to 6 but may experience some difficulty in areas with cool summers and a reduced growing season. Pawpaws can grow in full sun or partial shade and are best planted without too much root disturbance in a protected site that

receives ample heat throughout the growing season. The foliage turns a soft yellow in autumn. Plants are pest and disease resistant. Pawpaws are propagated from fresh seed that should not dry out. Named selections are budded or grafted on species rootstock.

Design tips: The pawpaw gives a tropical effect to the acidic garden. The early purplish flowers combined with the unusually shaped fruit command attention. The fruit resembles papaya in appearance and tastes like a cross between a melon and a banana. It can be used in natural settings with other Carolinian trees such as tulip tree, *Liriodendron tulipifera*, and sweetgum, *Liquidambar styraciflua*, or as an exotic addition to a cottage garden.

BETULA
Birch

Birch are easily recognizable trees of the northern temperate and boreal forests. Approximately 60 species are distributed throughout the northern hemisphere. The white bark species embody elegance and grace as they sometimes appear in vast stands among the northern forests of North America, Europe, and Asia. Birch range from small shrubs of the tundra, such as *Betula michauxii*, to large trees that exceed 25 metres tall. The more ornamental species have a graceful stature, often multi-stemmed, with exfoliating bark ranging from golden yellow to pinkish cream to alabaster white. All species are deciduous and, in autumn, paint the forest canvas with tints of copper and gold. All are monecious with both male and female flowers in the form of yellow to green, narrow catkins that are developed just before

Asimina triloba

Betula papyrifera

or during the spring flush of leaves. Most species prefer cooler climates and moist but well-drained, slightly acidic soils. Full sun is best. Propagation is primarily by seed. Birch can be susceptible to a variety of pests and diseases if they are sited in stressful growing conditions.

Four primary native birch species in eastern North America may reach 20 or more metres in height. The most common and widespread is paper birch, *B. papyrifera*, the provincial tree of Saskatchewan and the state tree of New Hampshire. The white bark of this species peels into papery sheets. Its leaves are dark green, triangular with toothed edges, and turn golden yellow in autumn. River birch, *B. nigra*, resembles paper birch in appearance but its leaves are oval, glossy, and veined. River birch turns buttery yellow in autumn. The selection Heritage® was selected for its superior peeling, multi-toned bark, drought tolerance, and disease and pest resistance. Yellow birch, *B. alleghaniensis*, has glossy, veined, oval-shaped leaves and distinct golden, exfoliating bark. Gray birch, *B. populifolia*, is a little smaller in size, up to 15 metres tall, with smooth white bark and triangular, narrow-tipped leaves. From East Asia comes Himalayan birch, *B. utilis* var. *jacquemontii*, reaching 8 to 12 metres in height, with brilliant white bark. The cultivar 'Snow Queen' has the most visually striking white bark of any landscape tree. The above birch are hardy to zone 3, except for Himalayan birch, which is rated hardy to zone 4.

Design tips: The visual interest of the bark of these birch species makes them indispensable in the winter garden, providing contrast with the bark of *Cornus sericea*. All provide dappled light for understorey woodland species such as trilliums, trout lilies, ferns, and smaller Rhododendrons. Birch are also popular as stand-alone lawn specimens.

CARPINUS
Hornbean
Most of the 30 species of *Carpinus* in the world hail from Asia. In cultivation, the two most common species are the American hornbeam, *C. caroliniana*, and the European hornbeam, *C. betulus*. Both have pyramidal to oval crowns. Their leaves are oval to ovate, sharply serrated, and ribbed. Bright green in summer, American hornbeam leaves turn orange red in autumn, while European hornbeam leaves turn golden yellow. Plants are monoecious; both sexes produce catkins just as the leaves unfurl. The females later develop catkins with elongate, arching bracts, a feature that separates them from hop-hornbeams, *Ostrya*, whose bracts overlap and catkins appear more sacklike. *Carpinus* prefer evenly moist, acidic, organically rich soil preferably in partial shade. They are not particularly fond of dry conditions. American hornbeam, hardy to zone 3, typically reaches 8 to 10 metres in height, while European hornbeam, hardy to zone 4, grows taller, reaching 15 to 20 metres. Propagation is by seed.

Design tips: Hornbeam may be pruned as a large hedge or grown as a stand-alone lawn tree. American hornbeam is a slow grower and small enough in stature to be grown as an understorey tree beneath taller trees.

Carpinus betulus, fall foliage

Castanea dentata

CASTANEA
Chestnut

Chestnuts are members of the Beech family with attractive toothed foliage and edible fruit. The Latin name is a reference to the town of Castania in Thessaly, Greece, where chestnuts were commonly grown. *Castanea dentata*, American chestnut, once occupied large tracts of the American forest system from Maine south to the Mississippi. Massive trees reached 30 to 40 metres in height, with an equal spread. In the early 1900s, chestnut blight, *Cryphonectria parasitica*, devasted the entire population, wiping out most of the trees throughout its range. Sizable trees still exist in eastern Canada, where the blight was not so prevalent. Chinese chestnut, *Castanea mollissima*, is resistant to chestnut blight and is recommended as a substitute. Its foliage emerges as reddish burgundy in spring, turning a lustrous dark green in summer and becoming bronzy yellow in autumn. Its fruit has a curious, prickly husk covering shiny brown nuts. Fruit, produced in copious quantities, present a cleanup issue. Both species prefer acidic, well-drained soil in full sun. Plants are usually propagated from seed. Both are hardy to zone 4.

Design tips: Position Chinese or American chestnut as a specimen tree in the background on large properties. Male flowers, while not showy, are pleasantly aromatic. The seeds, when roasted, are edible.

CERCIS CANADENSIS
Eastern redbud

One of the true gems of the eastern woodland, *Cercis canadensis*, Eastern redbud, graces the early spring woodland with reams of rosy pink, pea-shaped flowers cloaking bare branches and trunks, a condition called cauliflory. Green leguminous pods house seed later in the season. After flowering, reddish purple heart-shaped foliage emerge, expanding to 6 to 12 centimetres long, then turning a dark green for the summer, followed by chartreuse to buttery yellow tints in the fall. Plants produce a small solitary or multi-stemmed tree approximately 3 metres tall and wide. Redbuds like a woodland setting, enjoying well-lit, sheltered sites in an evenly moist woodland soil. Redbuds have an extensive north to south range, from southern Ontario to northern Florida, west to Texas, and into northern Mexico. Species hardiness is displayed in seed provenance, with plants from northern strains surviving into zone 4. Redbuds are propagated from seed, with named selections generally grafted or budded.

Of the many named selections, 'Alba' is a white-flowered form. The hardiest is 'Northland Strain', developed by the University of Minnesota. The spring foliage of Rising Sun™ is a mix of yellow, apricot, and orange, turning chartreuse in summer. 'Hearts of Gold' has yellow summer foliage, while 'Forest Pansy' has dark purple foliage. If weeping trees are your fancy, try 'Covey' or 'Ruby Falls', the latter has purple-red summer leaves.

Design tips: Unparalleled for early spring impact in the garden, the Eastern redbud lights up woodland gardens with floral displays. Plant with early spring bulbs, ephemeral perennials, and woodland shrubs such as *Pieris* and *Rhododendron*. This species is perfect as a small specimen plant or small groups in woodland settings.

Cercis canadensis

CHIONANTHUS VIRGINICUS
Fringe tree

Fringe tree is one of the finest additions to any garden. These trees are sufficiently and surprisingly hardy to zone 4 despite their native range, which is from New Jersey to Florida and into Texas. Plants grow slowly and eventually form a small tree 6 to 9 metres high, growing in moist, acidic soil in full sun or partial shade. Leaves are elliptical, 20 centimetres long by 10

Chionanthus virginicus

centimetres wide, medium to dark green, turning a buttery yellow in late autumn. Fringe trees are generally dioecious, with the male trees having slightly more elegant flowers. Creamy white panicles are produced in June on the previous season's growth. Its slightly fragrant flowers are four-petalled, 20 to 25 centimetres long, with a soft, fleecy appearance. The fruit produced on the female trees are dark purple, egg-shaped drupes, ripening in August to October. Plants are generally propagated from seed but require a month-long warm period followed by a cold period of the same duration, followed by a final warm period to overcome double dormancy within the seed.

Design tips: This species deserves a place in any garden and is regarded as a choice plant. It can be used as a specimen tree due to its ornamental floral displays, unblemished foliage, and slow growth rate (to not outgrow its allotted space too quickly).

CORNUS
Dogwoods

This genus is comprised of mostly trees and shrubs with a few herbaceous and evergreen species. Dogwoods are best at home in woodland settings in humus-rich, well-drained soils. Many species tolerate moderate- to low-pH conditions. Ornamental attributes are species- and cultivar-dependent and include exquisite bark, long-lasting colourful bracts, handsome foliage, distinctive forms, and attractive fruit often relished by wildlife. The following species and selections tolerate low-pH conditions and are best positioned on sheltered sites.

Perhaps the most popular of the larger dogwoods are the flowering dogwoods, which include *C. florida* from eastern US, *C. nuttallii* from the Pacific Northwest, and *C. kousa* from East Asia. All three may reach 8 to 12 metres tall and wide, with paired oval leaves which turn shades of red and burgundy in autumn. *Cornus kousa* has the bonus of exfoliating bark. All three produce white to pink flowers. *C. florida* flowers as the leaves emerge in spring; the two others bloom just after the spring flush. Of the many named selections of *C. florida*, the 'Cherokee' series, 'Cloud Nine', and Red Beauty® are highly recommended. *Cornus kousa* 'Satomi' is one of the most popular pink cultivars of that species. 'Milky Way' is a white-flowered selection of *C. kousa*. Scarlet Fire® has the darkest pink flowers. 'Wolf Eyes' has white-variegated leaves; 'Summer Gold' has yellow-margined foliage. Extensive breeding of flowering dogwoods has been carried out at Rutgers University. Among the flowering dogwood cultivars developed is the Stellar series; Venus®, Starlight®, Hyperion®, Saturn®, and Rosy Teacups®. *Cornus kousa* is the hardiest, rated for zone 5, while *C. florida* is reliable in zone 6 and C. *nuttallii* in zone 7. Hybrids are generally best in zone 6 or warmer.

Two other large dogwoods are grown for their horizontal layered branching habit. From eastern North America is pagoda dogwood, *C. alternifolia*. It has elliptical, wavy-edged leaves that are dark green in

Cornus 'Cherokee Brave'

summer but become purple in fall. Small creamy flowers borne in clusters become bluish black fruit. Fruit is showy but short-lived, as it is a favourite of woodland birds. The cultivar 'Argentea' has white variegated foliage. The cultivar Golden Shadows® has leaves that are margined in yellow. Gold Bullion™ has yellow foliage that turns chartreuse under shady conditions. The foliage of Pinky Spot® is irregularly margined with cream and pink. Pagoda dogwood reaches 3 to 4 metres in height, making it ideal for smaller gardens. From East Asia comes giant dogwood, *C. controversa*, which reaches 10 or more metres in height but resembles pagoda dogwood in its foliage, flowers, and form. 'Variegata' is highly ornamental, with variegated green and white foliage. Pagoda dogwood is hardy to zone 4, while giant dogwood is rated for zone 5.

The last species of note is a European species, Cornelian cherry, *C. mas*. It is another small tree, 8 to 10 metres tall, and hardy to zone 4. Glossy elliptical leaves turn red in autumn. Small clusters of tiny yellow flowers are produced before the trees leaf in spring, followed by edible cherrylike fruit in late summer.

For maximum floral display, grow flowering dogwoods and Cornelian cherry in full sun, but partial shade is tolerated. Pagoda and giant dogwoods are ideal in partial shade and may be grown under taller trees. They all prefer organically rich, well-drained, acidic soil. Species may be grown from seed, which requires a winter stratification period. Species and named cultivars may also be grown from summer cuttings.

Design tips: These larger dogwoods can be used to naturalize woodland settings or as stand-alone lawn specimens. Cornelian cherry combines with spring bulbs and early flowering perennials such as hellebores and lungwort. With its lovely bark, *Cornus kousa* is valuable for the winter garden. Few trees can rival flowering dogwoods for their floral displays. All the larger dogwoods have excellent fall foliage displays.

FAGUS SYLVATICA
European beech

At maturity, the European beech is impressive in stature, with branching foliage and smooth, grey bark. European beech is considered a "long-term" plant, aging gracefully after several hundred years. Old specimens attain heights of 18 to 20 metres and widths of 20 metres are not uncommon. Longstanding specimens occasionally reach 30 metres tall. The attractive foliage is coarse textured, serrated, 5 to 10 centimetres long, and often silky in appearance when unfurling. Juvenile plants retain foliage over the winter months. Beeches prefer slightly acidic, sandy-loamy soils, in open, well-lit sites. The species and most cultivars attain substantial proportions as they mature, so plan for ample space. An species indigenous to North America, American beech, *Fagus grandifolia*, is a plant of equal beauty but not recommended due to its being plagued by infestations of beech bark disease, which devastates large stands of wild populations, disfiguring the smooth bark. The disease is caused by a scale insect, with secondary infections from *Neonectria* fungal pathogens. European beech seems resistant to the

Fagus sylvatica, fall colour

attractive green, dissected foliage. If space is limited, try the columnar forms: 'Dawyck Gold', with yellow spring foliage, 'Dawyck Purple', or 'Red Obelisk'. With gracing wide-sweeping, weeping branches are 'Pendula' in green and 'Purpurea Pendula' in purple. With strongly weeping branches and yet a narrow habit is 'Purple Fountain' and 'Aurea Pendula'. Finally, the dwarf 5-metre-tall 'Ansorgei' has purple, very narrow, threadlike foliage.

Design tips: European beech bark retains its smooth nature even as an old specimen. They are an arresting sight in winter, particularly after a dusting of snow outlines their stately forms. Those with unique coloured foliage or forms are particularly impactful in any large garden.

FRANKLINIA ALATAMAHA
Franklin tree

This attractive monotypic species is related to *Stewartia* but has a mysterious history. In 1765, botanists John and William Bartram first observed the species growing along the Altamaha River in Georgia. William Bartram returned several times to the same location collecting seeds and not until those seedlings began to flower in 1775 did he assign it to the genus *Franklinia*, in honour of close family friend Benjamin Franklin. In his publication, Bartram recorded the species' limited distribution and in 1803 the last account of the species in the wild was verified by John Lyon; it has not been recorded since. The cause for its extinction is unknown and all specimens in cultivation originated from the Bartram collection during the late 1700s. *Franklinia* grows into a small

affliction and is thus recommended as an appropriate alternative. This species is hardy to zones 4b to 5 but is not exceptionally heat-tolerant, struggling beyond zone 7 in southern climes. Propagation of the species is from seed. Select cultivars are usually budded or grafted onto the species rootstock.

Not surprisingly, there are many named cultivars. Most gardeners prefer the copper 'Cuprea' or the purple 'Purpurea' beech. 'Riversii' is nearly black purple. 'Tricolor' has purple leaves margined in white and pink, while 'Zlatia' has bright yellow spring foliage that turns bright green. 'Asplenifolia' has

Franklinia alatamaha

Halesia carolina

airy tree 6 to 8 metres tall at maturity. Its leaves are shiny green on top with pubescent undersides and 15 centimetres long by 8 centimetres wide. The leaves turn shades of reddish orange in late fall occasionally while in full flower in the north. Its white flowers with yellow centres and showy stamens are typical of other genera in the tea family, such as *Stewartia* and *Camelia*. The flowers are produced in September to November and are 8 to 9 centimetres in diameter. Plants like well-drained, acidic soils and a sheltered location. *Franklinia* is hardy once established, surviving in zone 5 but probably best in zones 6 to 7. Propagate from summer cuttings or fresh seed.

Design tips: *Franklinia* forms a small tree which offers the gardener late-season floral and autumn leaf displays. This small specimen tree combines well with other late-season plants of interest, especially against dark foliage conifers such as *Taxus*.

HALESIA CAROLINA
Carolina silverbell

Silverbell, an attractive small tree, enjoys lower-pH soils and sheltered woodland sites. The genus name honours Reverend Stephen Hales (1677–1761), an English physiologist and chemist. With its love for moisture, silverbell is ideally situated along streams, rivers, or lake margins. The plants are hardy to zone 5 and can grow to 10 metres tall with an equivalent spread. Dainty, whitish bell flowers are borne on long nodding stalks, usually in mid- to late May. Flowers emerge before or as the leaves emerge. The fruit is a greenish brown, four-winged hanging drupe that persists into early autumn. 'Wedding Bells' is a suggested cultivar with significantly larger flowers than those of the upright species, while 'Arnold's Pink' has delicate pink blossoms.

Design tips: This is an ideal small tree for planting near water features. Combine with woodland perennials, Rhododendrons, and mid-spring bulbs.

HEPTACODIUM MICONIOIDES
Seven-son flower

This small tree from China is gaining popularity. Specimens grow to about 7 metres high by 4 metres wide and are hardy to zone 5, but as they love summer heat, they perform better in warm, inland locations. Its dark green leaves remain late into autumn. Flower buds appear in late summer and open into creamy white, fragrant panicles in September. Its fruiting structures are striking, initially green but maturing to rosy pinkish purple. The bark begins exfoliating at a young age, revealing tan tones. Plants enjoy moist, well-drained, acidic soil in a sunny site. Propagation is from seed or semi-hardwood cuttings in summer.

Design tips: Seven-son flower provides a green background throughout summer. This species is perfect for late-season interest with its fragrant flowers that complement fall asters, *Chrysanthemum*, and other late-season perennials. The fruit displays extend the interest well into autumn. The scale of the tree fits well within the boundaries of small garden spaces. *Heptacodium miconioides* bark can embellish winter-interest gardens.

Heptacodium miconioides

ILEX
Holly

The recognizable 'Christmas Holly', *Ilex aquifolium*, forms a splendid pyramidal tree about 10 metres in height. Its leaves are 2.5 to 4 centimetres long, glossy, with an undulating serrated edge. The American holly, *I. opaca*, is similar in appearance but has duller foliage. Typical of all hollies, these species are dioecious, producing small whitish, male or female flowers in the leaf axils of separate plants. To obtain fruit, you must plant both a male and a female; however, one male can pollinate many females. English holly is hardy to zone 6, growing best in the cooler coastal areas of the eastern seaboard and the Pacific Northwest. It can be invasive along the Pacific coast. American holly is hardy to zone 5, but performs best in warmer inland areas. Both prefer moist, acidic, well-drained soil in full sun to partial shade.

Suggested cultivars of English holly include 'Hibernica', a female selection with smooth-edged foliage; 'Bacciflava' with yellow fruit; and 'Green Pillar' or 'Pyramidalis', both females with a narrow, pyramidal habit. Perhaps more popular are the variegated selections. With white-edged leaves are 'Argentea Marginata' and 'Silver Queen'. 'Ferox Argentea' is spiny and lower in profile, making it perfect for hedging. The leaves of 'Golden Milkboy' and 'Silver Milkmaid' have a large creamy yellow central blotch. English holly is the parent of many hybrids, including the

Ilex opaca

Liquidambar styraciflua

popular 'Blue Holly', *Ilex* X *meserveae* cultivars.

American holly cultivars have generally been selected for hardiness and berry production. Suggested female cultivars include 'Old Heavy Berry', 'Satyr Hill', 'Greenleaf', 'Miss Helen', and 'Jersey Princess'. 'Jersey Knight' is a popular male pollinator. These holly selections are propagated by late-summer or autumn cuttings.

Design tips: Both hollies make striking specimen plants especially when cloaked in red fruit. Plants can be sheared into tight hedges and are salt-tolerant. They are also used for cuttings for late-season containers and arrangements. The berries are attractive to fruit-eating birds, especially in winter. Many English holly cultivars, including some spectacular variegated selections, are suited for milder plant zones. For contrast, try combining either with *Chamaecyparis* or larger rhododendrons.

LIQUIDAMBAR STYRACIFLUA
American sweetgum

American sweetgum is native to eastern areas of North America from Connecticut to Florida with populations in Mexico and Central America. The name "sweetgum" is from the resin that oozes from the bark when the tree is wounded. Sweetgum can become a substantial tree, reaching on average a height of 15 to 20 metres and occasionally up to 40 metres high. The foliage resembles maple leaves, distinctly lobed with five to seven points. Its leaves are dark, shiny green, turning vivid shades of orange and copper in autumn. The dioecious flowers are insignificant but female flowers develop into spiky globose fruit. Plants are rated for zone 5 but sometimes experience dieback, as they tend to grow late in the season, especially when young. As a result, they perform best in long-growing-season regions. Plants prefer open sites with moist, acidic soils. The several variegated selections include 'Silver King' and 'Variegata'. 'Moonbeam' has creamy yellow spring leaves, while 'Lane Roberts' has green foliage with a dark crimson fall colour. 'Worplesdon' has fiery orange fall foliage; 'Slender Silhouette' forms a columnar spire perfect for space challenged sites. Plants are propagated from seed or summer cuttings. Named selections are budded or grafted onto the species rootstock.

Design tips: Plant sweetgums as specimen trees on a large property. Glossy, unblemished green foliage followed by autumn foliage displays light up the late-season landscape. Distinct corky bark and coarse texture provide an interesting winter-specimen tree.

LIRIODENDRON TULIPIFERA
Tulip tree

Tulip tree is an eastern North Amercian tree native from southern Ontario to Florida. It is the tallest tree in this region, reaching nearly 60 metres in height, although in gardens it

Liriodendron tulipifera

usually tops at 30 metres. The four-lobed oval leaves are bright green in summer and turn golden yellow in fall. When the trees mature, they produce solitary, 5-centimetre-high tulip-shaped flowers, yellow with an orange band at the base of each petal. They bloom after the trees have leafed and, with the size of the tree, are not very noticeable. Tulip trees, which are hardy to zone 5, prefer evenly moist, organically rich, acidic soil. Propagation is by seed. It is the state tree of Kentucky, Tennessee, and Indiana. 'Arnold' is a narrow-growing cultivar, while 'Aureomarginatum' has yellow-edged foliage.

Design tips: With its impressive size, this is not a tree for a standard garden; it needs a large, estatelike setting or park to be best appreciated.

MAGNOLIA
Magnolia

With some 200 species of mainly trees, this genus was named in honour of Pierre Magnol, a French botanist (1638–1715). *Magnolia* species range throughout parts of Asia, eastern North America, Central America, and into South America. The genus is one of the first angiosperms to emerge from the age of conifers, with fossil records dating to the Cretaceous period some 95 million years ago. Magnolia can be deciduous or evergreen. The latter tend to be tender and mostly confined to warmer regions. Depending on the species, they range from 4 metres to over 30 metres in height. Most species generally prefer a soil pH of 6 or less in rich, loamy soils with plenty of moisture throughout the growing season. Most species

Magnolia X *soulangeana*

and selections are best suited to growing in protected areas, out of the wind and where they receive summer heat, beneficial in ripening seasonal growth. All *Magnolia* species have a fleshy root system that is sensitive to disturbance. It is best to site them where they will remain.

Magnolias are one of the most exotic trees that can be grown in temperate colder zones. White is the most common flower colour but trees with yellow, pink, or purple flowers are also available. Flowers of many species often appear before the foliage emerges. Many of the Asian species produce pubescent flower buds that are present all winter and appear like giant pussy willow catkins. Their bare stems cloaked in flower buds are effective attributes for the winter garden. The size, colour, and shape of the flowers vary by species as well as bloom time. Many of the American species have large tropical foliage with flowers appearing after the foliage emerges. The flowers of many species have a fragrance reminiscent of citrus and ripe melons. Entire books have been devoted to this genus; the descriptions here are a simple introduction.

Perhaps the most striking magnolia are those that hail from East Asia. The hardiest and smallest statured is the star magnolia, *M. stellata*, reaching 3 to 5 metre tall. Plants can survive very low temperatures and are firmly hardy in zone 4. It is one of the first magnolias to flower; one downside is that it is subjected to the vagaries of unsettled spring weather. 'Royal Star' is a popular white-flowered cultivar, but 'Centennial' may be a better choice, with semi-double flowers and copious floral display. 'Rosea' and 'Waterlily' both have light pink flowers.

Magnolia kobus is almost as hardy as *M. stellata* and can reach 10 to 15 metres tall. The hybrid between *M. stellata* and *M. kobus*, *M. X loebneri*, is readily available, especially the cultivars 'Dr. Merril' (white) and 'Leonard Messel' (pink). Yulan magnolia, *M. denudata*, and lily magnolia, *M. liliiflora*, are also rare in cultivation but readily seen in their hybrids. The former has white gobletlike flowers and is hardy to zones 5b to 6. The latter has dark purple lilylike flowers and is hardy to zone 6. The hybrid between the two is the classic saucer magnolia, *M. X soulangeana*, 6 to 8 metres tall and wide, hardy to zone 5b, and available in white and shades of pink. By crossing *M. liliiflora* with *M. stellata*, the Washington Arboretum has produced magnificent results, notably the popular 'Little Girl' series. Other noteworthy Asian magnolia flower after the leaves have emerged, running no risk of being burned by late spring frosts. These include *M. sieboldii* (zone 5) and *M. wilsonii* (zone 6). They produce pendant, white, open, saucerlike flowers that have contrasting pink to red stamens.

The American species generally have smaller flowers, larger leaves, and grow much larger than their Asian cousins, some reaching 10 or more metres in height. They bloom after the leaves emerge. These include cucumber tree, *M. acuminata*; bigleaf magnolia, *M. macrophylla*; sweet bay magnolia, *M. virginiana*; and umbrella magnolia, *M. tripetala*. All are rated hardy to zones 5 to 6. While most have creamy white to white flowers, *M. acuminata* has pale yellow flowers. Crossing this species with the spring-blooming Asian species has resulted in popular yellow-flowered hybrids, including

'Butterflies', 'Yellow Bird', and 'Elizabeth'.

Design tips: The Asian species of magnolia herald the onset of spring, with flowers often coinciding with early spring bulbs, early-flowerings rhododendrons such as 'PJM', and forsythia. All may be grown as lawn specimens. Larger American magnolia species, especially those with large foliage, lend an almost tropical effect to the landscape.

MALUS SARGENTII
Sargent's crabapple

This short-statured species of crabapple is native to Japan. *Malus sargentii* forms a 2- to 3-metre-tall tree with a spread of 3 to 4 metres. Plants are hardy to zone 4 and recommended because it is resistant to typical apple diseases such as apple scab and Cedar apple rust. Sargent's crabapple prefers loamy acidic soils in full sun. Fragrant flowers are in profusion, pink in bud opening to pure white. Flowers are followed by an autumn display of pea-sized red fruit about 0.6 centimetres wide. The fruit persists into early winter. The cultivar *Malus sargentii* 'Tina' is an irregular weeping form generally top-grafted as a standard. Plants are propagated from seed or grafted.

Design tips: Sargent's crabapple is a small specimen tree that puts on a brief but visually attractive floral spring display followed by an autumn fruit display. Complement with blue or golden conifers or in front of dark foliage evergreens such as yew or boxwood. 'Tina' makes an irregular weeping specimen over time. The persistent fruit is a favourite of waxwings, thrushes, and other fruit-eating birds.

Malus sargentii

Nyssa sylvatica, fall foliage

NYSSA SYLVATICA
Black gum, tupelo

Black gum ranges from Ontario to Florida and into Texas. Plants are long-lived in the landscape, can reach a height of 10 to 15 metres, and are hardy to zone 4. Leaves are 10 to 15 centimetres long and 5 to 8 centimetres wide and radiant green with whitened undersides. Plants are pyramidal when young and spread to about 10 metres wide. Tupelo prefers a well-drained, moist soil with a pH of about 5.5 to 6.5. Propagation is generally from seed.

Design tips: *Nyssa sylvatica* is suited as a specimen tree or a component of a woodland garden preferring moist, sheltered sites.

Ostrya virginiana

OSTRYA
Hop-hornbeam

Of the nine species of *Ostrya*, the most commonly cultivated are the American hop-hornbeam, aka ironwood, *O. virginiana*, and the European hop-hornbeam, *O. carpinifolia*. American hop-hornbeam is found in eastern North America, extending south into areas of Central America. It forms a small 10- to 12-metre-tall tree with oval to lance-shaped leaves which are ribbed and sharply toothed. It turns golden yellow in autumn. European hop-hornbeam can reach 20 metres tall. Both species are monoecious, with both sexes producing elongate catkins just as the leaves unfurl. The female catkins later develop overlapping bracts and appear almost sacklike. As the common name suggests, the mature female catkins are similar in appearance to those of hops, *Humulus lupulus*. Both prefer well-drained, acidic, rich soil in partial shade. *Ostrya* is more tolerant of drought than the similar genus *Carpinus*. Propagation is by seed. The American species is hardy to zone 3, while the European is hardy to zone 5.

Design tips: American hop-hornbeam may be pruned into a hedge. Both species may be grown as lawn shade trees.

OXYDENDRON ARBOREUM
Sourwood
See description under Ericaceous Shrubs.

QUERCUS
Oaks
The oaks are some of the most iconic trees of the Temperate Forest Biome, with over 600 species. North America boasts the most species, followed by China. Many species have the oak's typical lobed margins and spirally arranged foliage. Oaks fall into deciduous and evergreen categories. Many of the deciduous species, like their relatives beech (*Fagus*), exhibit marcescence (not fully dropping foliage until spring). *Quercus* produce male and female catkins on the same tree, subsequently producing a nut, commonly called an acorn, a key identifier of the genus. Ornamentally and aesthetically, oaks are beautiful specimen trees, stately and magnificent at maturity. Many have vibrantly coloured foliage and autumn colour.

Quercus rubra

Four eastern North American species are notable for their performance under acidic soil conditions. All forms trees 15 to 20 metres tall that are pyramidal when young and become broad and rounded with maturity. White oak, *Q. alba*, is very hardy and can survive into zone 3. Leaves are deeply lobed, 10 to 20 centimetres long, dark green, and whitened undersides, turning russet red in autumn. Scarlet oak, *Q. coccinea*, is hardy to zone 4. Dark shiny green leaves, ranging from 5 to 15 centimetres long by 5 to 10 centimetres wide, are deeply cut with bristle-tipped lobes and slightly whitened on the undersides. In the fall, leaves generally turn reddish scarlet, hence the common name. Pin oak, *Q. palustris*, is a popular landscape species, used extensively in parks, golf courses, and streetscapes. This species tolerates wet heavy soils but prefers well-drained conditions. In high-

pH conditions, plants exhibit iron chlorosis. Pin oak has 10-centimetre-long foliage with deeply incised lobes, pointed tips, and noticeably long petioles. The leaves are glossy dark green on their top surface and mid- to light green on their undersides, turning orange bronze in late autumn. Pin oaks are hardy to zone 4 and are among the fastest growing of the genus. Red oak, *Q. rubra*, is also fast growing and hardy to zone 3. The leaves are glossy green, sharply lobed, with variable sinuses and about 10 to 15 centimetres long by 10 centimetres wide. Like many of the eastern oaks, the fall foliage is russet red.

Design tips: Oaks are best suited to large gardens and park settings. Use as overstorey specimens for spring ephemerals and woodland plants such as large-leaved rhododendrons, mountain laurel, and shade-loving perennials.

SASSAFRAS ALBIDUM
Sassafras

Sassafras is a native eastern North American tree distributed from southern Ontario to northern Florida. It has a conical outline, suckering habit, and can reach 10 to 35 metres tall. Branches have a distinct zig-zag pattern, most noticeable in winter. The 10- to 16-centimetre-long leaves are variable in shape, from oval to bilobed to trilobed. Dark green with pale undersides, they turn brilliant shades of yellow, orange, and red in autumn. Plants are dioecious with separate male and female trees. Flowers, which are small and greenish yellow, are produced in clusters just as the tree leafs. Female flowers develop into

small black fruit at the ends of red stems. The entire tree is aromatic with a citruslike smell. This tree prefers moist, acidic, organically rich, loamy soil. Propagation is by seed or sucker division. It is hardy to zone 4.

Design tips: Sassafras is valued for both its attractive fall foliage as well as its branching habit, which adds interest to the winter landscape. It is suitable for naturalizing into large colonies if space allows; otherwise, it can be grown as a lawn specimen if the suckers have been removed.

Sassafras albidum

SORBUS
Mountain-ash, rowan

Sixty or so species of *Sorbus* are distributed across the northern hemisphere, with most originating in China. All have pinnate foliage and flat-topped clusters of white or pale pink flowers followed by clusters of brightly coloured berries. In eastern North America, two ornamental species, *Sorbus americana* and *S. decora*, inhabit boreal, Acadian, and temperate forests of the east coast, with *S. decora* extending farther north and west. Both are often multi-stemmed and may reach 5 to 10 metres in height and width. Their fruit is bright orange red and favoured by winter fruit-eating birds. Its fall colour is a blend of yellow, orange, and red. Both are hardy to zone 2. European rowan, *S. aucuparia*, is often grown as a single-trunked tree. Its appearance is otherwise similar to that of *S. americana* and *S. decora*, but it has no appreciable fall colour. It is slightly tenderer, hardy only to zone 3. All perform best in full sun with acidic, well-drained soil. None are fond of hot, humid summers.

Sorbus decora

Stewartia pseudocamellia

Many attractive Chinese species of *Sorbus* are available but rarely seen in North American gardens. Most of these species form large shrubs or small trees, 3 to 8 metres tall. Although most have the classic white flowers of the native *Sorbus*, albeit in smaller clusters, *S. cashmeriana* and *S. rosea* have light pink blossoms. The Chinese species' leaves have smaller and more numerous leaflets than the North American and European species noted, with leaves appearing almost fernlike. Many have spectacular fall foliage in shades of red, burgundy, and purple. *Sorbus commixta* has particularly brilliant red foliage. But by far the most noteworthy feature is the fruit displays. Most of the Chinese species have white berries with some, such as *S. rosea, S. vilmorinii, S. pseudovilmorinii,* and *S. bissettii,* having pearl pink fruit. The hybrid 'Joesph Rock' is notable for its yellow berries. Most of the Chinese mountain-ash are hardy to zone 5 and prefer full sun to dappled shade and moist acidic soil that does not dry out. Like the larger species, none are fond of hot summer temperatures, performing best in cooler coastal regions. All *Sorbus* are grown from stratified seed.

Design tips: The large mountain-ash species are popular as lawn specimens and can provide dappled shade for woodland plants grown beneath them. Their exceptional hardiness makes them suited to northern climates. The fruit are important food sources for winter fruit-eating birds; the trees are ideal for wildlife gardens. All species have berry displays that can persist into the winter, lending them use in fall and winter landscapes.

STEWARTIA PSEUDOCAMELLIA
Japanese stewartia

Native to Japan, this small to medium tree reaches from 6 to 12 metres tall. The genus honours John Stewart, a 16th-century Scottish botanist. The trees are pyramidal when young, with distinctive zig-zag growth on smaller branches resembling that of *Fagus*. Beautiful 5- to 5.5-centimetre cup-shaped white flowers with yolk-coloured centres and orange anthers appear in late June and July. Individually they are short-lived but are produced in multitudes over several weeks. Japanese stewartia, hardy to zone 5, is one of the hardiest species within the family Theaceae (the Camellia family). As the specific epithet suggests, the plant resembles a camellia and occasionally is called the "summer camellia." Plants require evenly moist, acidic soils and thrive in sheltered well-lit woodland sites. Its leaves are dark green, turning tones of yellow, orange, burgundy, and purple in autumn. Small egg-shaped fruit appear later in the season, revealing five valved capsules. The exfoliating bark is highly ornamental, particularly when the plant matures. Propagate from stratified seed.

Design tips: As this small tree's bark exfoliates, it reveals varying tones of patchy patterns. It is an ideal companion for ericaceous shrubs and is chosen as a specimen tree for summer flowering. It comes into its own as it matures and is effective for its autumn leaf display and in winter landscapes.

Styrax japonicus 'Pink Chimes'

STYRAX
Snowbell

Two main *Styrax* species are grown in North American gardens. Both hail from East Asia and can form small trees 6 to 9 metres tall. Japanese snowbell, *S. japonicus*, has small, 5- to 7-centimetre-long, elliptical leaves. Clusters of white, lightly fragrant, pendulous flowers appear in late May through June. 'Pink Chimes' is an exquisite pink-coloured selection. Fragrant snowbell, *S. obassa*, has larger foliage, is oval in outline, and reaches 15 to 20 centimetres in length. Their fragrant white flowers are held in long pendulous chains. This species also has attractive exfoliating bark, grey but exposing cinnamon inner bark. Both species have muted yellow fall foliage, are hardy to zone 5, and prefer acidic, well-drained soil. In colder areas, provide a sheltered, sunny site; in areas with hot summers, protect these trees from afternoon sun. They may be propagated from summer semi-hardwood cuttings. Seed propagation is challenging as they have a double dormancy, requiring two seasons to germinate.

Design tips: *Styrax* are suited for woodland gardens. Trees are small enough to be sited near patios and decks where the dainty pendulous flowers can be best appreciated. They are perfect companions for azaleas, rhododendrons, and woodland perennials.

Abies balsamea 'Nana'

ABIES
Balsam fir

About 50 species of fir are distributed across the northern hemisphere. For large gardens experiencing acidic soil conditions, there are several choices. Balsam fir, *Abies balsamea*, is the widest-ranging North American species and the classic eastern North American Christmas tree. It can form a stately pyramidal tree up to 20 metres tall. It has 2-centimetre-long glossy green needles with whitened undersides and is hardy to zone 2. For smaller gardens, try the dwarf cultivar 'Nana', which rarely exceeds 1 metre. Fraser fir, *A. fraseri*, originates in the Appalachians of southeastern US, and is similar in appearance but only hardy to zone 4. Also hardy to zone 4 is Caucasian fir, *A. nordmanniana*, the European cousin to balsam fir. 'Golden Spreader' is a highly recommended dwarf golden-foliaged cultivar generally less than 1 metre tall. From East Asia comes Korean fir, *A. koreana*, with 9-centimetre-long cones and snow-white undersides on glossy needles. 'Horstmann's Silberlocke' is noted for recurved needles that impart a silvery blue colour to the foliage. Its dwarf conical habit, up to 4 metres tall, makes it suitable for the smaller garden. 'Silver Snow' is similar in appearance but can reach 6 metres. 'Prostrate Beauty' is more green than silver and produces cones at an early age. Its maximum height is less than 1 metre but can spread to 3 or more metres wide; it is hardy to zone 5. The silvery dwarf 'Ice Breaker' forms a globe less than 1 metre tall. 'Aurea', a dwarf, 2-metre-tall conical selection whose foliage is golden-hued in winter, is hardy to zone 5.

All of the firs listed prefer acidic, evenly moist but well-drained soil, preferably in full sun. None tolerate urban pollution and are best suited to rural areas. As these conifers dislike heat and humidity, they are not suggested for areas south of zone 7. Propagation of species is from seed, while named cultivars are either grown from fall cuttings or grafting.

Design tips: All firs are ideal landscape evergreens and may be grown as lawn specimens. The many dwarf selections lend themselves to rock gardens and combining with other dwarf conifers or as contrasts for ericaceous shrubs. They are valuable in the winter garden.

CEPHALOTAXUS HARRINGTONIA
Japanese plum yew

This dark foliage conifer resembles yew, *Taxus*, but with longer, flattened needles up to 5 centimetres long. Plum yews, native to Japan, are found in semi-shaded woodland environments. Plants are slow growing, preferring moist, well-drained, acidic soils in semi-shade to shade in sheltered sites. Plants can eventually reach 10 metres tall by 5 metres wide and are hardy to zone 6. If space is limited, grow 'Fastigiata', which has upright stems and remains compact, reaching about 3 metres tall. On the other end of the spectrum is 'Prostrata', which remains less than 1 metre tall but can spread to 2 metres. Plum yews

Cephalotaxus harringtonia 'Fastigiata'

are more heat-tolerant than *Taxus* and grow better farther south. Plants are dioecious, with the female producing oblong fruit, which are pale green but ripen to olive brown. They are propagated from seed but also from late-autumn to winter hardwood cuttings.

Design tips: Plum yews work well in shade gardens as a winter-interest plant and equally well in conifer collections where foliage and texture are design considerations. 'Prostrata' is an ideal ground cover in shady areas.

CHAMAECYPARIS
False cypress

Only six species of *Chamaecyparis* exist, but hundreds of cultivars are available. The wild types may reach 55 metres in height! Thankfully, most of the readily available selections are less than 10 metres tall. False cypress has scalelike foliage generally presented in flat sprays. Some plants retain needlelike juvenile foliage; this attribute has been selected for and is represented in some named cultivars. The plants are monoecious, with separate male and female cones appearing on the same plant. Male cones are insignificant, but the females may produce their round cones in clusters. False cypress can grow in a variety of conditions; most prefer moist, well-drained, acidic soils. Many named selections have foliage with vivid colours and a myriad of textures and sizes. False cypress can fit almost any garden design, from impressive, tall specimens to minute dwarf selections for alpine gardens and containers. The genus generally grows best in areas where the growing season is not too hot and moisture is adequate. Most are hardy from zones 4 to 8.

CHAMAECYPARIS LAWSONIANA
Lawson's false cypress

This elegant species, native to the Pacific Northwest of Oregon and California, is

Chamaecyparis lawsoniana

named in honour of Charles Lawson, a Scottish nurseryman from the mid-19th century. Specimens in the wild can reach an impressive 20 metres tall. Plants, which are hardy to zones 5b to 6, prefer moist, well-drained, acidic soils on sheltered sites. The foliage is composed of sprays of green scalelike, waxy leaves with glaucous overtones. Plants grow at a medium rate, are conical when young, and mature into pyramidal specimens with ascending branches. Selections number into the hundreds, with countless shapes, colours, and textures. Among the taller cultivars are 'Ellwoodii' (green, tight columnar habit), 'Erecta' (green, dense columnar), 'Intertexta' (green, broad spreading habit), 'Lutea' (yellow foliage, pyramidal habit), 'Oregon Blue' (silvery blue, conical habit), 'Pembury Blue' (silvery blue, conical habit), 'Stewartii' (yellow foliage, conical habit), 'Winston Churchill' (golden foliage, columnar habit), and 'Wisselii' (deep green, columnar habit). Among the smaller upright forms are 'Albospicta' (white-tipped foliage), 'Aurea Densa' (golden foliage), 'Columnaris' (blue green), 'Fletcheri' (grey green), 'Lutea Nana' (golden), or 'Minima Aurea' (golden). Those with small, globular habits are 'Gimbornii' (blue green), 'Green Globe' (green), 'Minima Glauca' (blue green), 'Pygmaea Argentea' (white-tipped foliage), and 'Snow White' (white-tipped foliage). The named selections are raised from winter hardwood cuttings, which are best rooted under mist and bottom heat.

Design tips: This species makes an impressive specimen plant for most gardens. The taller forms are restricted to large estates and parks but the compact upright selections are ideal for foundation plantings. The dwarf forms are perfect for large rock gardens or dwarf conifer collections.

CHAMAECYPARIS OBTUSA
Hinoki false cypress

One of the most attractive of the *Chamaecyparis* species, the Hinoki is a slow growing species native to Japan. Beautiful bright green foliage is arranged in spiraling sprays. In the wild, pyramidal trees can reach 20 to 30 metres tall by 5 to 10 metres wide. Plants are hardy to zone 5 and prefer moist, well-drained, acidic soils in full sun. Mature plants produce small, solitary orange-brown cones. Most of the many named selections are relatively small, less than 3 metres. Those with upright, conical habits include 'Crippsii' (golden), 'Ericoides' (green), 'Gracilis' (green), 'Filicoides' (green), 'Nana Aurea' (golden), and 'Tetragona Aurea' (golden). With more globular habits are 'Chaboyadori' (green, twisted, feathery growth), 'Golden Sprite' (gold), 'Green Cushion' (green), 'Hage' (green), 'Juniperoides' (green), 'Kosteri' (green), 'Mariesii' (white-tipped), 'Minima' (green), 'Nana Gracilis' (green), 'Pygmaea' (green), 'Templehof' (green), and 'Verkade's Sunburst' (yellow). Notable cultivars with dwarf but irregular habits include 'Aurea Nana' (yellow), 'Coralliformis' (green, weeping, twisted, threadlike growth), 'Fernspray Gold' (yellow), 'Lycopodioides' (blue green), and 'Reis Dwarf' (green). Named selections can be propagated from winter cuttings under mist and bottom heat.

Design tips: Hinoki false cypress makes a superb specimen plant in most garden

Chamaecyparis obtusa 'Crippsii'

CHAMAECYPARIS PISIFERA
Sawara false cypress

The Sawara false cypress is one of the hardiest of the genus *Chamaecyparis*, performing well into zone 4. Plants are pyramidal when young, opening slightly as they mature. This species, native to Japan, reaches over 30 metres tall by 10 metres wide in the wild. The dark green foliage is in plumes of feathery scalelike leaves with whitish undersides. The small cones are brown and wrinkled. The Sawara false cypress has three distinct foliage forms from which many cultivars have arisen. The *Filifera* form has filament-like strings of compressed scalelike leaves that hang in threads. *Plumosa* resembles the species but is more plumelike, with additional awl-like foliage. The third form, the *Squarrosa* type, is composed mainly of soft juvenile foliage and is often referred to as moss false cypress. The foliage has glaucous blue overtones and is soft to the touch with a billowy appearance. Notable cultivars include 'Boulevard' (steel blue, conical, squarrosa-type), 'Filifera Aurea' (yellow, pyramidal, filifera-type), 'Golden Mop' (yellow, globular, pisifera-type), 'Plumosa Aurea' (yellow, conical, plumosa-type), 'Squarrosa Intermedia' (steel blue, globular, squarrosa-type), and 'Sungold' (yellow, globular, filifera-type). These plants are generally propagated from cuttings in late fall or early winter under mist and bottom heat.

Design tips: Given its height, Sawara false cypress is perhaps best suited as a background specimen plant if the species is used. The cultivar list is extensive, with many selections with diverse forms, foliage types, colours, and textures.

scenarios. Beautiful foliage and habit make it a desirable addition to conifer collections. Numerous selected forms are available with interesting forms, textures, and foliage colour. Many are scaled-down versions of the species, emphasizing spiraling foliage and tight pyramidal shapes, and are suitable for smaller gardens and alpine collections.

Chamaecyparis pisifera 'Filifera Aurea'

Chamaecyparis thyoides 'Heatherbun'

CHAMAECYPARIS THYOIDES
Atlantic white cedar

This species of *Chamaecyparis* is indigenous to the US eastern seaboard, ranging from Maine to Georgia. Plants mature to 20 metres tall by 3 to 6 metres wide and are hardy to zone 4. The plants are densely pyramidal when young, with bluish green scalelike foliage. Trees produce small globose cones. These plants tolerate very wet to boggy sites and low-pH conditions. Many horticultural forms are becoming popular in the trade. 'Glauca Pendula' is a tall selection with weeping, blue-green foliage; 'Blue Sport' has lacy blue foliage and a denser pyramidal habit. The dwarf forms are more popular; classics include 'Heatherbun', with a globular habit and soft grey-green foliage that turns purplish in winter; 'Andelyensis', semi-dwarf columnar form with blue-tinted foliage; 'Top Point' and 'Little Jamie', both with a dwarf columnar habit and grey-green foliage; and 'Ericoides', a compact pyramid with grey-green foliage tinted purple in winter. Plants are propagated from seed and late-season cuttings using methods like those described for other *Chamaecyparis* species.

Design tips: Atlantic white cedar is a good choice for natural wet sites as it has a high tolerance for wet soil. The many selections on the cultivar list focus on bluer foliage, juvenile foliage, and weeping forms. Some are desirable for alpine gardens or textural gardens like conifer/heath and heather collections.

Cryptomeria japonica 'Vilmoriniana'

CRYPTOMERIA JAPONICA
Japanese cedar

This graceful, stately conifer species is native to China and Japan. The medium to dark green foliage is awl-shaped with a spiral orientation. Plants form pyramidal trees with pendulous branches that reach 10 to 15 metres in height by 9 metres wide. Japanese cedar enjoys moist, acidic soils and is hardy to zone 5b. Globular terminal cones are relatively small and inconspicuous. Most of the popular cultivars are small in stature. 'Black Dragon' reaches about 2 to 3 metres tall, with an upright, pyramidal habit and dark foliage. Another slender, pyramidal form is 'Yoshino', which is rated as one of the hardiest cultivars. 'Spiralis' and 'Rasen' have a denser mounding habit, with unique twisted stems. Among the smallest, globular forms are 'Tenzan' and 'Vilmoriniana', both of which turn bronzy in winter. Plants are propagated from seed and are also easily propagated from hardwood cuttings in late autumn or early winter under high humidity with bottom heat.

Design tips: *Cryptomeria* is a graceful tree with ascending pendulous branches with red bark, making it useful as a specimen tree. Several cultivars exist with variations on form, foliage colour, and needle arrangement. The dwarfs are ideal for rock gardens.

CUPRESSUS NOOTKATENSIS
Nootka cypress, yellow cedar

Nootka cypress, native from coastal Alaska south to Oregon, was once considered a *Chamaecyparis* but has been reclassified as *Cupressus*. Nootka cypress grows to 40 metres tall in the wild but is typically 5 to 15 metres tall by 5 metres wide under cultivation. The trees form a distinct pyramidal crown. Pendulous, drooping branches with flattened sprays of scalelike bluish green foliage give it a stately effect. Copious amounts of small globular cones with several raised points turn dark purple at maturity. Native to the coastal forests of the Pacific Northwest, this conifer prefers moist soil that never dries out. 'Glauca' is a selection with blue-tinted foliage. Perhaps the most popular cultivar is 'Pendula', with dramatic, strongly weeping branches. 'Green Arrow' is similar but extremely narrow in its form, rarely exceeding 2 metres wide at its base. Nootka cypress is hardy, surviving in sheltered sites in zone 4. Plants are propagated as described for *Chamaecyparis*.

Design tips: This species is deservingly a specimen plant in gardens. In particular, the weeping 'Pendula' is a choice specimen for any landscape.

Cupressus nootkatensis

JUNIPERUS
Juniper

Juniperus comprises approximately 60 species of conifers throughout the northern hemisphere, with several species growing in some of the harshest environments on the planet. Junipers come in a wide range of sizes and forms, from upright trees to sprawling ground covers. They grow in a variety of habitats, tolerating extremely nutrient-poor soils, low to high pH, and, in some cases, drought conditions. Many are valuable landscape plants with interesting foliage colour, texture, and forms. The foliage has two distinct types: awl-shaped needles and scales. The cones are small, fleshy, overlapping scales which form a fruitlike structure. They are light green when immature and turn a dark purple when mature. The cones of some species are used as flavouring in commercial gin production.

Although many junipers tolerate alkaline soil, several perform best when grown in acidic, well-drained soil in full sun. Most of these are low-growing, spreading species. Common juniper, *J. communis*, is a tough, variable conifer tolerant of harsh growing conditions. It is found in north and central Europe, the Himalayas, and across Canada and the eastern US. Common juniper has both upright and spreading forms. Forms in harsh northern climates tend to be prostrate and spread 1 to 3 metres. In much of central Europe, they form small, upright trees up to 3 metres tall. As this species has sharp, awl-shaped foliage, handle with care. Plants are exceptionally cold hardy to zone 2 but not very heat-tolerant, preferring areas north of zone 7. Popular cultivars include 'Gold Cone', with a tight columnar habit and yellow spring foliage; 'Suecica', with a similar habit but blue-green foliage; 'Depressa Aurea', with year-round golden foliage and a prostrate habit; and 'Berkshire', which forms tight globular mounds which are blue green in summer and turn purplish in winter.

Creeping juniper, *J. horizontalis*, is a North American species with blue-green scalelike foliage that forms extensive procumbent mats spreading slowly up to 2 to 3 metres wide. Among the most popular blue, prostrate cultivars are 'Bar Harbor', 'Wiltonii' ('Blue Rug'), and Icee Blue®. With greener foliage are 'Prince of Wales' and 'Emerald Spreader'. 'Mother Lode' and 'Gold Strike' are notable for their golden foliage. With a slightly taller, more mounding habit are 'Youngstown', 'Yukon Belle', 'Hughes', and 'Blue Chip'. This is another exceptionally hardy species, to zone 2.

Juniperus communis 'Gold Cone'

From Western China, single seed juniper, *J. squamata*, has prickly awl-like foliage ranging from greenish grey to glaucous blue. Plants are hardy to zone 4 but do not tolerate high temperatures or excessive humidity. 'Blue Star', a dwarf mounding selection with steel-blue foliage, is among the most popular. 'Holger' is similar but has yellow-tipped new foliage, while 'Dream Joy' has yellow-tipped foliage that turns grey green. Perhaps the most striking is 'Blue Cream Star', whose blue foliage has creamy yellow speckles. 'Meyeri', with blue-green foliage, and 'Loderi', with grey-green foliage, produce a fountainlike effect up to 2.5 metres wide.

The species and selected forms are best propagated from cuttings taken in fall or early winter under mist with bottom heat.

Design tips: The prostrate nature of many junipers, along with their variable colour forms, make them popular ground covers for sunny, dry embankments. They are suited to rock gardens or large containers or cascading over retaining walls.

LARIX
Larch
Larch, a group of deciduous conifers native to the northern hemisphere, are exceptionally

Larix laricina 'Emerald Curtain'

cold hardy but are not fond of heat and humidity. They endure acidic, poor soils and may grow under considerably hostile conditions. Species like *Larix laricina* grow to and beyond the tree line, often forming low prostrate shrubs induced by extreme environmental conditions. Larch produce small cones which are vividly coloured, often bright green or magenta, when they first develop. Soft, emerald green to blue-tinted needles turn golden yellow late in autumn. Mature trees are dramatic in a winter landscape. The following species are very hardy and fast growing and tolerate low-pH soils.

Tamarack or eastern larch, *L. laricina*, is native across North America, extending well into the Arctic Circle. It has attractive blue-green needles and tolerates wet soil conditions, but trees are generally not symmetrical, often leaning to the east. 'Newport Beauty', derived from a witches-broom, is known for its slow, irregular mounding growth, suitable for rock gardens. 'Emerald Curtain' is a prostrate form that is ideal on embankments and over retaining walls. European larch, *L. decidua*, and Japanese larch, *L. kaempferi*, are fast-growing, upright trees reaching 20 to 30 metres tall. *Larix decidua* 'Pendula' is a 2-metre-tall, graceful specimen that can be a cascading focal point plant in smaller gardens. 'Varied Directions' is a dramatic selection with irregular weeping and ascending branches. *Larix kaempferi* 'Blue Rabbit' has blue foliage and a pyramidal habit. A distinct selection, 'Diana' has twisted and contorted branches. Eastern larch is hardy to zone 2, European to zone 3, and Japanese to zone 4. None are fond of heat and humidity, so restrict their

use south of zone 7. Propagation is by seed or, in the case of named selections, grafting or from mid-summer cuttings.

Design tips: European and Japanese larch are suitable lawn specimens for large gardens. The golden fall foliage is a noteworthy characteristic. Eastern larch is the most wetness-tolerant of any conifer. The dwarf selections are ideal for rock gardens or foundation plantings and blend well with other dwarf evergreen conifers as well as with heaths and heathers.

METASEQUOIA GLYPTOSTROBOIDES
Dawn redwood

The genus *Metasequoia* existed across the northern hemisphere during the Tertiary Period, 66 to 3 million years ago. Previously known only as fossil specimens, the discovery of a living specimen in a Chinese monastery in 1944 took the botanical world by storm. Like larch, dawn redwood is a deciduous conifer. Soft, bright green needles emerge in spring in opposite pairs, turning darker green in summer and a russet brown in autumn before dropping. Plants become large on suitable sites, growing up to 30 metres tall by 8 metres wide. Small globe-shaped cones dangle at the branch terminals. Plants are fast-growing. Pyramidal when young, they have an identifiable straight, tapered trunk and develop a buttressed base with age. Dawn redwood prefers moist, well-drained, acidic soil but is tolerant of heavy wet soils. It is surprisingly hardy, surviving into zone 4b. A golden foliage selection, 'Gold Rush' has golden chartreuse foliage. Dawn redwood can be propagated from stratified seed or semi-

Metasequoia glyptostroboides 'Gold Rush'

hardwood cuttings with rooting hormone under high-humidity conditions.

Design tips: This species is worth growing for its botanical history, its stature, and winter interest. Dawn redwood is effective as a stand-alone specimen as well as in groupings. Mature specimens have furrowed bark with large boles and buttresses.

PICEA
Spruce

The spruce are a large group of conifers with approximately 35 species native throughout the northern hemisphere. The species occupy many habitats, from dry mountain areas to northern sphagnum bogs. Many species play integral roles in the success of native fauna, providing habitats and food for a myriad of species. The following selections tolerate acidic, impoverished soils. As a group, they dislike high heat and humidity, so they are suggested mostly for areas north of zone 7.

Where space allows, Norway spruce, *Picea abies*, is among the largest and fastest growing spruce, reaching 40 metres in height. Needles are dark green; graceful pendulous branches have distinct hanging curtains of foliage. Long cylindrical cones start lime green and turn brown as they mature, persisting into winter. It is native to northern and central Europe and is exceptionally winter hardy, surviving into zone 3. Most of the named cultivars are dwarf. 'Acrocona', which reaches 3 metres tall, has bright red young cones. 'Cupressina' is a semi-dwarf fastigiate form reaching 3 metres tall and a little more than 1 metre wide. 'Pendula', a weeping form with branches that strongly sweep to the ground, is stunning in its architectural form. 'Repens' has trailing stems and, while short, can spread horizontally. Nest spruce 'Nidiformis' is rounded in shape and popular for foundation plantings. Among the smallest is 'Little Gem', another dense, rounded form with slow growth and small needles. Another notable European species is Causasian spruce, *P. orientalis*. This zone 4 tree can reach 20 metres tall. Among the most popular cultivars is 'Skylands', which is narrow with golden needles.

White spruce, *P. glauca*, ranges from Alaska to Newfoundland and is cold-tolerant to zone 2. As it can reach 30 metres tall, it requires plenty of space. Needle foliage is generally a glaucous green with bluish overtones. 'Densata' has a dense conical habit up to 12 metres tall. 'Pendula' has blue-tinted needles, a narrow habit up to 5 metres tall, and strongly weeping branches. Perhaps the most popular dwarf form is the dwarf Alberta spruce 'Conica', with a dense conical habit slowly reaching 4 metres. 'Sander's Blue' is similar in appearance but with blue-tinted foliage. 'Echiniformis' is dwarf with a rounded

Picea abies

habit to only 60 centimetres tall. If the soil is too wet, try black spruce, *P. mariana*. It is native across northern North America and is hardy to zone 1. It has dark green, blue-pointed needles and a narrow growth form, reaching a height of 10 metres. 'Ericoides' is often called blue nest spruce or Black Hills spruce. Its appearance resembles that of a smaller version of *Picea abies* 'Nidiformis' but with blue foliage. 'Nana' has short needles and an irregular mounding habit, generally less than 30 centimetres high.

All of these spruce species are propagated by seed. Named selections are either grafted or grown from cuttings (taken late fall to early winter) rooted within a bottom-heated mist chamber.

Design tips: The species spruce are tall and suitable only for large gardens or parklike settings, where their strong conical forms can be appreciated. The smaller cultivars are suited to rock gardens as foundation plants, or in combination with other conifers.

PINUS
Pine

The pines comprise approximately 125 species of conifers, the majority of which grow 5 to 80 metres tall. Most species are long-lived with some, such as the bristlecone pine (*Pinus aristata*), the oldest living members in the plant kingdom, exceeding 5,000 years. Pines are distinguished from other conifers by their needled foliage bundled together in clusters of 2, 3, or 5. Plants are monoecious, producing separate male and female cones on the same tree. They are distributed mainly in the northern hemisphere and occupy a

Pinus strobus 'Blue Shag'

wide range of habitats, with some species inhabiting subtropical zones. Pines are important timber plants and provide food and shelter for a wide variety of wildlife species. Many pine species are highly ornamental, offering the gardener beauty and function through habit, structure, and colourful foliage. Many species are drought-tolerant and tolerate low-nutrient soils with a range of pH conditions. Although most pines tolerate acidic soil conditions, several grow best in acidic soil.

Eastern white pine, *P. strobus*, is found from Newfoundland south to Georgia. These hardy zone 3 trees can reach 25 metres in height. The soft, light blue-green needles are bundled in clusters of five. Elongate cones reach 15 centimetres long. Named smaller selections include 'Blue Shag', a round, compact form reaching about 2 metres tall and boasting soft blue needles. Smaller still is 'Sea Urchin', which forms a globe only 50 centimetres in diameter. 'Fastigiata' is a slow-growing, narrow, slender form suited to tight garden spaces. It reaches 8 metres high by 4 metres wide. 'Pendula', a graceful weeping form that can reach 12 metres tall, is suitable as a specimen focal point; its form is dependent on training. Also from eastern North America is red pine, *P. resinosa*, with 15- to 18-centimetre-long dark green needles in bundles of two and small rounded cones. This hardy zone 2 tree is large at maturity. Jack pine, *P. banksiana*, is a northern pine, hardy to zone 2. The species has paired, short yellow-green needles and can grow under the most adverse conditions. Notable cultivars include the dwarf weeping 'Uncle Fogy' and the prostrate form 'Schoodic'.

Scots pine, *P. sylvestris*, is native throughout Europe and naturalized in parts of North America. Trees have short blue-green needles in bundles of two. This species is hardy to zone 3 and, when mature, is 10 to 15 metres tall with a similar spread. Young trees are pyramidal in shape but can become flat-topped and irregular at maturity. Old trees have exfoliating bark, showing cinnamon inner bark. For smaller gardens, try 'Fasigiata' or 'Sentinel', both narrow columnar selections which are perfect as accent specimens. They can reach 8 metres tall but only 1 metre wide. 'Hillside Creeper', a prostrate selection, creeps and undulates along the ground. 'Gold Coin' is a compact 6-metre-tall selection with brilliant yellow needles. 'Watereri' has blue-green needles and a dense, flat-topped form; it also reaches 6 metres tall.

Pines require full sun, well-drained soil and, once established, can be quite drought-tolerant. The species noted prefer cooler climates and are not recommended south of zone 7. As they do not tolerate salt or urban pollution well, they perform best in rural settings. Species are propagated from seed, while named selections are grafted.

Design tips: The species are statuesque trees suitable for large landscapes. Their falling needles naturally acidify the soil beneath them, creating ideal woodland conditions for a variety of acid-loving plants. With their dense habit, these pines may be planted as windbreaks. White pine may be pruned into hedges. Smaller gardens can use compact selections; the most dwarf selections are suitable for rock gardens and in combination with other dwarf conifers.

Pseudolarix amabilis

PSEUDOLARIX AMABILIS
Golden larch

Golden larch, a deciduous conifer from eastern China, is similar to true *Larix* but has longer needles and is more heat-tolerant. The plants are hardy in zones 4b to 5 and mature to 15 metres tall by 10 metres wide, but unlike *Larix*, its growth rate is slow. Soft, slightly curving, emerald needles turn chartreuse to amber gold in autumn. Plants prefer moist, acidic soil. Glaucous solitary cones are produced in spring and turn light brown as they mature. Plants are propagated from fresh seed without stratification.

Design tips: This is an alternative to *Larix* in more southerly climates, grown for its seasonal foliage change, picturesque stature, and low-pH tolerance.

SCIADOPITYS VERTICILLATA
Japanese umbrella pine

This conifer species is endemic to a few locations in Japan. Its long, thick, dark green, needlelike foliage is arranged radially in whorls reminiscent of miniature umbrellas.

Sciadopitys verticillata

Plants, hardy in zones 5 to 7, slowly grow as pyramidal spires in their early years; mature specimens attain a height of 30 metres by a width of 20 metres. Large green cones, up to 10 centimetres long, turn brown as they mature. Plants prefer moist, acidic soils with sun but tolerate more shade than most conifers. 'Joe Kozy', a compact fastigiated form, may reach up to 8 metres tall; 'Picola', a globular dwarf, is rarely more than 30

centimetres wide. Plants propagated from fresh seed need moist stratification for three months. Cuttings are slow to root, often taking more than eight months.

Design tips: Plant Japanese umbrella pine as part of a conifer collection or as a stand-alone specimen plant. Its unusual texture makes it an effective winter landscape plant.

TAXUS
Yew

An ancient group of conifers, yews originated in the Cretaceous Period, 145 to 65 million years ago. Species vary from 1 to 20 metres tall. They are long-lived, with some specimens over 900 years old. All have flat, dark green needles. Most are dioecious. Males have small cones, while females produce a minute cone that eventually develops into a specialized cone called an aril, which contains a single seed, surrounded by soft, pulpy, cherrylike flesh. All parts of yew are poisonous except for the pulp surrounding the seed. The nine known species of yew are distributed throughout the northern hemisphere, extending into the subtropics. Some botanists claim that there is only a single species, *Taxus baccata*, with the other species simply being subspecies. Of the over 400 named cultivars, *T. baccata*, *T. cuspidata*, and their hybrid *T. X media* are the most popular. Although yew are not obligate to acidic soil, they are very tolerant to it and for completeness in the conifer descriptions, have been included here.

English yew, *T. baccata*, is a slow-growing species native to Europe and Asia. Large specimens can reach 10 or more metres in height, with an equal spread. This species is hardy only to zone 5b. 'Fastigiata', often called the Irish yew, has a strong, upright habit and may reach 9 metres tall. 'Fastigiata Aurea' is the golden-needled form. For smaller gardens, try 'Standishii' or 'Goldener Zwerg', which are narrow golden forms topping at 2 metres. 'Repandens' is a low but wide-spreading form that may reach 4 metres wide.

Japanese yew, *T. cuspidata*, is the hardiest yew, to zone 4. It is similar in habit to English yew but its needles are light green. 'Capitata' is among the most popular selections, often clipped into a distinct pyramidal form. 'Densiformis' has a dense, globular habit up to 1.2 metres tall and is often clipped into formal globes. 'Emerald Spreader' has a vaselike habit, reaching 2 metres tall by 3 metres wide. Perhaps the most visually striking is 'Nana Aurescens', with a low, spreading habit and brilliant golden foliage.

More popular than either parent is the hybrid between English and Japanese yew, *T.* X *media*. This hybrid is used for formal hedging; the cultivar 'Hicksii' is the most common for this purpose. Cultivars 'Brownii' and 'Densiformis' are clipped into formal globes; 'Hillii' is the best to prune into pyramids. 'Andersonii' has a low but wide-spreading habit, popular for foundation plantings. It is hardy to zone 4.

All yews perform best with full sun and well-drained soil. However, they are among the most shade-tolerant of conifers. None tolerate open exposed sites, droughty conditions, or salt. Propagation is by late-fall to early-winter cuttings.

Taxus cuspidata 'Nana Aurescens'

Design tips: English and Japanese yew may be grown as specimens in large gardens and parks, forming large globular trees. Most are grown as formally clipped subjects, pruned into globes, boxes, or pyramids. The narrow, fastigiate forms in particular provide striking architecture to the landscape.

THUJOPSIS DOLOBRATA
Japanese staghorn cedar

Japanese staghorn cedar, native to Japan, is hardy to zone 5. The name *staghorn* arises from the antler-shaped compressed scales of each branchlet. The foliage is glossy green with silvery undersides. Trees form a dense pyramid and are capable of reaching a height of 20 to 30 metres at maturity. It is slower growing than *Thuja* and of a coarser texture. 'Nana' has smaller foliage than that of the species but an irregular rounded habit which is 30 centimetres tall by 60 centimetres wide. Seeds are difficult to germinate but cuttings are generally easy to root as a winter cutting under mist and bottom heat.

Design tips: This conifer is for the collector's garden and an ideal addition to the winter landscape. The form 'Nana' is suited to alpine gardens.

TSUGA CANADENSIS
Eastern hemlock

Eastern hemlock grows throughout eastern North America, usually in sheltered north-facing ravines. Eastern hemlock is hardy to zone 4 but dislikes exposure to cold winter winds. Short green needles with glaucous undersides cloak branches that weep slightly at the tips, giving this species its characteristic graceful appearance. Small green cones appear in spring, singularly at the tips of branches, and turn brown later in the season. Eastern hemlock prefers moist, well-drained, acidic soils and often grows along streams in mixed woodlands. It is among the most shade-tolerant conifers. This long-lived species is often seen in old-growth stands, reaching ages over 500 years. Trees mature into large specimens sometimes exceeding 30 metres in height with a 20-metre-wide spread. Of the numerous dwarf forms, 'Cole's Prostrate' is completely ground-hugging. 'Pendula' has a strongly weeping habit and can reach 4 to 5 metres tall. 'Jeddeloh' and 'Gracilis' are smaller versions of 'Pendula'. 'Everett Golden' is upright, up to 3 metres tall, with yellow foliage. Eastern hemlock can be propagated from seed; most germinate without stratification. Selected forms are usually grafted onto the species rootstock but can also be rooted under mist with rooting hormone.

Design tips: Try this species as a specimen plant in sheltered woodland sites. Its shade tolerance makes it suitable in areas where other conifers would not survive. Plants can be successfully grouped or used as a formal hedge. The numerous dwarf forms are ideal for rock gardens or for cascading over retaining walls.

Thujopsis dolobrata 'Nana'

Tsuga canadensis 'Pendula'

Abelia X grandiflora

ABELIA X GRANDIFLORA
Glossy abelia

The genus *Abelia* has about 30 species, most native to East Asia. The genus name honours Dr. Clarke Abel (1780–1826), a British physician and naturalist who collected seeds of this plant in China in 1817. Only one hybrid is commonly grown as a garden ornamental, *A.* X *grandiflora*, a hybrid between *A. chinensis* and *A. uniflora*. In the northern regions of its hardiness zone, it forms a spreading deciduous shrub up to 1.2 metres tall, while in warmer locations it may reach 2 metres tall and be semi-evergreen. Its elliptical leaves are often red-tinted when they emerge but later turn glossy green. Its fall colour is purple red. The trumpetlike white, pink-tinted flowers, produced from late spring and throughout the summer, are in axillary clusters. The calyx, often red-tinted, remains even after the flowers have fallen.

Of the many named cultivars, 'Rose Creek' is compact and bushy, with pure white flowers; the compact 'Sherwoodii' has pale pink flowers. 'Francis Mason' has yellow-edged foliage, while 'Kaleidoscope' has yellow-edged leaves and contrasting red stems. The compact yellow-variegated cultivar Golden Anniversary™ reaches 30 to 90 centimetres in height. Radiance™ is a compact cultivar with white-variegated foliage. 'Goldsport', 'Goldspot', and 'Goldstrike' all have pure yellow leaves. 'Edward Goucher' has lilac-pink flowers.

Glossy abelia prefers acidic, humus-rich, evenly moist but well-drained soil. Full sun provides the most flowers, but partial shade is tolerated. In its northern range, it is apt to die back significantly in winter, but it can be pruned hard in spring, as it blooms on new wood. It is not seriously affected by pests or diseases. Propagation is by cuttings. The hardiness range is from zones 6 to 9.

Design tips: Glossy abelia may be used in a mixed-shrub border or as a foundation plant or an informal hedge in warmer regions.

AMELANCHIER
Serviceberry, Juneberry, shadblow

The majority of the about 20 species of *Amelanchier*, and its naturally occurring hybrids, are found in northeastern North America. Most are medium to large multi-stemmed deciduous shrubs but some are trained as small trees. Their heights range from 1 to 20 metres. Their leaves are typically oval to elliptical, with most turning shades of yellow, orange, and red in autumn. The flowers, produced in mid- to late spring, are white, in terminal clusters or racemes of 2 to 20 flowers. These develop into sweet, juicy, purple-black berrylike pomes.

The most popular species grown as trees

Amelanchier laevis

are *A. canadensis*, *A. laevis*, *A. arborea*, and *A.* X *grandiflora* (aka *A. lamarkii*). Notable cultivars include *A. canadensis* Rainbow Pillar®, which has an upright, narrow habit reaching 4 to 8 metres tall; *A.* X *grandiflora* 'Ballerina', whose spring foliage is bronze and habit is broad, reaches 5 to 10 metres tall; 'Robin Hill', whose flowers are pale pink on a plant reaching 4 to 8 metres tall; Spring Flurry®, whose habit is pyramidal at 5 to 10 metres tall; Autumn Brilliance®, whose fall foliage is fiery red on a 4- to 8-metre-tall tree; and *A. laevis* 'Snow Cloud', which has bronzy purple spring growth on a 8- to 12-metre-tall tree.

Among the shrubby types, the most recommended are *A. spicata*, up to 1.2 metres tall; *A. stolonifera*, to 2 metres; *A. bartramiana*, to 2.5 metres; and 'La Paloma', with outstanding bronzy purple spring growth, at 2 to 4 metres. The large shrub *Amelanchier alnifolia*, the prairie Saskatoon, can reach 4 to 8 metres tall; it is grown primarily for its fruit and has many named cultivars on the market. The most ornamental is 'Obelisk', which forms a columnar, upright shrub up to 8 metres tall.

Amelanchier are not restricted to acidic soil but many perform best under acidic soil conditions. The best soil should be organically rich and evenly moist. Some tolerate very wet soil. The exception is saskatoon, *A. alnifolia*, which is more adapted to alkaline, dry soil. Full sun produces the most flowers, fruit, and best fall colour but they do tolerate partial shade. Propagation is by seed or cuttings. *Amelanchier* are prone to several diseases, including rust (attacks the fruit), mildew, fungal spotting, and fire blight. Many moth larvae as well as leaf miners attack them. They may occasionally be browsed by deer and moose. They are hardy to zones 4 to 8, with *A. alnifolia* rated for zone 2.

Design tips: The tree forms of *Amelanchier* can be planted as stand-alone specimens. Ideal species for underplanting include *Dicentra*, *Epimedium*, *Pachysandra*, and/or *Tiarella*. The low shrubby *Amelanchier* are ideal for shrub borders or naturalizing under taller deciduous trees. As most are wetness-tolerant, they may be used in wet depressions or along the borders of lakes and rivers where periodic flooding may occur.

ARONIA
Chokeberry

The three species of *Aronia* are confined to eastern North America. All are deciduous shrubs with spoon-shaped leaves that turn shades of orange, red, and purple in the autumn. Clusters of white flowers with pink stamens are produced in mid- to late spring, becoming clusters of edible (if not tasty) berries in the fall. Red chokeberry, *A. arbutifolia*, the tallest, reaches 4 metres tall. Leaf undersides are white pubescent and the fruit are red. Black chokeberry, *A. melanocarpa*, grows to 1 to 1.5 metres tall and its leaves have smooth undersides and berries that become black. Purple chokeberry, *A. prunifolia*, is similar to the black chokeberry in appearance but its leaves have pubescent undersides and a suckering habit and its berries turn dark purple. Many botanists consider it a hybrid between the black and red chokeberry. The berries of all three often

Aronia melanocarpa 'Autumn Magic', fall colour

remain on the bushes all winter. Of the two selections of black chokeberry, 'Autumn Magic' was selected for its intense orange-red fall colour, while Iroquois Beauty™ was selected for both its fall colour and compact 1-metre-tall habit. 'Brilliantissima' is a selection of red chokeberry with red fall colour, abundant fruit, and a compact 2-metre-tall habit.

Chokeberries prefer organically rich, evenly moist, acidic soil but adapt to alkaline soils. They are also suitable for boggy soil. Full sun produces the heaviest fruit set and best fall colour. Propagation is by cuttings or seeds. Few pests or disease bother them. Black chokeberry is hardy to zones 3 to 9; the red and the purple are rated for zones 4 to 9.

Design tips: With their spring blossoms, fall colour, and berries that often remain all winter, these shrubs are ideal for a mixed-shrub border. They are suitable for naturalizing, as well as for wet depressions or rain gardens.

AUCUBA JAPONICA
Japanese laurel

In milder, acidic soil regions, *Aucuba* is a popular broad-leaved evergreen shrub. It is native to the woodlands and thickets of Japan and China. Plants typically reach 2 to 3 metres tall with a dense habit and leathery leaves up to 20 centimetres long. Plants are dioecious: both sexes produce small maroon flowers in mid- to late spring. Female plants then develop red berries, which often remain all winter. The selections most often grown are 'Varigata' (female) and 'Mr. Goldstrike' (male), both of which have yellow-peppered leaves.

Aucuba grow best in dappled shade; in warmer areas, full sun can burn the foliage. The soil should be organically rich and moist but well drained. Although acidic soil is not a necessity, they do perform well under such conditions. Once established, it is reasonably drought-tolerant. The site should ideally be sheltered from cold winds, especially at the northern end of the hardiness range. Propagation is by cuttings. Few pests and diseases bother *Aucuba*, but watch for scale, mealybugs, and fungal leaf-spots. *Aucuba* is hardy to zones 7 to 9 but has survived in sheltered sites in zone 6.

Design tips: Plant *Aucuba* for year-round interest. It is popular for foundation plantings and can be used as a hedge. It blends well with other broad-leaved evergreens such as *Skimmia, Osmanthus,* and holly. In colder areas, it may be grown as a container plant and brought into a cool sunroom during the winter.

BERBERIS
Barberry

The nearly 450 species of barberry are found mostly in South America and include both evergreen and deciduous species. Their common feature: the many spines located along the length of their stems. The leaves are simple, often rounded to ovate and generally smooth-edged on deciduous species but toothed and often spiny on the evergreen types. Their small yellow to orange flowers, produced in mid- to late spring, are single or in drooping racemes. They later develop into teardrop-shaped berries which are often red on deciduous species and blue on the evergreen. Barberry are closely related to Mahonia, the grape-hollies.

The most popular species, the deciduous Japanese barberry, *Berberis thunbergii*, has enjoyed a resurgence in popularity in recent years, with numerous new selections being released. Although the species may reach 2 to 3 metres tall, many of the newer cultivars remain less than 1.5 metres tall. The various purple-leaved forms are perhaps the most popular, but yellow, orange, and variegated forms are also available. Of the over 50 cultivars on the market, recommended are 'Rose Glow' (purple leaves mottled with pink and white, 2 metres), 'Harlequin' (similar to 'Rose Glow' but 1.5 metres), Royal Burgundy® (purple, 1 metre), 'Concorde' (dark purple, 60 centimetres), Cherry Bomb®

Aucuba japonica 'Variegata'

Berberis julianae

(bright purple, 1 metre), 'Crimson Pygmy' (purple, 1 metre), 'Helmund Pillar' (purple, 1.5 metre, narrow habit), Golden Ruby® (orange purple, 60 centimetres), Sunjoy® Tangelo (orange pink with golden edge, 1.2 metres), Sunsation® (yellow, 1.2 metres), Golden Nugget™ (yellow, 30 centimetres), Sunjoy Gold Pillar™ (yellow, narrow habit, 1.2 metres), 'Lime Glow' (chartreuse, 1.5 metres), and 'Kobold' (green, fruitless, 60 centimetres). Many of these cultivars have fall colours in shades of yellow, orange, and red.

Among the evergreen types, the most popular are *B. verruculosa* (yellow flowers, 2 metres), *B. gagnepainii* (yellow flowers, 2.4 metres), *B. julianae* (yellow flowers, 2.4 metres), and *B. darwinii* (orange flowers, 3 metres). All have small hollylike foliage with whitened undersides and blue fruit.

Barberry are generally care-free and easy to grow in full sun to partial shade and any well-drained soil. Acidic conditions do not pose a problem. They are also drought- and salt-tolerant. Pests and diseases are rare. Propagation is by cuttings or seed but named selections may not grow true to form if grown from seed. In suitable areas the species, *Berberis thunbergii* may become invasive. The cultivars are less invasive. Japanese barberry is hardy to zone 4. The evergreen species are less hardy: *B. verruculosa* and *B. gagnepainii*, zone 5; *B. julianae*, zone 6; and *B. darwinii*, zone 7.

Design tips: Barberry are popular as foundation plants and hedging or as accents in a shrub border. The dwarf selections may be mixed with heaths and heathers.

Calycanthus floridus

CALYCANTHUS
Allspice, sweetshrub

Calycanthus, like several other genera, has gone through taxonomic changes in recent years. Originally there were three species, two in North America and one in China. The Chinese species has now been moved into its own genus, *Sinocalycanthus*, but based on the more recognized name, the Chinese species is included here under *Calycanthus*. As hardy ornamentals, there are two species, the Carolina allspice, *C. floridus*, and the Chinese sweetshrub, *S. chinensis*. Both are broad, spreading deciduous shrubs up to 3 metres tall. The 7- to 15-centimetre-long leaves are oval to elliptical and turn yellow in autumn. Both have camellia-like flowers whose petals are actually petaloid sepals called tepals. Carolina allspice flowers are up to 5 centimetres wide, clove-scented, with a double row of narrow maroon red tepals. 'Aphrodite' is a brighter red-flowered cultivar. Chinese sweetbush flowers are up to 7.5 centimetres wide with broad blush pink to white tepals with an inner ring of smaller yellow tepals. Their flowers have no fragrance. Both produce solitary flowers in mid-spring to early summer.

Calycanthus prefer full sun to partial shade and organically rich, well-drained but evenly moist soil. Chinese sweetshrub demands acidic soil, but Carolina allspice is not as restricted. Both dislike dry situations. Propagation is by seed or cuttings. Promptly remove any suckers to maintain tidier plants. They are mostly free of pests and diseases, but watch for powdery mildew. Carolina allspice is hardy to zone 5; Chinese sweetbush, zone 6.

Design tips: *Calycanthus* are best used in a mixed-shrub border or naturalized under taller deciduous trees, especially in warm southern regions.

CAMELLIA
Japanese camellia

Camellia boasts over 100 species and thousands of hybrids, all native to Asia. The genus name honours George Joseph Camel, a German Jesuit missionary to the Philippines. Gardeners are mostly interested in *C. japonica*, *C. sasanqua*, *C. oleifera*, and their hybrids. For mild areas, *Camellia* are the quintessential acid-loving shrub, reaching up to 4 metres tall. Their elliptical leaves are evergreen and glossy green. The flowers, up to 12 centimetres wide, may be single or double and in shades of pink or red as well

as in white. Winter-blooming in the mildest regions, they may bloom into May at the northern end of their hardiness range.

Camellia need acidic, organically rich, well-drained but evenly moist soil. They are not fond of drought, wind, wet sites, or heavy clay soil. *Camellia* perform best in dappled shade; full afternoon sun can bleach their leaves. They can be finicky plants, dropping their buds if the temperature changes too abruptly. They are also prone to insects and disease. Watch for aphids, thrips, mealybugs, scale, and mites. Diseases include various leaf spots, blights and root canker, and rot. Propagation is primarily through cuttings. Camellia are grown primarily in zones 7 to 9, particularly the coastal Pacific Northwest and southeastern US. However, some recent *C. oleifera* hybrids have survived in zone 6 and are expanding the range of *Camellia* growing into the southern New England states.

Design tips: *Camellia* are popular as informal hedging or placed around house foundations. They may also be used in shrub borders, combining beautifully with

Camellia hybrid

rhododendrons and azalea and other acid-loving, broad-leaved evergreens. In colder climates, try growing them as container plants, kept indoors in cool conservatories or minimally heated greenhouses during winter.

CARAGANA
Peashrub

The close to 100 species of *Caragana* are native to northern Asia and Eastern Europe. Despite the number of species, only two are commonly grown as a garden ornamental: the Siberian peashrub, *C. arborescens*, and pygmy peashrub, *C. pygmaea*. The former is a 2- to 6-metre-tall coarse shrub with small pinnate leaves with round leaflets, short spines, and solitary or small clusters of 2-centimetre-long yellow, pealike flowers in late spring or

Caragana arborescens 'Pendula'

early summer. 'Sutherland' was selected for its narrower form. 'Lorbergii' has very narrow leaflets which impart a feathery look to the foliage. Two weeping forms of peashrub are top-grafted at 1.5 to 2 metres tall. Their branches weep to the ground. 'Pendula' has standard peashrub foliage, while 'Walker' has narrow leaflets similar to those of 'Lorbergii'. Pygmy peashrub, *C. pygmaea*, has small elliptical leaflets in tufts, can reach up to 1.2 metres tall, and has a rounded habit.

Siberian peashrub, an adaptable plant, tolerates salt as well as both acidic and alkaline soil. Even poor, dry soil is acceptable. However, it does not tolerate wet soil. Propagation is by seed or grafting. This tough plant is not bothered by pests or diseases. It is hardy to zone 2.

Design tips: The standard peashrub is rather coarse for most gardens but is useful as a living screen or windbreak. 'Lorbergii' is a little more ornamental and can be used in the back of a shrub border. The weeping forms are often used for foundations, as a specimen, or in a shrub border. They blend well with conifers and look particularly good if combined with an evergreen backdrop.

CHAENOMELES
Flowering quince

Flowering quince are among the most colourful spring-blooming shrubs. Ornamentals include Japanese quince, *Chaenomeles japonica*; Chinese quince, *C. speciosus*; and hybrids between them, referred to as *C. X superba*. Generally, flowering quince are broad-spreading shrubs. Their height, depending on the cultivar, ranges

Chaenomeles japonica

from 1 to 3.5 metres. Although their glossy deciduous leaves are attractive in summer, they have no appreciable fall colour. All have spines, making them effective barriers. The single or double apple-blossomlike flowers are produced in clusters, from March to May, just before or as the leaves appear. The flowers are in white or shades of pink, red, or orange. Later in the summer, the flowers become small crabapple-like fruit. Although they are not edible in a raw state, they can be used for making preserves.

Some suggested cultivars include 'Crimson and Gold' (crimson red), 'Rowallane' (dark crimson), 'Nicoline' (deep red), 'Pink Lady' (deep pink), 'Coral Sea' (light pink), 'Pink Storm' (double pink), 'Orange Storm' (double orange), 'Cameo' (semi-double light orange), and 'Jet Trail' (white).

Flowering quince grow admirably under acidic conditions. In fact, too high a pH can lead to leaf chlorosis. Although they appreciate well-drained, evenly moist soil, they tolerate brief periods of drought. Full sun produces the most flowers, but partial shade is tolerated. Propagation is by cuttings. Typical of most members of the rose family, flowering quince may be bothered by a host of pests and diseases. Aphids, scale, pearslugs, and leafrollers are the main insect pests; various fungal leaf spotting and fireblight are the main diseases. As they are early bloomers, avoid low-lying frost pockets. Chinese quince is hardy to zone 4, while Japanese quince and the hybrids are better in zone 5 or warmer.

Design tips: The taller cultivars of flowering quince may be used as informal hedging. Otherwise, they may be used in a mixed-shrub border. They are also suitable for cottage gardens.

CLETHRA
Summersweet, sweet pepperbush

Over 70 species of *Clethra* were named historically, but today it is generally accepted that there are fewer than 10. The genus name comes from the Greek *klethra*, alder, referring to the plant's alderlike appearance. Two main species are grown as garden ornamentals: the North American summersweet, *Clethra alnifolia*, found along the coastal plains from Nova Scotia to Texas; and the Japanese clethra, *C. barbinervis*, from China, Korea, and Japan. Both are deciduous, multi-stemmed, suckering shrubs. Their leaves are lance-shaped, distinctly veined with finely toothed edges. The fall colour is typically yellow. Fragrant flowers are produced in narrow, bottlebrush-like racemes during late summer and into autumn. Flowers are white or less commonly pink.

Summersweet is more popular than Japanese clethra, probably due to its smaller, hardier nature. The wild form reaches up to 2.4 metres tall with 10- to 15-centimetre-long flower spikes. The named selections include 'Hummingbird', which is very compact and floriferous, up to 1 metre tall; 'Sixteen Candles', which has very erect flowers on 1.2-metre-tall plants; Vanilla Spice™, whose flower spikes are up to 30

Clethra alnifolia 'Ruby Spice'

centimetres long; 'Pink Spire', with light pink flowers; and 'Ruby Spice', whose flowers are rose pink. Japanese clethra is more challenging to find. It generally grows much taller, reaching 3 to 6 metres. Its exfoliating bark is striking. Their flower spikes are generally held more horizontal than those of summersweet and are less fragrant.

All *Clethra* prefer acidic soil that is evenly moist and well drained. Summersweet tolerates wet soil. Although they grow best in full sun, they tolerate considerable shade, yet still produce blooms. Overall, they are care-free plants, with few insect or disease problems. Propagation may be by seed or, more commonly, by mid-summer cuttings. Summersweet is hardy to zone 3, while Japanese clethra is rated for zone 5b.

Design tips: Use *Clethra* as foundation plants, in a mixed-shrub border, naturalized areas, or understorey shrubs beneath tall deciduous trees. With its love of water, summersweet can be planted along water features or in rain gardens.

COMPTONIA PEREGRINA
Sweetfern

The single species of sweetfern, *Comptonia peregrina*, is a North American native found from Nova Scotia to Minnesota and south to northern Georgia. The genus name honours Henry Compton (1632–1713), a British patron of botany. Sweetfern is a suckering mounding shrub from 1 to 1.5 metres tall, with glossy, narrow dark green leaves that have large rounded notches. Overall, they are reminiscent of Asplenium fern fronds, hence the common name. There is no appreciable

Comptonia peregrina

fall colour. The leaves are fragrant when bruised. The plants may be monoecious or dioecious but the yellow-green, catkinlike flowers are insignificant. The female flowers develop into spiny burrs.

Sweetfern prefers peaty-sandy, acidic soil but is adaptable, tolerating wet or dry conditions along with wind and salt. It can even survive in impoverished soils with the help of nitrogen-fixing bacteria on its roots. Full sun is best but it tolerates partial shade. It is difficult to transplant once mature. Propagation is primarily by root cuttings. It has no serious pest or disease problems. It is hardy to zone 4.

Design tips: Sweetfern is not a well-known garden plant but it has potential due to its adaptability. It is best used in mass plantings or along foundations but may be used in naturalized gardens, coastal gardens, roadside plantings, and even rain gardens. The fine foliage contrasts well with coarser-foliaged plants.

CORNUS
Dogwood

Thirty to 60 species of dogwood exist throughout the hemisphere and range from low woodlanders such as bunchberry, *Cornus canadensis*, to small trees, such as flowering dogwood, *C. florida* and *C. kousa*, which can reach 10 metres tall. All tolerate acidic soil but a few demand it. The flowering dogwoods perform better under acidic soil conditions. For more details on them, refer to their description starting on page 125.

Bunchberry is a native understorey sub-shrub across northern North Amercia and looks more like a perennial than a woody shrub. Plants spread by rhizomes to form dense mats. Each stem produces a whorl of ovate leaves with distinct ribs. The flowers are tiny, produced in a cluster in the middle of four creamy white decorative bracts. These later develop scarlet fruit similar to a large raspberry in appearance. Bunchberry requires organically rich, well-drained, acidic soil under cool, shady conditions. Propagation is by division. It is hardy to zone 2.

Perhaps the most popular shrubby dogwood suitable for acidic soil is the red-osier or red-twig dogwood, *C. sericea*, also known in the literature as *C. stolonifera*, *C. siberica*, *C. sanguinea*, and *C. alba*. This shrub, native across the northern hemisphere, reaches 1 to 3 metres tall and was traditionally grown for its red stems, which show in winter. However, they do produce flat-topped clusters of white flowers in late May or June, followed by white or pale blue berries in autumn. Elliptical leaves typically turn a mix of yellow, orange, and red in autumn. Among the popular red-stemmed cultivars are 'Baileyi' (3

metres tall), 'Cardinal' (2.8 metres), 'Isanti' (1.8 metres), 'Midwinter Fire' (1.8 metres), 'Prairie Fire' (1.8 metres), Arctic Fire® (1.8 metres), Little Rebel™ (1.25 metres), Firedance™ (1.2 metres), and 'Kelseyi' (0.8 metres). Yellow-twigged selections include 'Flaviramia' (2.8 metres), 'Bud's Yellow' (2.8 metres), and Arctic Sun® (1.8 metres). With white-edged foliage are 'Elegantissima' (3 metres, red stems), 'Silver and Gold' (2.7 metres, yellow stems), Ivory Halo® (1.7 metres, red stems), and Crème de Mint™ (1.7 metres, green stems). With yellow-edged leaves are 'Gouchaulti' (3 metres, red stems) and 'Hedgerow Gold' (1.8 metres, red stems). Finally, with completely yellow foliage are 'Prairie Fire' (2.5 metres, red stems) and Neon Burst™ (1.5 metres, red stems).

Red-osier dogwoods grow well in full sun to full shade, but the best flowering and foliage colour is in full sun. Any reasonably fertile soil is suitable if it is evenly moist. They are moisture-lovers and thrive in damp depressions or along water features. The most common insect problem is leaf miners; fungal spotting, tip blight, and powdery mildew are commonly encountered diseases. Be forewarned that deer and moose love to browse red-osier dogwood. Propagation is primarily by either summer or hardwood cuttings. Red-osier dogwood is hardy to zone 3.

Design tips: Because bunchberry can spread quickly by underground rhizomes, they are popular as a ground cover in partial to full shade. Their small size means that they can also be used in a rock garden. Red-osier are popular as foundation shrubs or in mixed shrub borders and particularly valued for their winter display. The variegated selections are often grown as a stand-alone specimen.

Cornus sericea 'Elegantissima'

Corylopsis pauciflora

CORYLOPSIS
Winter hazel

The 30 or so species of *Corylopsis* are all native to eastern Asia. The genus name translates from the Greek as hazel-like, referring to the foliage. As a group, they are broad deciduous shrubs with ovate, sharply toothed, distinctly veined leaves that turn yellow in autumn. The flowers are lemon yellow and bell-like and are produced in nodding clusters before the leaves unfurl in March or April. Most are lightly fragrant. Perhaps the most impressive for flowers and fragrance is *C. spicata*, which can reach 3 metres tall and 4 or more metres wide. It can have up to 12 flowers on 5-centimetre-long racemes. 'Golden Spring' is a yellow-foliaged selection, while 'Variegata' has irregular streaks and patches of white. Similar is *C. glabrescens*, which is also fragrant. 'Lemon Drop', a smaller selection, tops at 2 metres tall. *Corylopsis chinensis* is taller than the previous two species, reaching up to 5 metres. Its flowers are only lightly fragrant but are in denser clusters. 'Spring Purple' has purple-tinted foliage and its fall colour is a blend of yellow, orange, red, and purple. *Corylopsis pauciflora*, one of the smallest species, reaches 2 metres tall. The lightly fragrant flowers are produced in small clusters of two to five blossoms on short racemes up to 4 centimetres long.

Corylopsis prefer soil that is evenly moist but well drained, acidic, and humus-rich. Full sun produces the most flowers, but partial shade is tolerated. They are not well suited to windy locations, and as its early flowers are susceptible to late frosts, avoid frost pockets. Overall, they have few pest or diseases. Propagation is by cuttings or seed. *Corylopsis spictata* and *C. glabrescens* are hardy to zone 5, while *C. sinensis* and *C. pauciflora* are tenderer, zone 6.

Design tips: *Corylopsis* are related to *Hamamelis* and combine wonderfully with them along the borders of a woodland, as an understorey shrub beneath tall deciduous trees, or in naturalized areas. Also consider combining with Japanese maple, *Amelanchier*, and dwarf *Sorbus*.

CORYLUS
Hazel

About 15 species of *Corylus* are scattered across the northern hemisphere. The name comes from the Greek *korylos*, helmet, referring to the shape of the husk surrounding the fruit. All have rounded leaves with distinct ribs and sharp, double-toothed margins. Its fall colour is typically yellow. They grow as medium to large, rounded, suckering shrubs. Plants are monoecious with separate male and female flowers on the

Corylus avellana 'Red Dragon'

same plant. Female flowers are inconspicuous, but the males are elongate catkins 5 to 12 centimetres long that bloom before the leaves unfurl. The fruit, a nut, is edible in some species. Most species naturally grow along the margins of forests, streams, or lakesides. There are only a few ornamental species.

The European hazel, *C. avellana*, is a common hedgerow plant throughout Europe. There are four named ornamental selections. 'Contorta', often called Harry Lauder's walking stick or corkscrew hazel, is a medium shrub up to 3 metres tall. This grafted plant has distinct twisted stems and contorted leaves. 'Red Dragon' and 'Red Majestic' are striking purple-leaved versions. 'Pendula' is a green-leaved, weeping version that is top-grafted and usually grown as a standard. Also from Europe is the giant hazel, *C. maxima*, which reaches a height of 10 metres. The most commonly grown form for gardens is 'Purpurea', which has dark purple foliage. The commercial filbert or hazelnut is a hybrid between *C. avellana* and *C. maxima*, both of which have many named selections. The North American native beaked hazelnut, *C. cornuta*, and American hazel, *C. americana*, both reach up to 2.5 metres tall and are grown mostly for their edible nuts.

Hazels perform best in acidic, humus-rich, evenly moist soil. Full sun is best, but they tolerate partial shade. In the garden, remove suckers to maintain more tidy plants. Pests and diseases are not common, except for filbert blight, which can be problematic on commercial hazelnut varieties. Propagation is by grafting or cuttings. The above are all hardy to zone 4.

Design tips: Our native hazels and the European hazel are mostly naturalized along the margins of woodlands but may also be grown as living screens. The purple-leaved selections provide contrast in a shrub border. Weeping forms of *C. avellana* offer winter interest and are often grown as an isolated specimen where their unique form can be best appreciated.

COTINUS COGGYRIA
Smokebush, smoketree
In the wild, *Cotinus coggyria* is found from southern Europe to central China. It generally forms a large rounded shrub or small tree up to 4.5 metres tall. The blue-green leaves are distinctively round, with relatively long petioles. Its fall colour is typically a mix of yellow, orange, and red. The flowers are insignificant but the pink-grey seed heads are large, airy, and fluffy, appearing like puffs of smoke from a distance, hence the common name.

Cotinus coggygria 'Golden Spirit'

'Daydream' is the most popular blue-green-leaved selection. Perhaps more popular are the purple-leaved cultivars. 'Royal Purple', 'Velvet Cloak', and 'Norcutt's Variety' are similar and reach 4.5 metres tall, with wine-purple foliage, purple "smoke," and brilliant red fall foliage. In colder regions, try 'Nordine', which is a little hardier. The leaves of 'Grace', a hybrid between *C. coggyria* and *C. obovatus*, are a little brighter purple red than those of 'Nordine' and its fluffy seed heads are up to 30 centimetres wide and long. If space is limited, try Winecraft Black®, a dark purple-leaved selection that reaches just 1.5 metres tall. 'Ancot', also known as Golden Spirit®, has bright yellow summer foliage and a fall colour which is a mix of orange and red. It reaches 4 metres tall.

Smokebush prefers full sun to develop the best foliage colour and the most seed heads. It is not fussy about the soil type or pH as long as it is well drained. It performs better in poorer soils than in rich. It is very drought-tolerant once established. Pests and diseases are rare, although verticillium wilt can occur. Propagation is by cuttings. It is hardy to zone 5, although 'Nordine' may be tried in sheltered areas of zone 4.

Design tips: Smokebush may be grown as a stand-alone specimen or, more commonly, it is used in a mixed-shrub border or an informal hedging or screen.

DIERVILLA
Bush honeysuckle

Bush honeysuckle, *Diervilla lonicera*, is native primarily to the eastern half of North America. From southeastern US comes

Diervilla lonicera

the similar *D. sessilifolia*. The genus name honours a French surgeon named Dierville who introduced the plant to Europe around 1700. *Diervilla* has only recently been investigated for its potential as a garden ornamental. Multi-stemmed and suckering, *Diervilla* reaches about 1 metre tall. The lance to elliptical leaves are bronzy green when they emerge, becoming glossy deep green, and then turning yellow, orange, and/or red in autumn. In late spring to early summer, they produce small clusters of yellow tubular flowers which are relished by hummingbirds and butterflies. Named selections of *D. lonicera* include 'Copper', with coppery red spring foliage, and Kodiak® Orange, with its glowing orange fall colour. Selections of *D. sessilifolia* include 'Butterfly', with a compact habit, and Cool Splash™, which has white-edged leaves.

Bush honeysuckle, a tough, resilient plant, copes well with poor, rocky, acidic soil. Grow it in full sun or partial shade. It is drought-tolerant once established. Few pests or diseases bother it, but occasionally powdery mildew can be problematic. Propagation is by cuttings or, more commonly, through sucker removal. Although *D. lonicera* is hardy to zone 3, it does not cope well with high heat and humidity, so is not recommended south of zone 7. For warmer areas, try *D. sessilifolia*, which is rated for zones 5 to 8.

Design tips: Use bush honeysuckle as a ground-cover shrub for areas with too much shade or dry, poor soil. It is a little too aggressive for use in most gardens but it is an ideal subject for wildflower gardens. It combines well with *Viburnum*, *Hamamelis*, *Cornus*, *Corylus*, and *Corylopsis*.

FOTHERGILLA
Dwarf fothergilla, witch alder

The genus *Fothergilla* has two species: *F. gardenii* and *F. major*. The genus name honours English physician and botanist Dr. John Fothergill (1712–80). *Fothergilla gardenii*, the smaller of the two, forms a mounding, suckering, deciduous shrub that remains less than 90 centimetres tall. It is native to the coastal plains and wetlands of the southeast US, from the Carolinas to Alabama and Florida. *Fothergilla major* is larger, reaching 3 or more metres tall, and although native to the same geographic area, it prefers more mountainous terrain. Both have thick-textured, oval leaves that are ribbed

Fothergilla gardenii 'Blue Mist', fall colour

with distinct toothed edges along their outer half. Their summer foliage is often tinted blue green and typically produces fall colours in shades of red, orange, and yellow. Plants are monoecious with separate male and female plants. Just before (*F. gardenii*) or shortly after (*F. major*) the leaves unfurl, the plants produce fragrant, white, bottlebrush-like flowers up to 5 centimetres long. Selections of *F. gardenii* include 'Suzanne', which rarely exceeds 60 centimetres tall; 'Harold Epstein', dwarf at 40 centimetres; 'Blue Mist', which had distinct blue-tinted foliage; and 'Appalachia', chosen for its fall colour. The most common selection of *F. major* is 'Arkansas Beauty', which is more compact than the species, with glossier green foliage and better drought tolerance. Hybrids between the two species are also known. 'Mount Airy' is the standard, selected primarily on its easy rootability; it can reach 1.8 metres tall. 'Red Monarch' and 'Red Licorice' were both selected for their reliable red fall colour. 'Sea Spray' has bluer foliage than the norm, while 'Blue Shadow', a sport of 'Mount Airy', has powder blue foliage. 'Windy City' has uniform green leaves but is hardy.

Fothergilla prefer evenly moist, acidic, organically rich but well-drained soil in full sun; however, in hot locations some afternoon shade is appreciated. *Fothergilla major* tolerates some drought. These care-free shrubs require little pruning and are rarely bothered by pests or disease. Propagation is by fall-sown seed or mid-summer cuttings. Despite the native location of these species, both are surprisingly hardy to zone 5, with 'Windy City' hardy to zone 4.

Design tips: With their early flowers and fall colour, choose *Fothergilla* as specimens, accents in shrub borders, or among rhododendrons, along foundations, or even as an informal hedge. Plant near the front of a border so that their fragrant flowers and fall colour can be best appreciated.

HAMAMELIS
Witch hazel

Of the six species of *Hamamelis*, four are from the Americas and one each from China and Japan. The genus name comes from the Greek words *hama*, at same time, and *melon*, fruit, in reference to the plant's having both fruit and flowers at the same time. The flowers of all species are axillary, with four narrow straplike but often curled petals and four short but noticeable maroon-purple sepals. The flowers are often fragrant and typically in shades of yellow, bronze, orange, and red to purplish. The flowering season varies from late fall, through winter to early spring, depending on the species. The foliage is oval, slightly ribbed, and sharply toothed. The fall colour ranges from yellow to orange to red.

The most popular American species are *H. vernalis* and *H. virginiana*. The former has late-winter or early-spring flowers in a variety of colours, while the latter produces yellow flowers in late fall just as the leaves drop. Both grow 2 to 3 metres tall and generally have a yellow fall colour. They are native to the mountainous areas of the eastern US. The named selections of *H. vernalis* include 'Sandra' (yellow), 'Quasimodo' (orange), 'Amethyst' (purplish pink), and 'Autumn Embers' (yellow with multicoloured fall foliage).

Hamamelis vernalis

Far more popular is the hybrid *H. X intermedia*, created between the Asian species *H. mollis* and *H. japonica*. It typically grows larger than the American species, reaching 3 to 5 metres tall. Its flowers are a little larger than those of the America species and it blooms from mid-winter to early spring. Its fall colour is generally more striking than that of its American counterparts. Of the numerous named selections, the most easily found are probably 'Sunburst' (pale yellow), 'Primavera' (light yellow), 'Arnold Promise' (bright yellow), 'Barmstedt Gold' (golden yellow), 'Jelena' (orange), 'Diane' (orange red), and 'Ruby Glow' (red).

Witch-hazel prefer acidic, well-drained, humus-rich soil in sun or partial shade. Too dry soil can lead to leaf scorch. As many of the *H. X intermedia* hybrids are grafted, promptly remove any suckers that form. If pruning is required, do so in spring. Pests and diseases are generally not a problem but they are occasionally bothered by Japanese beetle, leafrollers, and, if grown in too sheltered a site, powdery mildew. *Hamamelis virginiana* is the hardiest, rated for zone 3; *H. vernalis*, zone 4; and *H. X intermedia*, zone 5.

Design tips: Plant *Hamamelis* along the edges of woodlands or as understorey shrubs beneath high-canopy deciduous trees. They are also suitable for use as a specimen plant in mixed-shrub borders or natural areas or even as a screen.

HIBISCUS SYRIACUS
Rose-of-Sharon

Native to China, Rose-of-Sharon is valued mostly for its late-season flowers. The wild form can reach 4 metres tall and has 7-centimetre-wide pink flowers with red "eyes" from mid-summer to fall. Each flower lasts but a day or two. The glossy deciduous leaves are three-lobed and coarsely toothed but have no appreciable fall colour. Popular cultivars include 'Minerva' (lavender pink), 'Blue Bird' (lavender blue), 'Mathilde' (pink), 'Aphrodite' (pink), 'Red Heart' (white, red "eye"), and 'Diana' (pure white). Double-flowered selections include 'Collie Mullen' (pink), 'Lucy' (deep pink), 'Blushing Bride' (pale pink), and the Chiffon™ series in

Hibiscus syriacus 'Lady Stanley'

blue, lavender, pink, and white. If space is a consideration, try one of the Lil' Kim® series, which top at 1.2 metres tall.

Rose-of-Sharon is easily grown in most soil types but does not tolerate wet soil. Full sun is best for maximum flower production. Propagation is by cuttings. The main diseases are various fungal leaf spotting, rust, or canker. Aphids may sometimes be problematic, but the most serious pest is Japanese beetles, which can defoliate the plant. It is hardy to zone 5, but at the north end of its range it appreciates a warm, sheltered site.

Design tips: Rose-of-Sharon is often grown as a stand-alone specimen or along foundations and among mixed-shrub borders. It is also used for hedging or as a screen.

HYDRANGEA
Hydrangea
Only five of the 70 species of hydrangea are commonly grown as garden ornamentals: *H. macrophylla*, *H. paniculata*, *H. arborescens*, *H. quercifolia*, and *H. anomala* ssp. *petiolaris*. The common feature is the combination of both small fertile flowers and larger sterile flowers among their inflorescence. As there are hundreds of cultivars on the market, each is described in generalities.

From Asia comes *Hydrangea macrophylla*, the popular mophead and lacecap hydrangea. The mopheads typically have a large, rounded head of mostly sterile flowers, while the lacecaps are flat-topped with fertile inner flowers surrounded by outer sterile flowers. Occasionally the names *Hydrangea macrophylla* ssp. *serrata* or *Hydrangea serrata*

are used to reference the hardy mountain hydrangea. "Wild" forms can reach 3 metres tall, while most modern cultivars are 1.5 to 2 metres tall. The flower colours of these hydrangea are affected by soil pH. Most gardeners prefer the rich blue colour which is achieved under acidic soil conditions. Near pH 7 (neutral), the flowers are purple; under alkaline conditions, they are pink. 'Nikko Blue', one of the oldest cultivars, is still widely available. Now it is mostly superseded by the Endless Summer® series, which have repeat blooms from mid-summer through fall. For smaller gardens, consider the dwarf Cityline® and Seaside Seranade® series, as most top at about 1 metre tall. Among the lacecaps, the older standard cultivars are 'Blue Wave' and 'Blue Bird'; newer selections are more compact, with repeat blooms, such as Twist-n-Shout®. If you prefer double flowers, try the Double Delights™ series, whose sterile flowers are double.

Also from Asia is the panicle or Pee-Gee hydrangea, *H. paniculata*. The largest of the shrubby garden hydrangea, it reaches potentially to 8 metres tall, although most modern cultivars are less than 3 metres. They have large cone-shaped flower heads that generally start white and turn pink as they age. The blooming season begins in July in the south but as late as September in the north. 'Grandiflora' is the oldest and tallest cultivar with nearly 100 per cent sterile flowers. This cultivar is often trained to a single stem to create a tree form. Other large cultivars include 'Phantom' and Strawberry Vanilla®. Many of the more recent cultivars have flowers that turn nearly red as they age, including Fire Light®, Quick Fire®, Pinky

Hydrangea arborescens Invincibelle® Spirit

Winky®, and Zinfin Doll®. If space is a consideration, try one of the dwarf cultivars: 'Little Lamb', Little Quick Fire®, Bobo®, or Diamond Rouge®. For something a little different, try one of the green cultivars: 'Limelight', reaching nearly 3 metres tall, or Little Lime®, which is half that size.

Smooth hydrangea, *H. arborescens*, is unique among the garden hydrangea: they bloom on new wood and can be hard-pruned each year. Native to the eastern US, the wild form produces large rounded heads of white flowers nearly 20 to 25 centimetres wide. It can reach 1.5 metres tall and blooms from early summer into autumn. As they age, the flowers may turn light pink or green. 'Annabelle', the oldest selection, is still popular. Incrediball® has large flowers sometimes exceeding 30 centimetres wide. Invincibelle® Spirit has smaller flower heads, around 15 centimetres wide, but open pink; Invincibelle® Ruby flowers are deep reddish pink. White Dome® has domed flower heads of mostly fertile flowers with just a ring of larger sterile flowers, giving a lacy effect.

From the southeastern US comes oak-leaf hydrangea, *H. quercifolia*, whose leaves are nearly as ornamental as its flowers. As the common name suggests, it has distinctly oak-shaped leaves that are lobed and coarsely serrated. The fall foliage is the best of any hydrangea, turning from orange to red to burgundy. Its white flowers, a combination of fertile and sterile, are held in conelike clusters similar to those of Pee-Gee hydrangea. Most selections reach 1.8 to 2.5 metres tall. 'Snow Queen' is a tall, white-flowered selection; 'Pee Wee' and 'Munchkin' are dwarf versions, at 1.2 metres and 1 metre tall respectively.

'Snowflake' is grown for its double sterile flowers. 'Amethyst' is a taller selection whose flowers age from light pink to dark reddish pink; 'Ruby Slippers' is a similar but compact 1.2-metre-tall selection. 'Little Honey' is a dwarf 1.2-metre-tall selection grown primarily for its golden yellow to chartreuse leaves.

The hydrangea prefer organically rich, well-drained soil. They are not fond of drought. Although acidic soil is needed to keep mopheads and lacecaps blue, pH does not affect the colours of either type. Full sun is best for Pee-Gee hydrangea but the others grow well in partial shade. Oakleaf hydrangea tolerates the most shade. Propagation is by cuttings. Few pests or diseases bother them, but powdery mildew is occasional if they are grown in sheltered sites. PG and smooth hydrangea are hardy to zone 3, and while rated hardy to zone 5, the oakleaf, lacecaps, and mopheads are more reliable bloomers in zone 6 or warmer.

Design tips: Hydrangea are versatile in the garden, as specimens, along foundations, in wildflower gardens, and in mixed-shrub borders. The dwarf cultivars are popular for patio containers.

ILEX
Holly
The tree hollies, *Ilex aquifolium* and *I. opaca*, are described starting on page 131. Among the shrubby hollies, the most important is blue holly, *Ilex* X *meservae* hybrids. This hybrid of English holly and the hardy Chinese species *I. rugosa* was done by Kathleen Meserve, who made it possible

Ilex verticillata

to grow hardy evergreen hollies in the northeast. The hybrids bearing her name, *Ilex X meservae*, generally have a broad, bushy habit with foliage akin to that of English holly. Most are dark green with shiny foliage. Popular male-female combinations include 'Blue Boy' and 'Blue Girl', 'Blue Prince and Blue Princess', China Boy® and China Girl®, and Blue Maid® and Blue Stallion®. Other cultivars include Blue Angel®, 'Golden Girl' (yellow fruit), Castle Wall® (male columnar form), and 'Centennial Girl' (female columnar form). The female cultivar 'Honey Maid' has variegated white-margined leaves.

Ilex cornuta, from China, is similar to American or English holly but not as hardy. The most popular cultivar is 'Dwarf Burford', a female which forms a bush up to 2 metres tall. Its leaves generally have smooth margins.

It is often sold as a pot plant at Christmas. Other American/English holly look-alikes are *I. pernyi* and the hybrid *I. X aquipernyi*, both of which have diamond-shaped, spiny leaves on large 3- to 7-metre-tall shrubs.

Box-leaved holly, *I. crenata*, is evergreen but its leaves are rounded and lack spines. It forms a rounded 1.5- to 3-metre-tall bush. The females have black fruit. Popular cultivars include 'Sky Pencil' (columnar female), Sky Pointer™ (pyramidal male), 'Helleri' (dwarf rounded female to 1.2 metres tall), 'Hetzii' (similar to 'Helleri'), 'Dwarf Pagoda' (dwarf male to 60 to 100 centimetres), 'Green Dragon' (very dwarf male to 45 centimetres), and 'Drops of Gold' (a yellow-leaved mutation of 'Hetzii').

Native to eastern North America is inkberry, *I. glabra*, a rounded, suckering evergreen 1.5- to 2.5-metre-tall bush. The females have smooth-edged, spoon-shaped leaves, and black fruit. 'Shamrock', 'Densa', Nordic®, and Green Gem® are compact cultivars, reaching about 60 to 90 centimetres tall. Winterberry holly, *I. verticillata*, a deciduous eastern North American native, is often found along streams and pond margins. It is grown for its orange berries, which remain on the naked stems all winter. Cultivars are available with yellow, orange, or red fruit. With a similar distributional range is mountain holly, *I. mucronata* (formerly *Nemopanthus mucronata*). This deciduous species can reach 2 to 5 metres tall and has yellow fall foliage; the females have long-stemmed matte red fruit.

The above holly prefer humus-rich, evenly moist, acidic soil. Inkberry, winterberry, and mountain holly tolerate wet sites. Full sun is best but partial shade is tolerated. Propagation is by cuttings. Few pests or diseases bother holly. Both male and female plants must be grown near each other in order to obtain fruit. Mountain holly is hardy to zone 2; winterberry holly, zone 3; inkberry and *Ilex* X *meservae*, zone 4; box-leaved holly, *I. pernyi*, and *I.* X *aquipernyi*, zone 6; and *Ilex cornuta*, zone 7.

Design tips: Blue holly is popular as a foundation plant but may also be used in a mixed-shrub border. The eastern North American natives may be used in wet depressions or along water features. Box-leaved holly may be used as a substitute for boxwood and as a clipped shrub in more formal settings. Any of the compact holly cultivars may be container plants in milder climates.

Itea virginica 'Little Henry'

ITEA VIRGINICA
Sweetspire

Most of the 10 species of *Itea* are evergreens from China. A single deciduous/semi-evergreen species from eastern North America, Virginia sweetspire, *I. virginica*, is native from Pennsylvania south to Texas. This plant is an arching, loose, suckering shrub that can reach 1 to 2 metres tall. The shiny leaves are lance-shaped and turn a mix of yellow, orange, and burgundy red in the fall. In the southern part of the plant's range, the leaves are semi-evergreen. In early to mid-summer, these plants produce narrow, 5- to 10-centimetre-long bottlebrush-like fragrant white flowers. 'Henry's Garnet' is a compact 1-metre-tall cultivar with burgundy fall colour and flower sprays up to 15 centimetres long. 'Little Henry' is even more compact, often reaching just 70 centimetres tall.

Virginia sweetspire may be grown in full sun or full shade; however, the most vibrant fall colour and heaviest flower production occurs under brighter light conditions. The soil should be acidic, humus-rich, and evenly moist; however, it adapts to a variety of soil types. It tolerates dry and wet soil. Propagation is by sucker division or cuttings. It has no serious pest or disease problems. It is hardy to zone 5.

Design tips: Virginia sweetspire is so adaptable that it may be used just about anywhere. The fall colours of the named cultivars make them suitable for mixed-shrub borders or as foundation plantings. Virginia sweetspire can also be used for naturalizing along the edges of water features or rain gardens.

LITHODORA DIFFUSA

Blue lithospermum, purple gromwell

Lithodora, a genus of flowering sub-shrubs, is now known botanically under the genus *Glandora*. For purpose of this book, they are included under their more familiar name *Lithodora*. *Lithodora* comes from the Greek meaning stone gift, which refers to the rocky, gravelly soils they inhabit in their native Mediterranean regions. Plants form low creeping mats of grey-green pubescent foliage and displays of blue flowers. Flowers are produced from mid- to late spring on plants that are 10 to 15 centimetres high and 50 to 100 centimetres wide. Plants can flower periodically in summer and well into late fall.

Well-drained acidic soils are a must for this group; poorly drained clay soils cause the plants' demise. Plants may experience some

Lithodora diffusa

foliar burn during sunny cold springs but generally recover quickly with a light pruning. In colder zones, plants benefit from snow cover or a mulching of evergreen boughs. *Lithodora diffusa* is the most seen species; cultivars include 'Heavenly Blue' (brilliant blue flowers), 'Grace Ward' (medium blue), 'Crystal Blue' (pale ice-blue flowers), 'Alba' (white), and 'White Star' (two-tone blue and white).

Propagation is by semi-hardwood cuttings under mist, taken in mid-summer. Few pests and diseases affect *Lithodora*, but excessive summer heat and extended periods of high humidity in southern zones are not recommended. Plants are generally trouble-free and hardy to at least zone 6; they are worth trying in zone 5 with winter protection.

Design tips: *Lithodora* is recommended as a ground cover, tumbling over small retaining walls, or scrambling through crevices and around boulders in rock gardens. Plants are eye-catching additions to heath and heather gardens.

MAHONIA
Oregon grape, grape-holly

The 70 species of *Mahonia* are native to Central and North America and eastern Asia and the Himalayas. They are closely related to *Berberis* (barberry) and are now included in that genus, but as they are so well known by their former name, they are described separately. As a group, they are suckering evergreen shrubs with spiny-tipped, compound leaves and terminal racemes of small, often yellow flowers which later

Mahonia aquifolium

develop into blue or black fruit. There are only a small number of commonly grown ornamental species. Perhaps the most popular is Oregon grape, *M. aquifolium*. This western North American species, native from British Columbia to northern California, can reach 1 to 2 metres tall. New foliage is often red-tinted and turns glossy deep green. Mildly fragrant yellow flowers are produced in April or May, becoming blue berries. More widespread in the Rockies of western North America is one of the smaller species, the creeping Oregon grape, *M. repens*. It is a short 30-centimetre-tall version of Oregon grape but its flower clusters are more compact and its leaves dull green. From Asia come *M. japonica* and *M. bealei*. These are similar in appearance and can reach 3 metres tall with large compound leaves reaching up to 45 centimetres long. The flowers are arranged in narrow racemes with several radiating like the spokes of a wheel from the terminus of the stems. *Mahonia bealei* is now naturalized in areas of Maryland and south to northern Florida. Very popular in milder areas is the hybrid *M. X media* and its selections 'Charity', 'Winter Sun', and 'Lionel Fortescue'. All grow to 3 metres tall with long leaves and large sprays of yellow flowers, often in late winter or early spring. Plants are reminiscent of a dwarf palm and impart a tropical effect.

Mahonia prefer acidic, humus-rich, evenly moist soil in full to partial shade. Full sun can lead to leaf scorching, especially in winter. They also prefer a sheltered site, as they are prone to winter burn. Unless you plan on naturalizing plants, excessive suckers should be removed to keep the plants within bounds. All *Mahonia* fruit best if two or more plants are grown together. There are no serious pests or diseases. Propagation is by cuttings. The hardiest species is creeping Oregon grape, which is hardy to zone 4. Oregon grape is hardy to zone 5. The Chinese species and hybrids are the tenderest, suitable for zones 7 to 9.

Design tips: As most *Mahonia* are tender, they are best used in sheltered sites away from winter sun. As such, they combine well with plants of similar needs such as *Sarcoccoca*, *Skimmia*, and *Aucuba*.

MITCHELLA REPENS
Partridgeberry

Only two species of *Mitchella* exist: *M. repens* in North America and *M. undulata* in eastern Asia. The genus honours John Mitchell (1711–68), an English physician who

Mitchella repens

lived in America and gave Linnaeus much valuable information on North American flora. It is partridgeberry, *M. repens*, that is most likely to be grown as a garden plant. It is a dwarf 5-centimetre-tall sub-shrub with trailing stems and pairs of leathery, evergreen, rounded leaves. In late spring, it produces pairs of white, often pink-tinted, fuzzy, fragrant, four- or five-petalled, starlike flowers. These later become two-eyed bright red berries that often remain on the plant all winter.

Partridgeberry requires humus-rich, acidic, evenly moist soil. It performs best in partial to full shade. It can be challenging to establish. Propagation is by layered stems that root on their undersides. Pests and diseases are rare. It is rated hardy to zone 3.

Design tips: Partridgeberry is most often grown as a ground cover under trees and shrubs,; consider planting on the edge of water features or in a shady rock garden.

MORELLA PENSYLVANICA
Northern bayberry

Northern bayberry is native to eastern North America from Newfoundland west to Ontario and south to North Carolina. It was once classified as *Myrica pensylvanica* and is still known by that name in much of the literature. This dense mounding shrub varies from 1 to 3 metres tall, rarely to 4.5 metres. The leaves are spoon-shaped, leathery, glossy, and fragrant when bruised. They hold on to their leaves late into the fall but have no appreciable fall colour. Plants are dioecious with insignificant flowers, but female plants develop stemless grey-blue berries in autumn, which remain on the plant all winter. The wax from the berries is the source of bayberry fragrance in candles. Silver Sprite™ is a compact selection which rarely exceeds 1.5 metres tall. Bobbee™ is also compact but has larger, wavy-edged foliage.

Bayberry prefer acidic, sandy-peaty, evenly moist soil but tolerates wet to dry soil, wind, and salt. Nitrogen-fixing bacteria on its roots allow it to survive in very poor soils. Plant at least one male to pollinate the females. Full sun is best, but it tolerates partial shade. Propagation is by seed or cuttings. Overall a care-free plant, it is rated hardy to zone 4.

Design tips: Although it is not commonly grown as a garden ornamental, bayberry is suited to areas unsuitable for other acid-loving shrubs, such as salty roadsides, coastal gardens, or wet depressions. It can also be used on embankments and in a mixed-shrub border.

Morella pensylvanica

Osmanthus fortunei 'Variegatus'

OSMANTHUS
False holly

The 30 or so species of *Osmanthus* are found mostly in the warm subtropical to tropical regions of Southeast Asia and Central America. The name comes from the Greek *osme*, fragrant, and *Anthos*, flower. Only two species are reasonably hardy for the temperate regions of North America: *O. armatus*, from western China, and *O. heterophyllus*, from Japan and Taiwan. These dense shrubs can reach 5 or more metres tall but more commonly are kept at 1 to 3 metres. From a distance, the plants look like English holly, *Ilex aquifolium*, but the leaves are opposite on *Osmanthus* and alternate on *Ilex*. The shiny evergreen leaves are stiff, oval in outline, and spiny-tipped. Plants are dioecious, with both sexes producing tiny but fragrant white flowers in the upper leaf axils in autumn. Selections of *O. heterophyllus* include 'Purpureus', which has purple new foliage that turns deep green; 'Variegatus', which has white-edged leaves; and 'Aureomarginatus', which has yellow-edged leaves. 'Goshiki', aka 'Tricolor', has pink-tinted new foliage and mature leaves that are heavily mottled with creamy white. *O. X fortunei*, a hybrid between *O. heterophyllus* and *O. fragrans* (a tender species), is similar to a plain green-leaved *O. heterophyllus*, but the spiny-tipped leaves have much smaller teeth. 'San Jose' is a popular selection, with narrower, finely serrated leaves.

Osmanthus prefer organically rich, evenly moist but well-drained soil. It grows well under acidic conditions but acidic soils are not requisite. In cooler coastal areas, it may be grown in full sun, but in warm summer regions, partial or afternoon shade is appreciated. Once established, it is reasonably drought-tolerant. Pests and diseases are not a problem. Propagation is by cuttings. Pinching the growing tips helps maintain bushier plants. It is hardy to zone 7 but worth trying in sheltered areas of zone 6.

Design tips: *Osmanthus* accepts pruning and thus can be grown as a hedge in milder regions. Otherwise, grow it in a shrub border. It blends well with other broad-leaved evergreens such as *Ilex*, *Skimmia*, *Rhododendron*, and *Aucuba*. In colder areas, it may be grown as a container plant and overwintered in a cool sunroom. *Osmanthus* X *fortunei* is also suitable as a living screen.

PACHYSANDRA
Spurge

Of the five species of *Pachysandra*, four are from eastern Asia and one from eastern North America. The genus name comes from

Pachysandra terminalis

the Greek *pachys*, thick, and *andros*, stamen, referring to the thick white filaments of the blossoms. All are suckering evergreen sub-shrubs which reach up to 30 centimetres tall. Their leaves are oval to spoon-shaped and often crowded toward the ends of the stems. The flowers, produced in mid- to late spring, are small, white, and bottlebrush-like. What they lack in ornamental value, they make up for in being highly fragrant. Japanese spurge, *P. terminalis*, has highly glossy foliage and terminal flower spikes; *P. axillaris* flowers arise from the upper leaf axils. Allegheny spurge, *P. procumbens*, has scalloped-edged leaves that emerge mottled brown and pale silver but later become plain green.

Pachysandra prefer humus-rich, evenly moist but well-drained soil. The Chinese species require acidic soil, while the Allegheny spurge is not as restricted. Both *P. terminalis* and *P. procumbens* tolerate some drought once established. All prefer partial to full shade; leaves may burn in full sun, especially in winter. Propagation is by sucker division. Although they are generally care-free, they are susceptible to leaf blight. *Pachysandra procumbens* is rated for zone 4; *P. terminalis*, zone 5; and *P. axillaris*, zone 6.

Design tips: All *Pachysandra* spread quickly by suckers, making them suitable as ground covers in partial to fully shaded areas. They blend well as an underplanting beneath deciduous azaleas, oak-leaf hydrangea, and viburnums.

PHYSOCARPUS OPULIFOLIUS
Ninebark

The genus name *Physocarpus* comes from the Greek *physa*, a bladder, and *karpos*, fruit, referring to the inflated dry fruits that this plant produces. Of the about 10 species of *Physocarpus*, eastern North American native *P. opulifolius* is the only one grown as an ornamental. The wild species can reach 3 metres tall and has bright green

Physocarpus opulifolius 'Amber Jubilee'

maplelike foliage. The autumn colour is not significant. In late spring, it produces 6- to 10-centimetre-wide hemispherical heads of tiny white or pale pink flowers. The uniform green-leaved form is not often grown in gardens, as the coloured forms are preferred. Among the oldest is 'Aurea', with yellow foliage. An improvement is 'Dart's Gold', with brighter yellow foliage and a more compact habit at 1.8 metres tall. 'Diablo', one of the older dark purple-leaved selections, has light pink flowers. Summer Wine® is more compact, at 1.8 metres tall, with arching stems and nearly black foliage. Fireside® has leaves that emerge red but later turn purple. Little Devil™ has dark purple foliage but its leaves are small; the plant tops at 1.2 metres tall. Tiny Wine® is similar to Little Devil™ but is more floriferous. Coppertina® has coppery orange foliage, while Amber Jubilee® is a combination of various orange tones. Both reach 2.5 metres tall.

A care-free shrub, ninebark grows in most soil types: organic to rocky, sandy to clay, acidic to alkaline. It requires only a well-drained site. It is also drought- and salt-tolerant. Although it flowers and, in the case of the coloured-leaf forms, performs best in full sun, it is surprisingly shade-tolerant. Pests and diseases are rare. Propagation is by cuttings. Although it is hardy to zone 3, it does not grow well in high heat and humidity; therefore, it is not recommended for south of zone 7.

Design tips: Use ninebark in a mixed-shrub border. They may also be planted as stand-alone specimens. Dwarf cultivars are also suitable for patio containers or as foundation plants.

POLYGALA CHAMAEBUXUS
Shrubby milkwort

Hundreds of species of *Polygala* are found throughout much of the world; however, the one most likely to be encountered as a garden ornamental in temperate climates is the shrubby milkwort, *P. chamaebuxus*, native to the European Alps and Carpathians. Shrubby milkwort is a suckering shrub with short stems up to 15 centimetres tall. Short-statured, the plants eventually form a dense, ground-cover-like mat. The small leaves are lance-shaped, dull green, thick-textured, and evergreen. The species name *chamaebuxus* means ground boxwood, and when not in bloom, the plants may be mistaken for a dwarf creeping boxwood. The 2.5-centimetre-long solitary or paired pealike flowers are produced in the upper leaf axils from late winter to late spring and sporadic at other times of the year. The wild form's white flowers have a bright yellow stigmatic

Polygala chamaebuxus

lobe. However, several named selections are magenta purple with a contrasting yellow stigma: 'Grandiflora', 'Kimniski', and 'Rhodoptera'.

Shrubby milkwort requires similar growing conditions to those required by heaths and heathers: humus-rich, evenly moist but well-drained, acidic soil. It grows best in full sun to partial shade but tolerates deep shade, although flowering is significantly reduced. As it dislikes excessive summer heat, it performs best along cooler coastlines or higher elevations. A care-free plant, it is easily propagated by division or summer cuttings. It is hardy from zones 5 to 8.

Design tips: Shrubby milkwort is small enough to use in a rock-garden setting, but as it spreads quickly, it can also be used as a ground cover. It combines well with heaths, heathers, *Cassiope*, and dwarf rhododendrons.

POTENTILLA FRUTICOSA
Shrubby cinquefoil

Among the 300-plus species of *Potentilla* found worldwide, three are woody types. Shrubby cinquefoil, *P. fruticosa*, is the only one commonly grown as a garden ornamental in temperate zones. The three woody species were moved to their own genus, *Dasiphora*; however, in the nursery trade, they are still known by their previous name. *Potentilla fruticosa*, found across the northern hemisphere, varies from being low and matlike to upright, 10 to 150 centimetres tall. Their pinnate leaves have no appreciable fall colour. The bark is shredded. The 2- to 3-centimetre-diameter flowers are produced in small terminal clusters from late spring

Potentilla fruiticosa 'Mango Tango'

through to fall. The wild form has bright yellow buttercup-like flowers, but modern cultivars are white and shades of yellow, orange, pink, and red. Of the over 130 named cultivars, some are more common in the trade than others. 'Abbotswood', 'Mount Everest', and 'White Lady' are the most popular white cultivars. 'Snowbird' is a double-flowered white cultivar. Of the numerous yellow selections, 'Coronation Triumph' is one of the oldest, with bright yellow flowers on 100-centimetre-tall plants. Other bright yellow cultivars include 'Elizabeth', 'Goldfinger', and Happy Face®, at 90 centimetres; and 'Gold Star' and 'Yellow Gem', at 30 to 60 centimetres. 'Yellow Bird' and Citrus Tart® have double yellow flowers on 90-centimetre-tall plants. Cultivars with pale creamy yellow flowers include 'Primrose Beauty', 'Katherine Dyke', and 'Summer Dawn'. Lemon Meringue™ has double soft yellow flowers with a darker yellow centre.

These all reach about 90 centimetres tall, with 'Primrose Beauty' having the bonus of silvery foliage. With orange flowers are 'Tangerine', Mango Tango®, and 'Orange Whisper'. 'Setting Sun' is peachy pink with a darker pink eye. Among the pure pink are 'Pink Beauty', 'Pink Whisper', and 'Pink Princess'. And with red flowers are 'Red Ace' and Marion Red Robin™, both brick red with orange tones. 'Red Lady' is one of the best truly red cultivars. The red cultivars reach 30 to 60 centimetres tall.

Shrubby cinquefoil are adaptable plants. They are not fussy about soil pH and grow well under acidic conditions. Although they prefer moist soil, once established they tolerate drought. Propagation is by cuttings. These are exceptionally care-free plants. Most are hardy to zone 3, and some to zone 2, but they are not fond of high temperatures and humidity; therefore, they are not recommended south of zone 7.

Design tips: Shrubby potentilla is indispensable in a mixed-shrub border, providing flowers throughout the entire summer. They are also popular for foundation plantings. The lower growing cultivars may be used in large rock gardens.

RHUS
Sumac
About 35 species of sumac are scattered across the northern hemisphere but only two are regularly grown as a garden ornamental in North America. Both are natives. The largest is *Rhus typhina* or the staghorn sumac, a large shrub or small tree up to 8 metres tall, native from the Great Lakes to the

Rhus typhina 'Lanciniata', fall foliage

Canadian Maritimes, south to Georgia. The wild form, with its large compound leaves, fuzzy stems, decorative rusty seed heads (on female plants), and scarlet fall colour, can be used in a naturalized setting, but with its suckering habit, it is a little too coarse for

commonly known as Tiger Eyes®. This yellow-foliaged sport of 'Laciniata' matures at 2 metres tall and is far less aggressive. With a similar distributional range is the fragrant sumac, *R. aromatica*. This suckering shrub reaches 1.2 to 2 metres tall, with trifoliate leaves. The leaves and stems are fragrant when bruised. 'Gro-low', a dwarf, wide-spreading selection, reaches 60 centimetres tall but up to 2 metres wide. Both sumacs noted above have exceptional fall colour in yellows, oranges, and reds.

To obtain the best fall colour, grow sumac in full sun. However, they do tolerate partial shade. The soil should be well drained; they do not tolerate soggy soil. They adapt to soil pH variations, with acidic soil causing no ill effects. Once established, both are drought-tolerant. *Rhus* are generally not bothered by insects, browsers, or diseases, although leaf spot and mildew may occur when plants are grown in sheltered locations. Propagation is by sucker removal or root cuttings. Both species are rated hardy to zone 3.

Design tips: Staghorn sumac is popular as a naturalized shrub or used in the back of a shrub border. Tiger Eyes® is suitable for use as a specimen or as a contrast in any landscape. Fragrant sumac may also be naturalized or even grown as an informal hedge. 'Gro-low' is ideal as a ground cover for problematic dry areas or embankments.

most gardens. A little more decorative is the selection 'Dissecta' (also known as 'Laciniata'), whose leaflets are further divided into more leaflets, resulting in a lacy foliage. It generally stays less than 5 metres tall but it can still sucker. The most striking is 'Bailtiger', more

ROSA RUGOSA
Rugose rose

Roses are not generally considered for acidic gardens; most perform best under neutral soil conditions. However, *Rosa rugosa* prefers

Rosa 'Henry Hudson'

highly fragrant flowers, up to 10 centimetres wide, are rose pink on the wild species, but modern selections are in shades of pink or purple and white, often with semi-double or double flowers. Blooming starts in late spring but can continue sporadically into late summer. In fall, orange-red hips are produced, which often remain on the plant all winter.

Suggested cultivars of *R. rugosa* include 'Alba' (single white), 'Hansa' (double lavender pink), 'Henry Hudson' (double white, dwarf), 'Roseraie de la Haye' (double magenta pink), 'Blanche Double de Coubert' (double white), and 'Scabrosa' (single pink). The Pavement series are ground-cover cultivars of *R. rugosa*. With small, fully double, carnation-like flowers are 'F. J. Grootendorst' (magenta pink), 'Grootendorst Supreme' (red), and 'Grootendorst Alba' (white). These three cultivars rarely produce hips and are not as fragrant as regular rugose roses.

As noted, rugose rose prefers acidic soil but tolerates adverse soil conditions such as clay soil, sandy soil, and drought. Full sun is best but it tolerates partial shade. However, it does not tolerate wet soil. Its excellent salt tolerance makes it indispensable for planting in coastal gardens. Propagation is by cuttings or sucker divisions. Unlike many roses, rugose rose is relatively disease-free, although powdery mildew can be a problem if plants are grown in a too-sheltered site. However, it may be attacked by aphids, pear slugs, or leafrollers. It is among the hardiest of shrubs, zone 2, making it the most reliable rose for the coldest regions of North America. However, it is not fond of high heat and humidity; therefore, unlike most roses, is not recommended south of zone 7.

acidic soil; if the soil is too alkaline, it quickly suffers from leaf chlorosis. Rugose rose is native to coastal regions of northern Japan and adjacent northern China and the Russian Far East. This old-fashioned rose, grown as an ornamental in North America for over 100 years, is now naturalized in many parts of the country. Although it is a little too coarse for a refined rose garden, it is perhaps the hardiest rose, making it useful in the cold Midwest and the Canadian Prairie provinces. Rugose rose is a suckering, thorny shrub that can reach 2 metres tall. The leaves are glossy and heavily veined. In autumn, they turn brilliant yellow; on some plants, they may be orange red. The

Design tips: Rugose rose can be grown as an informal hedge or planted along shorelines to help prevent erosion. Even though it may be used in a shrub border, it is invasive and needs ample space. An old-fashioned rose, it is ideal for cottage gardens.

SAMBUCUS
Elderberry

The about 25 species of *Sambucus* are distributed worldwide. As a group, they are large multi-stemmed shrubs with large pinnate leaves and clusters of white flowers that develop into small berries that are relished by birds. Several species, as well as numerous cultivars, are commonly grown as ornamentals in temperate gardens. Native to Europe is the black elderberry, *S. nigra*. In eastern North America is the similar American black elderberry, *S. canadensis*, referred to as *S. nigra* ssp. *canadensis* by some taxonomists. Both reach 3 to 4 metres tall and have flat-topped clusters of scented flowers in early summer followed by edible black berries. Several cultivars are grown primarily for their fruit production: 'York', 'Adams 1', 'Adams 2', 'Kent', 'Nova', 'Scotia', and 'Victoria'. These have plain green foliage. From an ornamental point of view, the most popular is 'Aurea', which has golden yellow foliage. 'Aureovariegata', 'Madonna', and Instant Karma® have white to yellow-edged leaves, while 'Pulverulenta' has white mottled leaves. Black Beauty® has dark purple foliage and pale pink flowers. Black Tower® has a fastigiated form, while Black Lace® has deeply cut lacy purple foliage. From western North America is *S. caerulea*, sometimes referred to as *S. nigra* ssp. *caerulea*. Although this plant has green leaves, its berries are an attractive powder blue.

Native across the northern hemisphere is red elderberry, *S. racemosa* (includes *S. pubens*). This 3- to 4-metre-tall shrub produces conical clusters of creamy white flowers in mid- to late spring, followed by bright red berries. The red elderberry does not have edible berries. 'Plumosa Aurea' has deeply cut bright yellow foliage. 'Sutherland Gold' has even lacier foliage. The dwarf Lemony Lace™ cultivar reaches 1.6 metres tall with lacy leaves. 'Golden Glow' is also 1.6 metres tall and has red-tinted spring leaves that later turn yellow. 'Goldenlocks' has lacy yellow leaves but very narrow leaflets.

Elderberries prefer organically rich, evenly moist, well-drained soil. It adapts to soil pH variations and grows well in acidic soil conditions. They tolerate wet soil. Full sun develops the best foliar colour on the yellow and purple-leaved cultivars but partial shade is tolerated. For cultivars with decorative leaves, a hard pruning is recommended every few years. This keeps the plants compact and less woody. Removal of excess suckers also maintains more compact plants. The fragile branches can be damaged by heavy snow loads. The main disease is powdery mildew if they are grown in a too-sheltered location, but cankers and leaf spot also occur. Although few insects bother them, watch for elder borer beetle, which can be devastating in some locations. Propagation is by cuttings. As red elderberry is not fond of excess heat and humidity, it is recommended for zones 3 to 7; black elderberry for zones 4 to 8.

Sambucus racemosa 'Lemony Lace'

Sarcococca hookeriana

Design tips: Cut-leaved selections such as Black Lace® and 'Golden Glow' are substitutes for Japanese maple in areas that are too cold to grow the latter. Their soft texture can be appreciated in any landscape. Those selections with decorative foliage may be grown as specimens or as contrasts in a shrub border. As all are relatively fast growing, they may be used as living screens. Their love of water makes them suited to rain gardens.

SARCOCOCCA
Fragrant sweetbox

This genus of about 20 species is native to eastern and southeastern Asia and the Himalayas. The genus name comes from the Greek *sarkos*, fleshy, and *kokkos*, berry, referring to the fleshy fruit produced by the plants. As a group, they are evergreen plants with shiny, lance-shaped leaves up to 10 centimetres long. The flowers are monoecious; therefore, plants are functionally male or female. The flowers of both are unassuming, white, axillary, spiderlike flowers. However, their lack of floral beauty is compensated by their intense fragrance. They also bloom early in spring, even in late winter in milder areas. Female plants produce wine red berries in late summer. The most popular species is perhaps *S. hookeriana* var. *humilis*, which forms a slow-growing suckering shrub up to 45 centimetres tall. Fragrant Mountain™ has broader, deeper green leaves, while Fragrant Valley™ has longer, narrower foliage. *Sarcococca hookeriana* var. *digyna* 'Purple Stem' has dark purple stems and red flower buds which open to white flowers. It grows a little taller than var. *humilis*, up to 60 centimetres. 'Winter Gem', of hybrid origin, appears like a shorter version of 'Purple Stem'. Also offered in the landscape trade are the species *S. ruscifolia* and *S. confusa*, both of which reach 90 centimetres or taller.

Sweetbox prefer partial shade but tolerate full shade. Too much sun bleaches the leaves. The soil should be organically rich, acidic, and evenly moist, although well-established plants tolerate some drought. They are seldom bothered by pests or disease. Propagation is mostly by cuttings. *Sarcococca hookeriana* and its selections are the hardiest types, suitable for zones 6 to 9. *Sarcococca ruscifolia* and *S. confusa* are listed for zones 7 to 9.

Design tips: *Sarcococca hookeriana* is often grown as a ground cover in shady areas or even trimmed as a low hedge. It can also be used in a container or along the front of a shrub border. It is ideal near the entrance to a house, where its sweet fragrance can be best appreciated.

SKIMMIA JAPONICA
Japanese skimmia

All four species of *Skimmia* are native to East Asia, where they grow as understorey shrubs. The only species likely to be found in North American garden centres, *S. japonica*, is the hardiest of this group of mostly tender plants. *Skimmia japonica* forms a rounded mound to 1.2 metres tall, with lance-shaped, deep green evergreen leaves that are slightly aromatic when bruised. Plants are dioecious; both sexes produce rounded terminal clusters of fragrant white flowers in mid- to late spring. Female plants then develop clusters

Skimmia japonica

of red berries that often stay on the plant through much of the winter. Of the several named selections, 'Rubella' is a compact male clone that reaches 75 centimetres tall; its red buds form in the fall and look attractive all winter. Recent introductions from Holland include Red Dwarf®, Pink Dwarf®, and White Dwarf® male clones which have red, pink, or creamy yellow winter buds on compact rounded plants, all ideal as pot plants for patios. Among the female clones are 'Nymans', which forms a larger plant; 'Chameleon', whose berries change from green to white to red; and 'Pabella', which is compact with abundant fruit production. 'Reevesiana', a hermaphroditic form, has both male and female flowers that produce fruit even as a stand-alone plant. However, fruit production is still better if a male plant is nearby. 'Temptation' is a more compact hermaphroditic form. For decorative foliage, try Magic Marlot® or Mystic Marlot®, both

of which have grey-green leaves with a white margin; these compact male plants have red overwintering buds.

Skimmia prefer well-drained, humus-rich, acidic soil in partial to full shade. Too much sun results in scorched leaves. In colder zones, plants are best sited where they will be to be protected from winter sun. It is suited to shrub borders, foundation plantings, and woodland settings. It is among the most shade-tolerant shrubs. It is overall a care-free plant, but in warmer areas mites may be a problem. Propagation is by cuttings. It is rated hardy from zones 6 to 8.

Design tips: *Skimmia* are ideal for the front of a shady shrub border or as a foundation plant on the east or north side of a building. They are ideal as container plants, especially in areas with mild winters. They blend well with other evergreen, mild-zone, acid-lovers such as *Sarcococca*, *Aucuba*, *Pernettya*, and *Mahonia*.

STEPHANANDRA INCISA
Lace shrub

Stephanandra incisa, native to Japan and Korea, forms a low but spreading shrub, 60 centimetres tall but 2 metres wide. Its arching stems have small maplelike leaves that are bright green in summer and orange yellow in autumn. These stems often root where they touch the ground, resulting in a ground-cover effect. Throughout the summer, plants produce small rounded clusters of white starlike flowers. 'Incisa', the standard cultivar, has deeply cut leaves.

Stephanandra prefers acidic, humus-rich soil that stays reasonably moist. Full sun

Stephanandra incisa 'Crispa'

produces the most flowers and best fall colour, but partial shade is tolerated. Plants respond well to shearing. Propagation is by cuttings. It is not bothered by any serious pests or diseases. It is hardy to zone 5, but as it is not fond of high temperatures and humidity, it is not recommended in areas south of zone 7.

Design tips: *Stephanandra* is ideal for growing over retaining walls, along foundations, or on embankments as a ground cover.

VIBURNUM
Viburnum

Over 150 species of *Viburnum* are native across the northern hemisphere, northern South America, and north Africa. They have opposite leaves and flat-topped clusters of white to pink flowers followed by small berrylike drupes that attract fruit-eating birds. Those from northern areas are deciduous, often with excellent fall colour; those from southern areas are evergreen. Numerous species and cultivars are grown in temperate gardens. The earliest to bloom are *V. grandiflorum*, *V. farreri*, and the hybrid between them, *V.* X *bodnantense*. These all have elliptical, ribbed foliage and nodding clusters of highly fragrant pink flowers in winter to mid-spring, usually blooming before leaves appear. All reach up to 3 metres tall, with the exception of *V. farreri* 'Nanum', which reaches about 100 centimetres. Among *V.* X *bodnantense* cultivars are 'Pink Dawn', 'Charles Lamont', and 'Deben', the latter with white rather than pink flowers.

Among eastern North American wild viburnums are witherod, *V. nudum*, and *V. cassinoides*. Both reach 4 metres and have glossy elliptical to lance-shaped leaves, flat-topped clusters of creamy white flowers in early summer followed by fruit that change from green to pink then finally blue black. Its fall colour is a mix of yellow and wine red. Brandywine™, 'Pink Beauty', and 'Winterthur' are the most popular cultivars. Similar but larger is nannyberry, *V. lentago*, which reaches 5 metres tall; rusty nannyberry, *V. rufidulum*, which can reach 6 metres; and blackhaw viburnum, *V. prunifolium*, which can also reach 7 metres. Also native to eastern North America is arrowwood, *V. dentatum*; this shrub reaches 3 metres tall and has ovate leaves that are ribbed with serrated margins. Clusters of white flowers are produced in late spring and become blue-black fruit in autumn. Its fall colour is a mix of yellow, orange, and red. Blue Muffin® was selected for its powder blue fruit on a compact 1.6-metre-tall plant. Chicago Lustre® and All that Glitters® have glossy foliage, while Autumn Jazz® was selected for its outstanding fall foliage. Bracted viburnum, *V. bracteatum* All That Glows®, reaches 2 metres and has blue-black fruit and glossy ovate leaves. Hobblebush, *V. lantanoides*, is yet another eastern North American native. This 4-metre-tall shrub has heart-shaped, ribbed foliage and clusters of white flowers in late spring followed by red fruit in fall.

European highbush cranberry, *V. opulus*, and American highbush cranberry, *V. trilobum* (now *V. opulus* var. *trilobum*) both reach 4 metres tall and are grown for their white flowers, attractive red fruit (edible on *V. trilobum*), and excellent red fall colour. These viburnum have a combination of smaller fertile flowers surrounded by larger sterile ones. Snowball bush, *Viburnum opulus* 'Roseum' (aka 'Sterile'), has all sterile flowers held in a globular cluster but it does not produce fruit. The European wayfaring tree, *V. lantana*, can grow to 5 metres tall and has oval to elliptical foliage that is densely hairy on its undersides. Creamy white flowers develop into red fruit. 'Mohican', a compact cultivar, reaches 2.5 metres tall.

A number of garden-worthy viburnums hail from Asia. Leatherleaf viburnum, *V. rhytidophyllum*, can reach 3 metres tall and has elliptical to lance-shaped, wrinkled and leathery leaves that are evergreen in the south, semi-evergreen in the north. White flowers produce red fruit that eventually turn black. 'Cree' is a popular, slightly hardier, cultivar. The hybrid between leatherleaf viburnum and wayfaring tree, *V.* X *rhytidophylloides*, is similar to leatherleaf viburnum but more deciduous. 'Alleghany' and 'Willowwood' are popular cultivars. The newer Red Balloon® was selected for its better fruit set. Linden viburnum, *V.*

dilatatum, reaches 3 metres tall, with rounded foliage, white flowers, and red fruit; it has good fall colour in a blend of red, bronze, and burgundy. 'Erie' and 'Asian Beauty' are popular cultivars, while Cardinal Candy® is a dwarf, free-fruiting selection reaching 1.6 metres tall. *V. dilatatum* hybrids include 'Emerald Triumph', 'Oneida', and 'Fugitive'. Siebold's viburnum, *V. sieboldii*, reaches 6 metres tall and has white flowers and fruit that change from red to black. Doublefile viburnum, *V. plicatum*, has ovate leaves with sharply toothed margins. Like highbush cranberry, its flowers are also composed of small fertile inner flowers that are surrounded by larger sterile flowers. Its fruit is red. Reaching up to 4 metres tall and often even wider, this species has distinct layered branches that add architectural elements to the landscape. 'Mariesii' is the most popular taller cultivar; 'Shasta' is more dwarf, at 2.5 metres tall; and 'Watanabei', at 2 metres. 'Summer Snowflake', at 2.5 metres, has its main flower flush in late spring but blooms sporadically all summer. 'Popcorn', at 2.5 metres tall, has all sterile flowers held in a rounded cluster that looks similar to the common snowball bush.

Also of Asian origin are the fragrant snowball viburnums. The most important species is Koreanspice viburnum, *V. carlesii*, whose pink buds open to white, highly fragrant snowball-like clusters in late spring. Their leaves are rounded and covered in stiff hairs. Several hybrids have been developed from *V. carlesii*, including *V.* X *juddii* (*carlesii* X *bitchiuense*), *V.* X *burkwoodii* (*utile* X *carlesii*), and *V.* X *carlecephalum* (*carlesii* X *macrocephalum*), and 'Eskimo'. All are similar, reaching 2 to 3 metres tall, with white, fragrant, round flower clusters. The similar

Viburnum plicatum 'Sterile'

Viburnum X *pragense* (*utile* X *rhytidophyllum*) has semi-evergreen glossy foliage and round but only slightly fragrant flower clusters. A final Asian species of note is *Viburnum davidii*, a dwarf 100-centimetre-tall evergreen species with glossy, ribbed, elliptical leaves, white flowers, and blue fruit.

Viburnum as a group prefer evenly moist, organically rich, well-drained soil. They adapt to a range of soil pH levels and grow well under acidic conditions. Full sun develops the best flowers, fruit, and fall colour, but partial shade is tolerated. As many are partly self-sterile, better fruit production occurs when two or more plants are grown near each other. Propagation is by cuttings. The most serious pest is viburnum leaf beetle, which, after several years of attack, completely destroy the plant. Thin-leaved viburnums such as *V. opulus*, *V. plicatum*, and *V. dentatum* are the most

susceptible. Powdery mildew can attack all of them if they are grown in too sheltered a site. Hardiness is variable among the species and hybrids. *Viburnum opulus* is hardy to zone 2; *V. lentago*, *V. cassinoides*, *V. prunifolium*, and *V. dentatum*, zone 3; *V. lanatana*, *V. lantanoides*, and *V. sieboldii*, zone 4; all the fragrant snowballs, *V.* X *bodnantense*, *V. dilatatum*, *V. nudum*, *V. rufidulum*, *V. plicatum*, and the leatherleaf types, zone 5; *V. bracteatum*, zone 6; and *V. davidii*, zone 7.

Design tips: Plant *Viburnum* in mixed-shrub borders or as living screens. In milder regions, combine *V. davidii* with *Aucuba* and *Skimmia*. The native North American species are also useful in more naturalized settings and may be grown as understorey shrubs beneath taller deciduous trees. With its layered branches, the doublefile viburnum is best given plenty of space and grown as a specimen.

Andromeda polifolia

ANDROMEDA POLIFOLIA
Bog rosemary

Only a single species of *Andromeda*, *A. polifolia*, a bogland plant, is found throughout the northern hemisphere. North American populations were formerly known as *A. glaucophylla* but are now known as *A. polifolia* var. *glaucophylla*. The genus was named by Carl von Linnaeus in 1732 as a tribute to the Greek goddess Andromeda. Bog rosemary, a small often suckering shrub, varies from 10 to 50 centimetres tall, with narrow, rugose, evergreen leaves that vary from dark green to grey green to blue green. It often takes on purple tones in winter. The nodding, urn-shaped, white to pink flowers are borne in loose terminal clusters in late spring or early summer. Of the named selections, 'Compacta', a dwarf form, is usually less than 15 centimetres tall; 'Macrophylla' has larger, wider leaves than the norm. 'Kirigamine', often misspelled as 'Kiri-Kaming', is a compact form whose grey-green leaves often have a fine red margin. 'Blue Ice' is a larger plant up to 30 centimetres tall selected for its consistent blue-green foliage. Derived as a sport from 'Blue Ice' in 2010 was 'Blue Lagoon', whose foliage is silvery blue.

Bog rosemary, as the name suggests, requires sandy-peaty, acidic, consistently moist soil. Plant in full sun to maintain compact plants and maximize blooms.

Plants may be lightly trimmed to maintain a more rounded habit. It is rarely bothered by pests or disease. Propagation is by cuttings. Although it is rated hardy from zones 2 to 6, it dislikes warm summer temperatures; therefore, it is likely to perform better along cooler coastlines than inland.

Design tips: The blue foliage of *Andromeda* contrasts with heaths, heathers, and dwarf rhododendrons. It may also be used as an edger in an acid shrub border, in a rock-, bog-, or rain-garden setting, or along water features.

ARCTOSTAPHYLOS
Bearberry, kinnikinnik, manzanita

The 66 species of *Arctostaphylos* are distributed mostly in the western mountains of the Americas, with one species extending into Eurasia. The Latin name means grapes of the bear, as the fruit of this genus is popular as an autumn food source for bears. The most common species grown in gardens is *A. uva-ursi*, which is the most widely distributed species, the only one to naturally extend into Eurasia. This species has trailing stems and forms a dense spreading mat with spoon-shaped evergreen leaves that are often tinted wine red in autumn. The urn-shaped white to pink flowers are produced in terminal clusters in late spring. These become bright red berries in fall that often remain on the plant through the winter. Of the named selections, 'Massachusetts', the oldest selection, is grown for its abundant flowers and fruit, disease resistance, cold hardiness, and slightly more compact habit. The similar 'Vancouver Jade' stays greener in winter. 'Wood's Compact',

Arctostaphylos uva-ursi

the densest selection, tolerates more shade than the others. 'Point Reyes', a California selection, is distinguished by its leaves being produced in whorls and its taller habit, reaching up to 45 centimetres.

Less commonly seen in gardens are the manzanita hybrids *A.* X *media* and *A.* X *coloradoensis*. The former is a hybrid between *A. uva-ursi* and *A. columbiana*. 'Peter Ehrlich', a named selection, forms a mounding shrub up to 90 centimetres tall with terminal clusters of pale pink flowers that develop into red berries. The latter, a hybrid between *A. uva-ursi* and *A. patula*, is similar to bearberry but more upright and less spreading, reaching 20 to 60 centimetres tall. The 'Panchito' and 'Chieftain' selections were released by Plant Select in Colorado.

As a group, *Arctostaphylos* prefer full sun to light shade. They are not fond of excessive wetness and, once established, tolerate some drought. Well-drained, sandy-peaty soil is best. Bearberry is the hardiest, zones 2 to 7, with afternoon shade required in warmer zones. An exception, 'Point Reyes' is not particularly hardy, zone 5, but tolerates more heat and is suitable for coastal areas to zone 9. Pests and diseases are rare but excessive moisture or heat can lead to a variety of fungal leaf problems. The hybrid *A. X media* is not particularly hardy, rated for zones 7 to 9, but it is drought- and heat-tolerant for acid-plant growers in warm regions. The hybrid *A. X coloradoensis* is much hardier, zones 4b to 8. It too is drought-tolerant but prefers some afternoon shade.

Design tips: As bearberry is very salt-tolerant, it is ideal for coastal gardens. Alternatively, it may be grown in a rock garden, over retaining walls, as a ground cover in sun or shade, or along the edge of a shrub border. The manzanita hybrids are suitable for the front of shrub borders or for xeriscapes.

ARCTOUS ALPINA
Alpine bearberry

This genus was once included among the *Arctostaphylos*, but foliar differences make *Arctous* unique, so they were separated into their own genus. The Latin name comes from the Greek *arktous*, northern, referring to the natural distribution of the genus. Two species are native to North America. The most likely species to be encountered is alpine bearberry, *A. alpina*, which is found across northern Canada as well as northern Eurasia. It extends as far south as New Hampshire and Maine, atop the highest mountains. This completely prostrate plant forms a low twiggy mat with rugose shiny foliage that turns red in autumn.

Arctous alpina, fall foliage

The small, often solitary creamy urn-shaped flowers, which are produced just as the leaves appear, become shiny purple-black berries.

With its natural distribution, alpine bearberry is not fond of excessive heat; the best chance of growing this plant is along cooler coastal regions where it still should be grown with some afternoon shade. As it prefers sandy, gravelly soil, it is best grown in a rock-garden setting. It does not tolerate either drought or excessive moisture. Pest and diseases are generally not a problem. Propagation is by seed or cuttings. It is hardy to zone 1 but tolerates zone 7 if it is not exposed to excessive heat. Overall, it is a challenging plant to find and grow.

Design tips: With its low habit, alpine bearberry is ideal for a sunny rock garden or along the edges of the heath/heather planting. It is also a suitable subject for an alpine trough.

CALLUNA VULGARIS
Heather

A single species, *C. vulgaris*, exists within the genus *Calluna*. The genus name comes from the Greek *kalluno*, to clean, referring to the plant's historical use as a broom. This species is native across northern Europe to Siberia and is now naturalized in parts of New England, Atlantic Canada, and the Pacific Northwest. This evergreen shrub has tiny overlapping scalelike leaves arranged in four rows along its wiry stems. The flowers are produced in terminal one-sided racemes from mid-summer through fall. Individual flowers are typically purple pink, bell-shaped, and small but noticeable. Popular as a garden plant for hundreds of years, over 800 named cultivars are now available. Some have been selected for their foliage colour, which can range from grey through various shades of green, yellow, orange, red, or chocolate, with some changing colour throughout the season. Flowers range from white through every imaginable shade of pink and purple, as well as nearly red. Several cultivars have fully double miniature pompomlike flowers. "Bud-type" heathers (also "bud bloomers") whose flower buds colour up but never open are often sold as fall pot plants in local florist shops but are perfectly hardy to grow outside in the proper hardiness zones. These "bud-types" remain attractive into late fall and even into early winter in milder areas. Plant habit is also variable. Typically, the plants form matted clumps with upright stems up to 60 centimetres tall, but many of today's cultivars are bushier, often less than 30 centimetres, with some completely prostrate and less than 10 centimetres tall. The most popular cultivars are listed in the appendix on page 252.

Heathers require acidic, sandy-peaty, well-drained but evenly moist soil. They do not tolerate droughty soil. Full sun maintains the most flowers and best foliar colour. Plants

Calluna vulgaris 'Darkness'

should be trimmed each spring to remove the old flowers and maintain a bushier habit. Propagation is by cuttings. Heathers are not usually bothered by pests and diseases. Heathers dislike hot, humid weather. In eastern North America, they are suitable only in zones 4 to 6; however, in coastal regions of the Pacific Northwest, they can be grown south to zone 8.

Design tips: Heathers are often grown in their own dedicated gardens, sometimes in combination with other ericaceous shrubs such as heaths, bell heather, and mountain heather. They also combine well with dwarf rhododendrons and dwarf conifers. The smaller prostrate cultivars are also useful in rock gardens.

CASSIOPE
Mountain bell heather

The nine species of *Cassiope* are found in Arctic regions and points farther south atop the highest mountains. Considered snowbed species—plants that grow beneath late-lying snow where they are mostly protected from the freeze-thaw cycle of fall and spring— they are challenging to cultivate. Plants are matlike, 10 to 20 centimetres tall, with prostrate stems and evergreen, overlapping, scalelike leaves. The nodding, white, lily-of-the-valley-like flowers, often with contrasting red calyxes, are solitary near the stem tips. Blooming occurs from mid- to late spring. Three main species are grown as garden plants: *C. mertensiana* (Alaska to California), *C. lycopodioides* (Alaska, BC, and northern Washington state), and *C. selaginoides* (Himalayas). The named cultivars 'Muirhead',

'Randle Cook', and 'Beatrice Lilley' were selected for their freer flowering habit, as many *Cassiope* are shy bloomers.

Cassiope require similar conditions as those for heaths and heathers: acidic, sandy-peaty, well-drained soil and full sun. In hotter summer areas, some afternoon shade is appreciated. They do not tolerate drought. Propagation is by cuttings. Few pests or diseases bother them. In the wild, they may grow in zone 2; in areas with no reliable winter snow cover, they are best in zones 5 to 7. As they dislike excessive summer heat, they are easiest to grow in cooler coastal areas of the Pacific Northwest and northeast North America.

Design tips: Grow *Cassiope* with heath, heather, and other similar plants such as *Phyllodoce* and *Daboecia*. They may also be combined with dwarf rhododendrons and miniature conifers. They are suitable for rock-garden settings as long as the soil is not too dry.

Cassiope 'Muirhead'

CHAMAEDAPHNE CALYCULATA
Leatherleaf

The single species in the genus *Chamaedaphne*, *C. calyculata*, is commonly called leatherleaf or bog Andromeda. The genus name comes from the Greek *chamai*, dwarf or on the ground, and *daphne*, laurel. It is Holarctic in its distribution, found in bogs, along streams, or on moist barrens. This evergreen shrub has an open habit and can reach 1.5 metres tall. Oval leaves tend to be held erect along the arching stems. The leaves are dull grey green on the surface, pale with rusty scales on the undersides, and become brown-tinted in winter. The white, lily-of-the-valley-like flowers are produced in leafy, arching, terminal racemes in early to mid-spring. Although it is not common in cultivation, there are three named selections: 'Verdant' has greener foliage than is normal for the species; 'White Bells' is more compact, up to 50 centimetres tall, with larger, more abundant flowers; and 'Nana' is dwarf, at less than 30 centimetres.

Leatherleaf requires full sun and acidic, peaty-sandy, consistently moist soil. Propagation is by cuttings. This plant, toxic if ingested, is rarely bothered by pests or diseases. Trim the faded flowers to keep the plants tidy. This plant is rated hardy from zones 2 to 7.

Design tips: Grow leatherleaf with other moisture-loving ericaceous plants such as bog rosemary, bog laurel, and Labrador tea. However, leatherleaf tolerates drier conditions than most bog plants and may be used in more classic ericaceous settings among rhododendrons, azaleas, heaths, and heathers.

DABOECIA CANTABRICA
St. Dabeoc's heath

The sole species within the genus *Daboecia* is native to the coastal rocky cliffs and dry barrens of Ireland, UK, France, Spain, Portugal, and the Azores. Although the stems may reach 40 centimetres tall, they are generally prostrate, with the plants forming a loose mat up to 1 or more metre wide. The small 1-centimetre-long evergreen leaves have glossy green surfaces and white-felted undersides, with inrolled margins. The flowers are in loose terminal racemes. Individual flowers are urn-shaped, 10 to 14 millimetres long, and generally in shades of reddish purple. Plants have a prolonged blooming period from May until October. The over 50 named selections differ in their mature size and floral colour. Among the more popular are 'Atropurpurea', dark purple; 'Praegerae', rich pink; 'Cinderella', light pink; 'Amelie', magenta; 'Angelina', reddish pink; 'Vanessa', mauve; 'Snowdrift', white; and 'Alba', white. Unique is 'Bicolor', whose flowers are either magenta, white, or striped, all on the same plant. For decorative foliage, try 'Rainbow', whose leaves are flecked with yellow and its flowers purple pink.

Daboecia are closely related to heaths and heathers, combine well with them, and require similar growing conditions. The soil should be acidic, organically rich but well drained. Full sun is preferred in cooler regions but partial shade is appreciated in warm, inland areas. A light shearing each spring keeps the plants tidy. Pests and diseases are rare. Propagation is by summer cuttings. Tenderer than heaths and heathers, it is rated for zone 6.

Design tips: Use *Daboecia* as a companion plant for heaths, heathers, *Cassiope*, and dwarf

Chamaedaphne calyculata

Daboecia cantebrica 'Hookstone Purple'

rhododendrons. As it prefers cooler summer temperatures and naturally grows near the sea in its native range, it is ideal for coastal gardens.

ENKIANTHUS
Redvein enkianthus

The dozen or so species of *Enkianthus* are all native to eastern Asia. They are large shrubs or small trees with elliptical, finely serrated leaves that are often in whorls. Many have vibrant red and orange fall foliage. The nodding bell-like white to red flowers are produced in terminal clusters in late spring. The most frequently grown species is *E. campanulatus*. This Japanese species can reach 4 metres tall and has a narrow, upright form. The creamy white flowers have red veins. 'Red Bells' has flowers with reddish pink tips, while 'Lipstick' has hot pink flower tips. 'Showy Lantern' and 'Pagoda' have completely pink flowers. 'Bruce Briggs' has the darkest flowers of any selection, nearly red. *Enkianthus perulatus* is smaller than *E. campanulatus*, reaching 2 to 3 metres tall, with nearly pure white flowers. The most popular selection is 'J. L. Pennock'. *Enkianthus cernuus* var. *rubens* is also more compact, at 2 metres tall, but with a rounded habit. Its red bells are held in drooping racemes of up to 12 blossoms per raceme. These last two have a much slower growth rate than that of *E. campanulatus*.

All *Enkianthus* require acidic, organically rich, evenly moist but well-drained soil. Full sun produces the most flowers and best fall colour, but partial shade is tolerated and required in hotter climates. Propagation is by cuttings or seed. There are no serious pests or

Enkianthus cernuus var. *rubens*

disease problems. *Enkianthus campanulatus* is the hardiest, at zone 4. *Enkianthus cernuus* is rated for zone 5, while *E. perulatus* is rated for zone 6.

Design tips: *Enkianthus* looks good in a mixed-shrub border or combined with dwarf conifers and blends well with rhododendrons and azaleas. A particularly pleasing spring combination is planting it with bleeding heart (*Dicentra spectabilis*) and Solomon's-seal (*Polygonatum* species).

EPIGAEA REPENS
Trailing arbutus, mayflower

Of the three species of *Epigaea* in the world, one occurs in North America, one in the Caucasus Mountains, and the other in Japan. Trailing arbutus, *Epigaea repens*, is native to

Epigaea repens

eastern North America from Newfoundland south to Florida, where it commonly grows as an understorey plant beneath coniferous and mixed forest. The plant is completely prostrate and, if grown well, can form an evergreen mat. The matte green leaves are oval and leathery and the plant stems hairy. Five-petalled, white to pink and spicily fragrant tubular flowers are produced in terminal clusters in early to late spring.

Trailing arbutus is challenging to grow. It needs specific mycorrhizae fungi in order to survive. The best chance at success is to grow it under taller coniferous trees. The soil should be acidic, loose in texture with a high humus content. A yearly top-dressing of conifer needles is highly recommended. Dappled shade is best but it tolerates full shade. Winter sun can burn the foliage.

Propagation is by layering. It is not bothered by pests or diseases. It is hardy from zones 3 to 8.

Design tips: Trailing arbutus does not transplant well from the wild: start with a young plant. About the only garden situation where it might be successfully grown is naturalized under taller coniferous trees.

ERICA
Heath

Of the hundreds of species of *Erica*, most are from South Africa, and the few that are grown in Atlantic Canada are all natives of Europe. Their common feature is tiny needlelike leaves. They are either spring- or summer-bloomers. The more popular spring-blooming heaths start to bloom as soon as the snow melts in April and can continue into early June. They are important nectar plants for early emerging bees and butterflies. *Erica carnea* and *E.* X *darleyensis*, the main spring heaths, form low mounds 15 to 30 centimetres tall. Their narrow urn-shaped flowers are white, red, or purple or various shades of pink. Refer pages 256 and 266 for a list of popular spring-blooming heaths.

Among the summer-blooming heaths, the most common are *E. tetralix*, *E. cinerea*, and *E. vagans*. *Erica tetralix*, or cross-leaved heath, has grey-green, pubescent leaves and terminal clusters of nodding flowers from July through frost. *Erica cinerea*, or bell heather, also has terminal clusters of flowers, but the foliage is dark green. Cornish heath, *E. vagans*, has masses of tiny flowers nestled among the leaf axils along the branch tips. Hybrid summer-blooming heaths include

Erica vagans 'Valerie Proudley'

E. X watsonii, *E. X stuartii*, and *E. X griffithsii*. The table on page 256 describes the popular summer-flowering heaths.

Heaths require organically rich, well-drained soil and a position in full sun. They are often combined with heathers and dwarf rhododendrons, but the spring-blooming heaths may also be mixed with spring-flowering bulbs. Pests and diseases are uncommon, but hares can nibble the stems. Propagation is by late summer to fall cuttings. Most are hardy through zone 5, except *E. X griffithsii*, which is rated for zone 6.

Design tips: Heaths are indispensable companions for the other low ericaceous shrubs such as *Calluna*, *Cassiope*, *Daboecia*, and *Phyllodoce*. They also mix well with dwarf rhododendrons. The winter-blooming species and hybrids are must-haves for a winter garden. Try combining them with hellebores, snowdrops, and early primroses.

GAULTHERIA
Wintergreen

About 135 species of *Gaultheria* are found throughout North and South America, Asia as well as Australasia. The South American species were once placed in their own genus, *Pernettya*, but are now included in *Gaultheria*. *Pernettya mucronata* is so well known under its former name that it is included in this book under that name. The genus *Gaultheria* honours Jean-Francois Gaulthier, a Quebec physician and naturalist of the mid-1700s. The wintergreens are broad-leaved evergreens with nodding urn-shaped white to deep pink flowers in racemes or as solitary flowers. If fertilized, they develop into fleshy berries

Gaultheria miqueliana

which vary from white to pink to purple to blue or to black. Some are edible. The plant sizes vary from a few centimetres to over 5 metres tall. Only a few are hardy and of ornamental value as garden subjects. Perhaps the most recognized by North American gardeners is the American wintergreen or teaberry, *G. procumbens*, and the western salal, *G. shallon*. The former is a low 10- to 15-centimetre-tall shrub with stiff, glossy deep green foliage that emerges red-tinted in spring and often becomes red-tinted again in winter. Flowering commences in early summer, with edible red berries developed in late autumn. These berries often remain attached for up to a year. It is native from Newfoundland to eastern Manitoba and south to Alabama. It is commonly seen as an understorey plant of open forests. Salal is native from Alaska south to California, where it grows along forest edges, and as an understorey plant, of coniferous forests. It is also naturalized in the UK. It is a suckering shrub that reaches 2 metres tall with stiff, leathery, egg-shaped leaves. The flowers, produced in late spring, are in racemes and become dark blue edible berries in autumn.

From northern Japan, Sakhalin, and the Aleutian Islands comes Miquel's wintergreen, *G. miqueliana*. This suckering shrub reaches 20 to 30 centimetres tall and has oval, matte green, distinctly veined leaves. Clusters of white flowers are often hidden under the leaves but develop into large, decorative edible white berries in late summer and fall. *Gaultheria* X *wisleyensis* is a hybrid between *Pernettya* (*Gaultheria*) *mucronata* and *G. shallon*. They form dense shrubs up to 1 metre tall with ovate leaves, clusters of white flowers followed by showy red berries on 'Wisley Pearl' or purple-red berries on 'Pink Pixie'.

All *Gaultheria* require humus-rich, acidic soil that does not dry out. Dappled shade is best, but if the soil stays reasonably moist, they tolerate full sun. Deep shade is also tolerated but result in few flowers or fruit. Pests are not generally a problem but anthracnose and mildew can be problematic in certain regions. Propagation is by division, cuttings, or seed. American wintergreen is hardy to zone 3; Miquel's wintergreen, zone 5; salal, zone 6; and *Gaultheria* X *wisleyensis*, zone 7.

Design tips: While the above wintergreens are all suitable as a ground cover for semi-shaded to shaded locations, the most ornamental is *G. miqueliana*. Salal is popular as cut greenery for floral arrangements. American wintergreen is becoming increasingly popular as a pot plant at Christmas.

Gaylussacia baccata, fall foliage

GAYLUSSACIA
Huckleberry

The 50 or so species of *Gaylussacia* are confined to the Americas; the 10 North American species are confined to the eastern half. The genus was named in honour of French chemist Joseph Louis Gay-Lussac (1778–1850). Huckleberries are closely related to *Vaccinium* and some botanists suggest that they should be included with them. Popular for their harvested wild berries, they are not generally grown as garden ornamentals, although they are not without their merits. The only species seriously considered for its ornamental potential is box huckleberry, *Gaylussacia brachycera*. This

sphagnum bogs, they are difficult to grow under regular garden conditions. Worth attempting are black huckleberry, *G. baccata*, which has coral pink flowers, and bog huckleberry, *G. bigeloviana*, which has snow-white blossoms. These are both compact, 15 to 40 centimetres tall, with fiery red fall foliage.

Box huckleberry is the easiest to cultivate and needs acidic, humus-rich, well-drained soil under dappled light conditions. Black and bog huckleberry need full sun and sandy-peaty soil that stays consistently moist. Propagation is by seed or cuttings. Few pests and diseases cause any problem, although leaf miners periodically may be a nuisance. Box huckleberry is rated for zones 5 to 7, while dwarf and bog huckleberry are rated for zones 3 to 7.

Design tips: Grow box huckleberry as a ground cover under dappled shade conditions or as a substitute for periwinkle, bugleweed, or English ivy, all of which are often considered invasive species. Black and bog huckleberry are worth trying in a bog garden, combined with pitcher plants, sundews, and bog orchids.

low, suckering, mostly evergreen, 20- to 45-centimetre-tall shrub is an understorey plant beneath forests of the eastern US from Delaware to North Carolina and west to Tennessee. Its spring foliage is bronze-tinted, becoming glossy deep green in summer, then taking on burgundy tones through the winter months. In late spring, plants produce clusters of white, pink-tinted urn-shaped flowers. If two clones are planted near each other, it develops edible blue berries. Buried Treasure™, the selection currently on the market, rarely sets fruit on its own, as it is self-sterile. The other North American *Gaylussacia* are deciduous shrubs with often red fall foliage. As they typically grow in wet

KALMIA
Mountain laurel, bog laurel

The eight species of *Kalmia* are native to North America. The genus name honours Swedish botanist Peter Kalm (1716–79), who botanized in parts of eastern North America from 1747 to 1751. Although all have merit as garden plants for acidic soil, only one species has been widely cultivated as a garden ornamental, *K. latifolia*, the mountain laurel.

Kalmia latifolia 'Carousel'

This medium to tall, 3- to 9-metre-tall shrub is native from southern Maine to northern Florida and west to Indiana and Louisiana, primarily along the Appalachian Mountains. Plants have lance-shaped, dark green, glossy, evergreen foliage. Terminal clusters of saucer-shaped, 2.5-centimetre-diameter, white to red flowers are produced in early summer, generally just after the main rhododendron flowering season. Refer to the table on page 257 for a list of the most popular cultivars. Old plants can become gnarled, which adds character.

Over the years, many named selections have been developed. Most generally are less than 2.5 metres tall. Refer to the list on page xx for a description of the more common cultivars. Less commonly seen as a garden ornamental is the bog laurel, *K. polifolia*, found across much of Canada and the northeastern US. It is a low open shrub, less than 1 metre tall, with narrow, dark green, glossy foliage and terminal clusters of pink flowers in late spring. A particularly attractive white form is 'Leucantha'.

Mountain laurel require cool, moist, acidic yet well-drained soil. A peaty-sandy loam is perfect. Clay soil should be avoided. If your rhododendrons are successful, then mountain laurels should also grow well in your soil. The ideal light is dappled shade or at the least, shade from a hot afternoon sun. Bog laurel, on the other hand, demand full sun and peaty, consistently moist if not wet, soil. Little pruning is required for either, except dead-heading. Pests and diseases are rare. All parts of the plant are toxic if ingested by humans. Propagation is by cuttings. Mountain laurel is best grown in zones 5 to 8 but have survived in sheltered areas of zone 4. Bog laurel is hardy to zone 2.

Design tips: Flowering just after the main rhododendron season, mountain laurel combines well with rhododendrons to extend the season of interest. With their shade tolerance, they may be used as understorey shrubs beneath hgh-canopy deciduous trees, combining well with *Amelanchier*, *Hamamelis*, and *Clethra*. Bog laurel, as the name suggests, requires a bog-garden setting to flourish but have been known to grow well when combined with heaths and heathers if adequate soil moisture is maintained.

Kalmiopsis leachiana

KALMIOPSIS
Kalmiopsis

The two species of *Kalmiopsis* are rare endemics found in Oregon and discovered as recently as 1930. *Kalmiopsis leachiana* is exclusive to the Siskiyou Mountains, while *K. fragrans* is exclusive to the Cascades. Both are low bushy evergreen shrubs 15 to 30 centimetres tall, with small oval, glossy leaves. Pink flowers are in terminal clusters, from mid- to late spring. Individual flowers are saucer-shaped, 1.5 centimetres wide, and look much like those of the true laurels, *Kalmia*. The easiest way to differentiate the two species is by the length of their stamen filaments. Those of *K. leachiana* are less than 7 millimetres long; those of *K. fragrans* are more than 7 millimetres long. The older literature notes two cultivars of *K. leachiana* 'Le Pineac' or 'Umpqua'; both are now classified as *K. fragrans*.

Kalmiopsis are not easy to cultivate. The soil should be humus-rich but gritty and very well drained, as they do not tolerate wet soil. Full sun to partial shade is ideal but plants dislike excess summer heat. Propagation is by cuttings and it is bothered by few pests or diseases. It is rated hardy to zone 7.

Design tips: Those who have success with *Kalmiopsis* often grow it in an alpine trough or in pot culture. It is worth trying on the shaded side of a large boulder in a rock-garden setting. In cooler coastal areas, it can be combined with dwarf rhododendrons.

LEDUM
Labrador tea

As of 1990, the eight species of *Ledum* were all reclassified as *Rhododendron*. However, as they are so well known under the former name, they are described separately in this book. Members of the genus *Ledum* were all restricted to high northern regions of the

Rhododendron groenlandicum

consistently moist, acidic, peaty soil in full sun. However, they are adaptable for growing alongside more regular rhododendrons. Propagation is by cuttings. Pests and diseases are rare. Although *L. groenlandicum* and *L. palustre* are hardy to zone 2, they are not fond of hot, humid weather; they are best grown north of zone 6. *Ledum hypoleucum* is hardy to zone 4 and more tolerant of warmer summers.

Design tips: Because they are bog plants, Labrador tea is best suited for a bog garden, combined with bog rosemary and bog laurel. However, as they are adaptable, they can also be used along the front of a rhododendron border.

northern hemisphere. Only three are likely to be encountered as a garden ornamental. The common Labrador tea, *L. groenlandicum* (now *R. groenlandicum*), is found across Canada and the northwestern and northeastern US. It forms a small evergreen shrub generally less than 45 centimetres tall. Its leaves are elliptical with revolute margins. The undersides of the young leaves are covered in white indumentum, but this becomes cinnamon-coloured as the leaves mature. The foliage is aromatic when bruised. In late spring, the plants produce terminal rounded clusters of white flowers. *Ledum palustre* (now *R. tomentosum*) is a smaller, more northerly cousin found in northern Canada as well as in parts of northern Asia and Europe. *Ledum hypoleucum* (now *R. hyperleucum*), another look-alike, is native to northern Asia.

Bog plants, Labrador tea prefer

LEIOPHYLLUM BUXIFOLIUM
Sand-myrtle

As of 2008, *Leiophyllum* were reclassified as *Kalmia*, but in this book they are described by their more familiar name. *L. buxifolium* (now *K. buxifolia*), which has only a single species, is restricted to three locations in eastern US: the New Jersey Pine Barrens, the coastal plain of the Carolinas, and the southeastern Blue Ridge Mountains. Sand-myrtle is a low evergreen shrub, generally less than 30 centimetres tall. The round to elliptical leaves are about 1 centimetre long. Its glossy green summer foliage develops bronzy tones in winter. In late spring, the plants produce terminal rounded clusters of small, starlike, white or pink-tinted flowers. Of several cultivars, 'Prostratum' has trailing stems; 'Pinecake', a dwarf mounding habit; and 'Eco Red Stem', distinctive red stems.

Sand-myrtle requires full sun to partial

Leiophyllum buxifolium

shade and peaty-sandy acidic soil that retains some moisture yet is well drained. Propagation is by cuttings. It has no serious pests or diseases. It is rated hardy to zone 5.

Design tips: Sand-myrtle ideally grows with heaths, heathers, and dwarf conifers. Its small stature and slow growth rate make it ideal for rock gardens as well.

LEUCOTHOE
Drooping leucothoe, fetterbush

The 50 or so species of *Leucothoe* are distributed primarily in North America and Asia. They are deciduous or evergreen, 1- to 3-metre-tall shrubs with lance-shaped leaves and axillary drooping clusters of white urn-shaped flowers in late spring. Those that are commonly grown as garden ornamentals in temperate areas are the broad-leaved evergreen types. Perhaps the most well-recognized species is *L. fontanesiana*, native

to the Appalachians from New York to Georgia and Alabama. This species can reach 2 metres tall but is generally low, spreading, and about 1 metre high. In the wild, the similar *Leucothoe axillaris* grows closer to the coast rather than in the mountains. It is distributed from Virginia to Florida. There are several selections of both *Leucothoe* species and possibly hybrids too. As the species of the cultivars is often blurred, they are described here under their cultivar names. Scarletta® has red spring leaves that turn glossy green only to take on red and burgundy tones again in winter. The leaves of 'Rainbow', aka 'Girard's Rainbow', are irregularly steaked with cream and yellow. For small gardens, try 'Compacta', which is denser and bushier, reaching 1 metre tall, or 'Nana', which grows 30 to 60 centimetres tall. Both have red to burgundy winter colour. Leafscape™ 'Little Flames' is a dwarf cultivar whose spring leaves are red, winter leaves are wine, and, in summer, retain red tips on each stem, looking, as the name suggests, like flickering candles. Red Lips® is similar but retains a burgundy red colour all year long. Curly Red® is similar but has smaller, distinctly curled foliage. These last three dwarf cultivars rarely produce flowers. From northern California and Oregon comes *L. davisiae*, a suckering 30- to 60-centimetre-tall shrub with glossy bright green foliage and erect racemes of white flowers from late spring to early summer.

The most popular Asian species is *L. keiskei*. It is similar to a compact form of *L. axillaris*. Named cultivars include 'Halloween', 'Royal Ruby', and Burning Love®. These are all bushy 30- to 60-centimetre-tall shrubs with red spring growth, dark green summer leaves, and burgundy wine tints in winter. 'Halloween' is noted for its narrow foliage. These cultivars are grown primarily for their foliage, as they produce few flowers.

Most *Leucothoe* require evenly moist, acidic, humus-rich soil; an exception, *Leucothoe davisiae* tolerates reasonably dry soil. Dappled shade is ideal, but if kept moist, they tolerate full sun. Deep shade is also tolerated but both flower production and leaf colour are reduced. Propagation is by cuttings. These are care-free plants with few pest or disease problems, with the possible exception of leaf spotting if grown in a too-sheltered location. The above are all hardy to zones 6 and even zone 5 if provided some winter wind protection.

Design tips: *Leucothoe* may be used in a mixed-shrub border, especially one devoted to other ericaceae such as *Pieris, Enkianthus,* and *Rhododendron.* It is also popular as a foundation plant or grown as a ground cover below high-canopy deciduous trees. The compact cultivars may be used as container plants or in large rock-garden settings. *Leucothoe davisiae* is also suitable for a large rockery.

LYONIA
Maleberry, shining fetterbrush

The 35 or so species of *Lyonia* are native to Asia and North America. In eastern North America, three primary species are worthy for the acidic garden. *Lyonia lucida* is an evergreen with shiny, leathery, lance-shaped leaves and axillary clusters of pink urn-shaped flowers in April and May. This species is typically 1 to 1.7 metres tall. It is native to the US southeast. *Lyonia mariana* and *L. ligustrina* are deciduous, suckering shrubs. The former is generally less than 1.5 metres tall, while the latter may reach 2 or more metres. Both have oval to elliptic leaves and terminal clusters of nodding white urn-shaped flowers in June.

All need acidic, sandy, moist but well-drained soil. Partial shade is ideal but full shade is tolerated. *Lyonia lucida* is hardy only to zone 7; *Lyonia mariana*, zone 6; and *L. ligustrina*, zone 5.

Leucothoe fontanesiana

Lyonia ligustrina

Design tips: *Lyonia* is rangy for a formal garden but is suited to growing in the shade of taller trees and shrubs in a woodland setting.

MENZIESIA
Fool's huckleberry, false azalea, minniebush

Menziesia are, in fact, a type of *Rhododendron* and were reclassified as such in 2011. As they are more commonly known by their older name, they are described here separately. The genus was named in honour of Archibald Menzies (1754–1842), a Scottish physician and naturalist who travelled the Pacific Northwest with George Vancouver from 1791 to 1795. Two species are found in North America, with the remaining few found in Japan. These are deciduous 1- to 2-metre-tall shrubs, with an open habit. When they are not in bloom, they can be mistaken for a deciduous azalea. The flowers, however, differ from azaleas in that they are nodding, urn-shaped, and small at about 1 to 1.5 centimetres long. *Menziesia ferruginea* (now *R. menziesii*), from the mountainous areas of western North America, and *M. pilosa* (now *R. pilosum*), from the mountains of southeastern US, both have greenish yellow flowers, tinted bronzy purple. They flower just as their leaves unfurl. Their main claim to fame as a garden ornamental is their fall colour, a mix of yellow, orange, and red. If obtainable, the Japanese species have more showy flowers. Of note are *M. multiflora* (now *R. multiflorum*) and *M. ciliicalyx* (now *R. benhallii*), both of which have clusters of dusty purple-rose flowers up to 1.7 centimetres long. These compact shrubs, less than 1 metre tall, also have colourful fall foliage.

Menziesia require acidic, organically rich, well-drained soil—essentially the same soil conditions required by azaleas and rhododendrons. In the wild, they often grow as understorey plants; in the garden, they appreciate dappled shade. Propagation is by seed or cuttings. Few pests and diseases bother them. The Japanese species are rated hardy to zone 6; *M. pilosa*, zone 5; and *M. ferruginea*, zone 4.

Design tips: *Menziesia* combine well with rhododendrons and azaleas but may also be used in shady shrub borders. They are particularly effective when grown under tall deciduous trees.

Menziesia ferruginea

Oxydendron arboreum, fall foliage

OXYDENDRON ARBOREUM
Sourwood

A slow-growing outstanding tree species with an extensive range throughout coastal Appalachian regions from Pennsylvania to Florida, *Oxydendron arboreum* grows in gravelly nutrient-poor soils, in a low pH, usually near rivers and streams in full sun or partial shade. Plants in the wild form sizeable trees averaging 8 to 15 metres tall with a spread of 8 metres. Leaves are elliptical, about 10 centimetres long, and glossy green, turning shades of red in autumn. Drooping racemes of flowers are urn-shaped, resemble those of *Pieris japonica*, and appear in late August to September for several weeks. Plants are difficult to grow from cuttings but germinate easily from fresh seed.

Design tips: *Oxydendron arboreum* is a species relegated to specimen use in a woodland garden, ericaceous gardens, and rhododendron collections. It is chosen for its summer foliage, late-season bloom, and autumn foliage. Creamy greenish white developing seed capsules contrast with red fall foliage. This species complements broadleaf rhododendrons and azaleas and combines well with other key autumn foliage plants like *Hydrangea quercifolia* and *Rhus aromatica*.

PERNETTYA MUCRONATA
Prickly heath

A single species of *Pernettya*, *P. mucronata*, sometimes appears in North American

Pernettya mucronata

gardens. This species is native to the Andes of Chile and Argentina. Botanically this plant is now known as *Gaultheria mucronata*, but since it is so well known in the literature as *Pernettya*, it is described here under that name. This plant is a dense, suckering 45- to 120-centimetre-tall shrub, with small, shiny, evergreen, spiny-tipped leaves not unlike those of a miniature holly. And, like holly, these plants are dioecious. Both male and female plants produce small, white, urn-shaped flowers in late spring or early summer. Female plants, if pollinated, produce decorative pearl-like berries in shades of pink, red, magenta, or white in autumn. These fruit often remain through much of the winter, adding winter interest to the acidic garden. One male plant can pollinate several females, but at least one male is needed to assure good berry production. Named cultivars include 'Snow White' (white berries), 'Mulberry Wine' (magenta purple), 'Crimsonia' (crimson fruit), and 'Pink Pearl' (light pink fruit).

Pernettya require evenly moist, acidic, humus-rich soil in full sun or partial shade. It tolerates boggy soil. Plants may be trimmed to keep them denser and more compact. Their tough leaves make them unpalatable to browsers, and diseases are rare. Propagation is by cuttings. It is rated hardy for zones 7 to 9 but is not fond of intense summer heat, performing best near the coast or at higher elevations. Some strains are hardier and have been known to grow well in zone 6.

Design tips: *Pernettya* is a lovely plant to grow among dwarf rhododendrons, low evergreen azaleas, heaths, heathers, and its close relative *Gaultheria*. Keep them near the front of the border so that their decorative fruit can be fully appreciated.

PHYLLODOCE
Mountain heather

Depending on the botanist, four to eight species of *Phyllodoce* exist. The genus is named for a Greek mythological sea nymph. All are confined to the Arctic regions of the northern hemisphere, with some extending south along higher mountain ranges. In their natural haunts, they are considered snowbed species, growing where late-lying snow does not expose them to fluctuating freeze-thaw cycles. As a result, many can be difficult to cultivate in warmer climates. As plants, they are low-growing sub-shrubs, rarely exceeding 30 centimetres tall. Their leaves are needlelike and much like a larger version of spring heath, *Erica carnea*. The flowers are terminal, either solitary or in clusters, blooming in early summer. Individual flowers are urn- to bell-shaped, nodding and either creamy white or purple pink. Perhaps the easiest to cultivate is *P. glanduliflora*, which has clusters of cream-white flowers that are covered in sticky hairs. In the wild, it is native to subalpine and alpine habitats from Alaska south to Wyoming. With a similar range is *P. empetriformis*, whose purple-pink flowers are in clusters. Hybrids between these two species, *P.* X *intermedia*, exist. 'Fred Stoker', a named cultivar, has light pink urn-shaped flowers. Other species rarely encountered as garden ornamentals due to their difficult cultivation are *P. aleutica*, pale yellow; *P. caerulea*, pale purple pink; and *P. breweri*, purple pink with bell-like flowers and exerted stamens.

Phyllodoce need similar soil conditions as those of heaths and heathers—moist, acidic, and sandy-peaty with good drainage. Full sun is preferred, although afternoon shade is appreciated in warmer climates. Propagation is by cuttings. There are few pests or disease. Although it is hardy to zone 3, summer heat is more of a restriction. The best chance of

Phyllodoce empetriformis

success, outside their natural range, is the cool coastal areas of the Pacific Northwest or northeastern North America.

Design tips: In regions where the cultivation of *Phyllodoce* is possible, they are best combined with heaths and heathers, often bridging the blooming gap between those two plants.

PIERIS

Japanese andromeda

The seven species of *Pieris* are native to East Asia or North America. All are broad-leaved evergreens with glossy foliage and terminal clusters of nodding, white, urn-shaped fragrant flowers. Two species are commonly grown as garden ornamentals: Japanese andromeda, *P. japonica*, and to a lesser degree, mountain andromeda, *P. floribunda*. The latter is native to the mountains of southeastern US: North Carolina, Georgia, Tennessee, Virginia, and West Virginia. It can reach 2 metres tall, with elliptical leaves. The flower stems are erect and the newly emerging leaves are yellow green; both features separate it from the similar Japanese andromeda, whose flower stems are arching and newly emerging leaves are red-tinted. It blooms from late winter to mid-spring. The only cultivar is 'Millstream', which is compact, bushy, and generally less than 1 metre tall. Japanese andromeda is native from eastern China, Taiwan, and Japan. Although it is similar to mountain andromeda, it can reach up to 4 metres tall. It also blooms from late winter to mid-spring. This species has been extensively hybridized such that there are now many cultivars, ranging from dwarfs less than 1 metre tall, to those with red new foliage and even variegated cultivars. Refer to the table on page 259 for a list of the most popular cultivars. 'Brouwer's Beauty' is a hybrid between mountain and Japanese andromeda; its spring leaves are yellow green like those of mountain andromeda but its flowers are on arching stems.

Pieris require acidic, well-drained, humus-rich soil in full sun or partial shade. They do

Pieris japonica 'Valley Valentine'

not tolerate poorly drained sites. Propagation is by cuttings. All parts of Pieris are toxic if ingested; hence, they are not bothered by larger herbivores. The main disease is root rot, especially if the drainage is poor. Lace bug can devastate Japanese andromeda. The hybrid 'Brouwer's Beauty' is more resistant, while mountain andromeda is unaffected by lace bug. Mites and scale can occasionally be a problem. Both plants have brittle stems that can be damaged by heavy wet snow loads. Mountain andromeda is hardy to zone 4; 'Brouwer's Beauty', zone 5; while Japanese andromeda is reliably hardy to zone 6 but worth trying in sheltered areas in zone 5.

Design tips: Andromeda can be used in ericaceous shrub borders and blend well with rhododendrons and mountain laurel. Dwarf cultivars may be combined with heaths, heathers, and dwarf conifers and in milder areas make suitable container plants for patios. Foundation plantings, woodland gardens, and informal hedging are additional uses.

X PHYLLIOPSIS HILLIERI

Intergeneric plant crosses (hybrids between two different genera) are rare outside the world of orchids. Among the Ericaceae, the only intergeneric hybrid likely to be encountered as a garden ornamental is X *Phylliopsis*, a cross between *Phyllodoce* and *Kalmiopsis*. Although both genera are challenging to grow in gardens, the hybrid is far more amenable. This hybrid appears more like the *Phyllodoce* parent: it is a low 15- to 30-centimetre-tall mound with narrow, needlelike leaves. The flowers, produced in terminal racemes in early summer, may be urn-shaped or more open and bell-shaped but always a shade of purple pink. The three main hybrids are 'Coppelia', which is *P. emptriformis* X *K. leachiana*; 'Sugar Plum', *P. caerulea* X *K. leachiana*; and 'Pinocchio', *P. breweri* X *K. leachiana*.

Like most ericaceae, X *Phylliopsis* require acidic, sandy-peaty, evenly moist but well-drained soil. Full sun is preferred. Propagation is by cuttings. Pests and diseases are not a problem. They are rated hardy to zone 4 but dislike excess summer heat; they are best grown in cooler coastal areas.

Design tips: X *Phylliopsis* combines well with heaths and heathers but may also be combined with dwarf conifers and dwarf rhododendrons.

X *Phylliopsis* 'Pinocchio'

RHODODENDRON
Rhododendron

Over 1,000 species of *Rhododendron* are grown, in addition to thousands of hybrids. They are considered *the* most important group of ornamental flowering shrubs. Entire books have been devoted to this genus, so the following description does not do justice to the array of variety and flower colour that exists in this genus. For simplicity, rhododendrons are separated into five groups: Vireya rhododendrons of the tropics (beyond the focus of this book); large-leaved evergreen rhododendrons of the Elepidote group; small-leaved evergreen rhododendrons of the Lepidote group; evergreen azaleas; and deciduous azaleas. The azaleas are described separately.

Rhododendron hybrids

The classical large-leaved, large-trussed rhododendrons are what rhododendron taxonomists call the Elepidotes. These vary dramatically in their size. Some have small 2-centimetre-long leaves and are prostrate, less than 30 centimetres tall, but most have larger leaves, some with foliage up to 30 centimetres long on large shrubs up to 10 or more metres tall. Some have dramatic foliage covered in soft feltlike covering on their upper and lower leaf surfaces. The upper feltlike covering, tomentum, usually lasts only for the growing season, while the lower covering, indumentum, may last for several seasons. In zones 4 to 7, the majority of elepidote rhododendrons are less than 6 metres tall. Flowers may be in small trusses with clusters of only two to three flowers; others have head-sized, spherical clusters of flowers. Although white and pink to purple shades are the most common floral colour, a few have deep red, brilliant yellow or sunset tones. Flowering ranges from mid-spring to -summer. The hardiest of these, zone 4, are the Catawba or Ironclad hybrids. More recent are a series of Finnish hybrids which are equally hardy. For the best foliage, choose one of the "Yak" hybrids, derived from the species *R. yakushimanum*. The tables of elepidote rhododendron species and hybrids on pages 253 and 254 suggest some of the best and most widely available.

The lepidote rhododendrons typically have smaller leaves and flowers. Some of these are among the earliest rhododendron to bloom, in late winter in mild areas, yet others do not bloom until early to mid-summer. The floral colour range is more restricted and lacks reds and sunset tones. Many are dwarf, less than 1 metre tall, while others reach 4 or more metres. Among the taller lepidotes are the PJM series, many of which have leaves that turn bronzy to deep purple in winter. Also taller and early blooming are the *R. dauricum / mucronulatum* selections, which reach 2 or more metres tall and are semi-deciduous, losing many of their leaves over the winter. The tables on page 257 and 258 suggest some of the best lepidote species and hybrids.

Rhododendrons need full sun to partial shade and acidic, organically rich but well-drained soil. They do not tolerate drought, soggy soil, or salt. Retaining their leaves all winter, they need to be positioned in a sheltered location; otherwise, they risk significant winter burn. Few pests or diseases bother them, with the exception of root rot, which occasionally occurs, and root weevils, which cause scalloped leaf edges. Propagation is by fall cuttings. The Ironclads, Finnish Yak, and PJM hybrids are hardy to zone 4; the others are hardy to zones 5 or 6.

Design tips: The dwarf species and hybrids are small enough to use in rock gardens or combine with other low ericaceous shrubs such as heaths and heathers. The taller types combine well with mountain laurel and other taller ericaceous shrubs. They are also popular as foundation plants along houses and fences. Taller types are suited to shrub borders, especially useful for blocking unwanted views.

RHODODENDRON
Azalea

Two groups of rhododendrons are commonly called azaleas. The first group are broad-leaved evergreens. Many gardeners are familiar with florist azaleas, commonly sold in nurseries and box stores between Valentine's Day and Mother's Day. These azaleas are not reliably hardy and are more suited to the deep south of the US. However, several evergreen azaleas survive into zone 6. Far hardier are the deciduous azaleas. Azaleas vary in height from less than 45 centimetres to more than 3 metres. Some bloom as early as April or as late as August. Deciduous azaleas have larger trusses than the evergreen types, are fragrant, and have a wider range of colours, including bright yellow and orange. They have the bonus of red and orange fall colour. Royal azalea, *R. schlippenbachii*, and pinkshell azalea, *R. vaseyi*, are the earliest to bloom, flowering in May to early June before they flush leaves. Originating from Europe are the Gent, Knaphill, and Exbury hybrids, all hardy to zone 5. The hardiest of all are the Northern Lights series, which are available in a wide range of colours. The hybrids all have the word 'Lights' in their name: for example, 'Mandarin Lights' and 'Orchid Lights'. These are often hardy into zone 4. To extend the blooming season of azaleas, try the Weston hybrids. These are generally dwarf, up to about 1 metre tall, and bloom into August.

Like rhododendrons, azaleas need acidic, organically rich, well-drained but evenly moist soil. Full sun results in the most blooms, but most azaleas can tolerate some shade. Pests are not common, but powdery mildew can occur if the plants are grown in a too-sheltered location. Propagation is by summer cuttings. Most deciduous azaleas are hardy to zone 5, with the Northern Lights series rated for zone 4. Evergreen azaleas are most reliable in zone 6, but with good winter protection have survived in zone 5. Refer to tables on page 251 and 252 for suggested azalea hybrids and species.

Design tips: Azaleas may be utilized in the same way as that suggested for rhododendrons, with dwarfs used in rock gardens and the larger as foundation plants. Azaleas are also ideal for incorporating into open woodlands. By shedding their leaves, deciduous azaleas tolerate greater exposure variations than evergreen rhododendrons.

VACCINIUM
Blueberry, bilberry, lingonberry, cranberry

The genus *Vaccinium* is perhaps the most commercially important member of the Ericaceae. The cultivation of blueberries and cranberries is a multi-million-dollar industry which is only possible because the plants are grown with an acidic substrate. However, the focus here is on Ericaceae of ornamental value, and on this count, the genus *Vaccinium* is still noteworthy. Over 450 species of *Vaccinium* are found across the Holarctic region and south in mountainous areas into the southern hemisphere, with the exception of Australia. Only a small number of species are hardy north of zone 7.

Vaccinium typically have small, simple leaves which vary in shape from round to lanceolate. They may be evergreen or deciduous, the latter often turning brilliant shades of orange, red, or burgundy in the fall.

Azalea garden

Vaccinium vitis-idaea

The urn-shaped white to pink flowers may be solitary or in clusters. They later develop into edible white, pink, red, purple, blue, or black fruit.

Among the tallest of the hardy species is the highbush blueberry, *V. corymbosum*, which may reach 4 metres. More ornamental and smaller is the lowbush blueberry, *V. angustifolium*, which rarely exceeds 60 centimetres. The hybrid between these two species contains a host of named hybrids such as 'Northcountry', 'Northsky', 'Northland', and 'Polaris'. These grow between 1 and 2 metres tall. Other similar low, deciduous species include *V. myrtilloides* and *V. myrtillus*. Bilberry, *V. uliginosum*, has round, blue-tinted foliage on a prostrate shrub less than 15 centimetres tall. All have edible blue fruit and leaves that turn brilliant red in the fall. The low species and hybrid blueberries are hardy to zone 3, while the highbush is best in zones 5 or warmer.

The evergreen species lingonberry, *V. vitis-idaea*, has red fruit and rarely exceeds 15 centimetres in height. Most have a low, tufted habit, making them ideal companions for heaths, heathers, and other low ericaceous species. The round foliage is glossy green in summer but newly emerging foliage has a red tint and plants often take on red to purple tones through the winter. The flowers are usually pale pink and the red fruit are tart but desirable. The fruit often remain on the plants throughout the winter. 'Koralle' is the most popular cultivar and also the tallest, reaching 30 centimetres.

Cranberry, *V. macrocarpon*, is also evergreen. It forms a low ground cover and typically requires wetter soil than can be achieved in most gardens, except for a bog garden. Its flowers are pink and similar in shape to a miniature *Cyclamen* flower. 'Hamilton', a compact, bun-shaped selection less than 15 centimetres tall, tolerates relatively dry soil and may be used among other low acid-loving shrubs. It is hardy to zone 2.

V. ovatum, the evergreen huckleberry, can reach 2 metres tall and has boxwoodlike foliage. Its pink, urn-shaped flowers develop into blue-black berries. The spring foliage is red, akin to the spring foliage of Japanese pieris. 'Thunderbird' is the most popular cultivar. This is among the tenderer *Vaccinium*, only rated hardy to zone 6.

All *Vaccinium* require highly acidic, organically rich soil. In the wild, many grow in pure peat. With the exception of cranberry, *Vaccinium* need well-drained soil that does not become too dry. All perform best with at least a half day of sun, with most preferring

Zenobia pulverulenta

full sun, especially in northern areas.

Design tips: The highbush blueberry and evergreen huckleberry are suitable companions for rhododendrons, azaleas, mountain laurel, and other taller ericaceous shrubs. They are also suited to woodland gardens. The lower species are ideal companions for heaths, heathers, and their relatives.

ZENOBIA PULVERULENTA
Honey-cup, dusty zenobia

A single species of *Zenobia*, *Z. pulverulenta*, is a suckering, twiggy, 1- to 3-metre-tall shrub native to the southeast US. The leathery elliptical to oval leaves may be up to 10 centimetres long. The summer foliage is often covered in a dusty grey-green to blue-green bloom. In fall, the foliage turns reddish purple, especially if grown in full sun. In mild areas, the plants are semi-evergreen but at the northern end of their range, they are deciduous. In late spring to early summer, these plants produce bell-shaped, lily-of-the-valley-like white flowers in nodding axillary clusters. The flowers have a strong anise fragrance. The selections 'Blue Sky' and 'Woodlander's Blue' are both chosen for their intense blue-grey foliage. 'Raspberry Ripple' has typical grey-green foliage but its claim to fame is its reddish pink-edged flowers.

Zenobia may be grown in full sun to partial shade, in a moist, sandy-peaty soil. Pests and diseases are generally not a problem but the stems are weak and may be damaged under heavy snow loads. Propagation is by cuttings or seed. It is rated hardy from zones 6 to 9.

Design tips: *Zenobia* may be used in a shrub border, placed near the front where the decorative foliage and fragrant flowers can be best appreciated. With its love for water, it may even be used in a bog or rain garden.

Hydrangea anomala ssp. *petiolaris*

HYDRANGEA ANOMALA SSP. *PETIOLARIS*
Climbing hydrangea

Climbing hydrangea, *H. anomala* ssp. *petiolaris*, is a climbing deciduous vine which clings to trees, brickwork, wood, and similar substrates via adventitious roots. This East Asian species can reach 16 metres in length but is often less than 10 metres. Its rounded to heart-shaped leaves turn yellow in autumn. Its fragrant, white, flat-topped clusters of flowers are produced from May to July. Like most hydrangea, the flower clusters are a mix of small fertile flowers and larger sterile flowers. 'Miranda' is a choice variegated selection with yellow-margined leaves.

Climbing hydrangea grow in full sun to considerable shade. It is perhaps the best flowering vine to grow on a north-facing wall. The soil should be fertile, acidic, and evenly moist. This care-free climber has few pests or diseases. Propagation is by summer cuttings. It is hardy to zone 4.

Design tips: A reliable vine for shady areas, consider planting climbing hydrangea so that it can grow up the trunks of larger trees. Growing on a wall, it provides a backdrop for any plantings featuring acid-loving plants.

LONICERA
Honeysuckle

The many species and hybrids of twining

Lonicera periclymenum 'Belgica'

honeysuckle may quickly reach 6 or more metres in length. The genus name honours German botanist Adam Lonitzer (1528–86). Common or European woodbine, *Lonicera periclymenum*, has waxy, deep green leaves with pale blue-green undersides. The two-lipped, tubular, highly fragrant flowers are produced in a terminal whorl from June to frost. Flowers open white and pink but turn golden yellow as they age, later developing into glossy red fruit. 'Serotina' and 'Belgica' are two established cultivars, the former with broader and shorter floral tubes than the latter. More recent cultivars include 'Heaven Scent', 'Graham Thomas', and 'Scentsation', both with white flowers that age to pale yellow. The hybrid *L.* X *heckrottii* 'Gold Flame' has two-tone deep pink and golden flowers. If variegated foliage is your preference, try *L.* X *italica* Harlequin™, whose leaves are edged in white.

Another group of twining honeysuckle has trumpet-shaped flowers in shades of yellow, orange, and red but lack any strong fragrance. These include *L. sempervirens* 'Major Wheeler' (reddish orange), *L. sempervirens* 'John Clayton' (bright yellow), *L. sempervirens* 'Blance Sandman' (pinkish red), and the hybrids *L.* X *brownii* 'Dropmore Scarlet' (deep orange red), *L.* X *brownii* Honeybelle™ (bright yellow), *L.* X *tellmanniana*, and *L.* 'Mandarin' (bright orange). Although all twining honeysuckle are attractive to butterflies, hawkmoths, and hummingbirds, this second group is a hummingbird magnet.

These honeysuckles bloom best if grown in full sun with organically rich, evenly moist soil. The most common disease is powdery mildew. Insect pests include small moth larvae, which can be particularly damaging to flower buds; plants can be prone to aphids during hot dry periods. Leafroller moths may also be problematic. Propagation is by summer or hardwood cuttings. All of the above are hardy to zone 4.

Design tips: The fast growth rate of twining honeysuckles make them indispensable for growing over arbours,

pergolas, trellises, or fences. Avoid growing them through shrubs or trees as they can be aggressive and literally strangle their hosts.

SCHISANDRA CHINENSIS
Schisandra, magnolia vine

Schisandra, sometimes spelled *Schizandra*, is a genus primarily from East Asia with some 25 species. The species most likely to be grown in North America is *Schisandra chinensis*. This twining species ranges from China into neighbouring Russia, growing in shady woodlands. Vines may reach 7 or more metres. The oval leaves are bright green in summer and turn bright yellow in autumn. Plants are dioecious with separate

Schisandra chinensis

male and female plants. Both produce small white to pale pink flowers in their lower leaf axils. Female flowers develop into decorative hanging clusters of bright red, edible berries.

In the wild, *Schisandra* often grows in woodlands; in the garden, they produce more fruit if they are grown in sunny areas. The best soil is slightly acidic. To obtain fruit, at least one male plant needs to be grown with several females. Powdery mildew can be a problem if plants are grown in too sheltered a location. Propagation is by seed or late-summer cuttings. It is hardy to zone 4.

Design tips: *Schisandra* has a dual purpose: the fruit display can be both attractive and edible. Plants may be grown on arbours, pergolas, and trellises or allowed to scramble up the trucks of trees, an ideal quality for woodland gardens.

SCHIZOPHRAGMA HYDRANGEOIDES
Japanese hydrangea
Closely related to climbing hydrangea, Japanese hydrangea, *Schizophragma hydrangeoides*, is a self-clinging, deciduous plant with sharply serrated, heart-shaped leaves. Like climbing hydrangea, it turns bright yellow in autumn. Plants can reach 12 metres in height if given the proper support. Its adventitious roots stick to any rough surface, especially brick and stonework. Flowers are much like those of climbing hydrangea—flat-topped clusters of white flowers are a mix of small fertile flowers and larger sterile ones. The cultivar 'Moonlight' has silvery green leaves with dark green veins, while Burst of Light® has white-mottled leaves. 'Roseum' has white flowers that age to pink.

Japanese hydrangea grow in full sun to considerable shade and in any fertile, evenly moist soil. Overall, it has a slower rate of growth than climbing hydrangea. It has few pests or diseases. Propagation is by summer cuttings. Not quite as hardy as climbing hydrangea, it is rated for zone 5.

Design tips: Japanese hydrangea may be grown as a substitute for climbing hydrangea and, with its slower growth rate, is suggested for smaller gardens.

WISTERIA
Wisteria
No climber is as impressive in bloom as a well-grown wisteria. The eight species of wisteria are native to Asia and eastern North America. The genus name honours Caspar Wistar (1761–1818), a professor of anatomy at the University of Pennsylvania. Wisteria are twining vines, up to 8 metres tall, with large pinnate leaves similar to those of ash. Shortly before or after they begin to flush leaves, plants produce 15- to 30-centimetre-long pendant sprays of purple-blue pealike flowers. The foliar fall colour is usually yellow. Wisteria are commonly grown over pergolas and arbours. Japanese wisteria, *W. floribunda*, needs hard pruning each fall or winter to keep it in check and encourage flowering. Popular cultivars of Japanese wisteria include 'Macrobotrys', 'Royal Purple', 'Issai', 'Alba', 'Black Dragon', 'Pink Ice', and 'Lawrence', the latter being the hardiest. Silky wisteria, *W. brachybotrys*, is similar to Japanese wisteria but its flower clusters are shorter. 'Okayama' has pale lilac flowers, 'Shiro-beni' pale pink, and 'Shiro-kapitan' white. Both Japanese and

Schizophragma hydrangeoides

Wisteria floribunda 'Rosea', standard

silky wisteria have fragrant flowers that start blooming just prior to leafing.

From eastern US is Kentucky wisteria, *W. macrostachya*. It is similar in appearance to the Asian species but it flowers after the leaves have emerged. It is apt to be a reliable bloomer but lacks the wonderful fragrance of the Asian species. However, it is significantly hardier and far less aggressive. 'Blue Moon' is a popular cultivar. Also similar and from the southeastern US is American wisteria, *W. frutescens*, whose flowers, in clusters up to 15 centimetres long, are lightly scented. 'Amethyst Falls' is the most popular cultivar.

Wisteria need full sun and slightly acidic, humus-rich soil. They do not appreciate droughty conditions. Hard pruning encourages flowering. Few pests or diseases bother them. Propagation is by summer cuttings. Kentucky wisteria is hardy to zone 4; American wisteria and the Asian species are rated for zone 5.

Design tips: Perhaps no other vine suitable for acidic soil conditions is as spectacular in full bloom as *Wisteria*. It is second to none for growing over arbours and pergolas. With proper pruing it can be trained to make an admirable standard.

A heather garden.

APPENDIX:
ERICACEOUS SHRUB SPECIES AND CULTIVARS

Blooming Code	Blooming Season
VE	Very early
E	Early
EM	Early midseason
M	Midseason
LM	Late midseason
L	Late
VL	Very late

A wide range of species and cultivars exist among the Ericaceous shrubs noted in this book. The tables in this appendix describe many of the most readily available types. Rhododendron and azaleas, in particular, bloom in various seasons. Please refer to the key at left for the bloom season codes used.

AZALEA HYBRIDS

Deciduous hybrids	Height (cm)	Hardiness	Bloom Season	Description
Appleblossom	180	5a	M	Pink and white with yellow flare
Arneson Ruby	150	5a	M	Ruby-red
Berryrose	180	5a	M	Vivid yellow
Cannon's Double	180	5a	M	Double light yellow
Fireball	180	5a	M	Orange-red
Gibralter	180	5a	M	Bright yellow-orange
Homebush	180	5a	LM	Double rose-pink
Irene Koster	250	6b	M	White, flushed pink
Klondyke	180	5a	LM	Deep orange
Koster's Brilliant Red	180	5b	LM	Reddish-orange
Millenium	150	4a	L	Dusty rose-red
Narcissiflora	180	5b	LM	Double yellow
Northern Lights	180	4b	M	Mixed colours
Old Gold	180	5a	LM	Light orange
Oxydol	180	5a	M	White, yellow flare
Persil	180	5a	M	White, yellow flare
Spek's Orange	120	5a	M	Orange-red
Weston's Innocence	120	4a	L	White
Weston's Lemon Drop	180	4a	VL	Bright yellow
Weston's Lollipop	150	4a	L	Silvery-pink
Weston's Parade	150	4b	VL	Deep pink
Weston's Pink and Sweet	150	4a	L	Light pink

Evergreen hybrids				
Blaauw's Pink	100	6a	E	Coral-pink
Encore Series	150	6a-7a	EM	Hardiness variable depending on hybrid; mixed colours
Girard's Hot Shot	150	6b	EM	Orange-red
Herbert	120	6a	EM	Purple-pink
Hino Crimson	100	6a	E	Crimson-red
Karen	120	5a	E	Lavender-pink
Rosebud	120	6a	ML	Double pink
Stewartstonium	150	5b	EM	Bright red

AZALEA SPECIES

Deciduous Species	Height (cm)	Hardiness	Bloom Season	Description
R. alabamense	160 to 300	6b	LM	White with yellow blotch; fragrant
R. albrechtii	150 to 250	5b	E	Purplish-red saucer-shaped flowers
R. arborescens	200 to 600	6a	ML	Small white to pale pink with dark pink filaments; fragrant
R. atlanticum	100 to 200	5b	M	Small white to pale pink; fragrant
R. austrinum	200 to 300	5b	E	Small yellow to orange with long floral tube; fragrant
R. calendulaceum	120 to 300	4b	L	Orange-red
R. canadense	75 to 150	4a	E	Grey-green foliage; rose-purple
R. canescens	200 to 600	6b	M	Small white to deep pink with long floral tube; fragrant
R. cumberlandense (bakeri)	200 to 500	5b	L	Orange-red
R. flammeum	200 to 300	5b	M	Orange to red
R. japonicum	100 to 200	4b	EM	Yellow, orange or red
R. luteum	150 to 350	5b	M	Yellow; fragrant
R. molle	100 to 200	5b	E	Yellow
R. occidentale	600 to 800	6b	M	White, salmon or pink with darker blotch; fragrant
R. periclymenoides	120 to 200	5b	EM	Small white to deep pink with long floral tube
R. prinophyllum	120 to 300	4b	M	Bright pink; fragrant
R. prunifolium	250 to 500	5b	VL	Orange to red
R. quinquefolium	250 to 600	6b	E	White bell-shaped flowers
R. schippenbachii	120 to 300	4b	VE	Light pink saucer-shaped flowers
R. serrulatum	250 to 500	6b	L	Small white with long floral tube; fragrant
R. vaseyi	200 to 400	5b	E	White or pale to deep pink saucer-shaped flowers
R. viscosum	300 to 500	5b	ML	Small white with long floral tube; fragrant
Evergreen Species				
R. kaempferi	180-250	6b	ML	White and pink to red shades
R. kiusianum	30-60	6a	M	Small-flowers; low spreading habit; white and pink to purple shades
R. nakaharae	30-60	6b	L	Low habit; mostly red shades
R. yedoense v. poukhanense	125-180	5b	E	Mostly purple shades

CALLUNA CULTIVARS

Cultivar	Height (cm)	Description
Alba	40	Bright green foliage; white flowers
Alba Plena	30	Mid-green foliage; double white flowers
Alexandra	30	dark green foliage; crimson bud-bloomer
Alicia	30	Bright green foliage; white bud-bloomer
Allegro	50	Dark green foliage; ruby-red flowers
Alportii	40	Dark green foliage; crimson flowers
Amethyst	30	Mid-green foliage; purple-pink bud-bloomer
Arran Gold	25	Gold summer foliage develops red tints in winter; mauve flowers
Athene	30	Dark green foliage; deep red bud-bloomer
Battle of Arnhem	65	Dark green foliage; bronze winter foliage; lilac-pink flowers
Beoley Gold	35	Yellow foliage year-round; white flowers
Blazeaway	35	Gold summer foliage turns red in winter; lavender flowers
Boskoop	30	Gold summer foliage turns orange with red tints in winter; lavender flowers
Clare Carpet	5	Light green foliage; prostrate habit; shell pink flowers
Corbett's Red	25	Dark green foliage; crimson flowers
County Wicklow	25	Mid-green foliage; double shell pink flowers

CALLUNA CULTIVARS con't.

Cultivar	Height (cm)	Description
Finale	40	Dark green foliage; amethyst flowers; late-flowering
Firefly	45	Brick-red foliage; deep mauve flowers
Flamingo	30	Dark green foliage; spring tips red; lavender flowers
Freya	30	Dark green foliage; shell-pink bud-bloomer
Glenfiddich	30	Copper to red foliage; mauve flowers
Gold Haze	30	Pale yellow foliage; white flowers
H. E. Beale	30	Dark green foliage; double shell pink flowers
J. H. Hamilton	10	Dark green foliage; prostrate habit; double deep pink flowers
Kinlochruel	25	Bright green foliage; double white flowers
Mrs. Ronald Grey	15	Dark green foliage; low spreading habit; mauve flowers
Mullion	20	Dark green foliage; lilac-pink flowers
Multicolor	10	Copper to red foliage; mauve flowers
Radnor	25	Bright green foliage; double shell pink flowers
Red Haze	50	Gold summer foliage turns orange-red in winter; lavender flowers
Red Wings	45	Dark green foliage; crimson flowers
Robert Chapman	25	Gold summer foliage turns orange to red in winter; lavender flowers
Ruth Sparkes	20	Yellow foliage; double white flowers
Selly	45	Dark green foliage; deep pink bud-bloomer
Silver King	25	Downy silver-grey foliage; white flowers
Silver Queen	40	Downy silver-grey foliage; lavender flowers
Sir John Carrington	20	Gold summer foliage turns red in winter; deep liac-pink flowers
Spring Cream	35	Mid-green foliage with cream spring tips; white flowers
Svenja	40	Mid-green foliage; rose-red bud-bloomer
Tib	30	Dark green foliage; double heliotrope-purple flowers
White Lawn	5	Bright green foliage; prostrate habit; white flowers
Winter Chocolate	20	Gold summer foliage turns chocolate-bronze in winter; lavender flowers

ELEPIDOTE RHODODENDRON CULTIVARS

Cultivar	Height (m)	Hardiness	Bloom Season	Description
Besse Howells	1.5	5a	EM	Compact habit with shiny foliage; frilled, purplish-red flowers, red blotch
Boule de Neige	1	4b	M	Compact plant; white flowers sparingly dotted with green and brown dots
Brown Eyes	2	5a	M	Deep green foliage; spreading plant; wavy pink flowers, light brown blotch
Calsap	1.5	4b	M	Light- green foliage on a dense plant; white wavy flowers, large wine blotch
Casanova	1.5	5a	M	Dark green foliage; compact plant; flowers pale yellow, flushed with pink
Catawbiense Album	2	4b	ML	Large plant; dark green foliage; flowers white, small green-brown blotch
Catawbiense Boursault	2	4b	ML	Dense dome-shaped plant; flowers lilac/purple, pale green-brown blotch
Catawbiense Grandiflorum	2.5	4b	ML	Large open plant; lavender flowers
Crete	1	5a	EM	Compact habit; dark pink buds open to light pink flowers that age white
English Roseum	2.5	4b	LM	Dense mounding habit; flowers lilac-rose pink with an orange blotch
Fantastica	1	5a	M	Dense compact plant with indumented foliage; flowers two-tone pink
Firestorm	1.5	5a	L	Dark green foliage flushes lime green on a spreading plant; flowers deep red
Florence Parks	2	4b	EM	Dark green foliage; vibrant purple flowers
Francesca	2	5b	LM	Broad plants with dark red flowers
Golfer	0.5	5b	EM	Dense compact habit with indumented foliage; appleblossom-pink flowers
Haaga	1.5	4b	L	Compact with glossy foliage; shell-pink flowers
Hellikki	1.5	4a	L	Compact with lightly indumented foliage; dark reddish-pink flowers

ELEPIDOTE RHODODENDRON CULTIVARS con't.

Cultivar	Height (m)	Hardiness	Bloom Season	Description
Helsinki University	2	4a	L	Glossy foliage; soft pink flowers
Henry's Red	1.5	4b	M	Open habit; flowers dark red flowers with a dark blotch
Holden	1	5a	M	Compact plant; dark reddish-pink flowers
Ingrid Mehlquist	0.5	4b	LM	Dense spreading form; dark green foliage; pink flowers fade to pure white
Janet Blair	2	5a	M	Dense; dark green foliage; rose-pink flowers, gold-bronze blotch
Kalinka	1.5	5b	LM	Compact habit; dark green, indumented foliage; dark reddish-pink flowers
Ken Janeck	1	5b	M	Compact habit; indumented foliage; pink buds; light pink flowers fade to white
Lee's Dark Purple	2	5a	LM	Broad mounding habit; flowers reddish-purple with orangey blotch
Mikkeli	2	4a	VL	Dome-like habit; pink buds open to white flowers with olive-brown spots
Mist Maiden	1.5	4b	M	Dense broad habit; deep pink buds open light pink aging to white
Nova Zembla	2.5	4b	M	Wavy dark green foliage; large upright plant; flowers cherry red, black spots
Percy Wiseman'	1	5b	M	Dark green foliage; compact plant; flowers dark pink, yellow and orange spots
Pink Parasol	1	5a	EM	Dense plant; indumented foliage; deep pink buds open light pink, age to white
Polarnacht	1	5b	LM	Wide growing habit; very dark purplish red flowers with dark red spots
Purple Passion	2	5a	LM	Domed habit; reddish-purple flowers
Roseum Elegans	2	4b	LM	Large spreading habit; lavender-rose flowers, small red-brown dorsal spots
Scintillation	2	5b	M	Large broad plant; flowers clear pink with a greenish yellow blotch
Teddy Bear	1.5	5a	EM	Dark glossy foliage; dense mounding plant; flowers pink fading to white
Vinecrest	1.5	5a	M	Upright; elliptical olive-green foliage; green-yellow flowers, light brown spots
Wojnar's Purple	1.5	4b	LM	Compact habit; dark purple flowers with blackish blotch

ELEPIDOTE RHODODENDRON SPECIES

Species	Height (m)	Hardiness	Bloom Season	Description
R. adenogynum	0.5-3	5b	EM	White with red spots; lanceolate, tan indumented leaves
R. argyrophyllum	1.5-3	6a	EM	White to pink, spotted; lanceolate, silvery indumented leaves
R. brachycarpum	1-2	4b	VL	White with yellowish green spots and large leaves
R. bureavii	2-3	6a	M	Pink fading to white; lanceolate, cinnamon indumented leaves
R. calophytum	1.5-4	6a	E	Pink; very long leaves
R. campanulatum	0.6-3	6b	EM	Light lilac to white; rounded, cinnamon indumented leaves
R. campylocarpum	1.5-4	6b	EM	Yellow; round foliage
R. catawbiense	2-5	4b	LM	Lilac purple, pink to white
R. cinnabarinum	1-2	6b	EM	Red nodding
R. decorum	2-4	6b	EM	White to pink; fragrant
R. degronianum	1-2	5b	EM	Pink fading to white; lanceolate cream indumented leaves
R. dicroanthum	0.6-1.2	6b	LM	Orange shades; oval, fawn indumented leaves
R. forrestii	0.5-1	6b	EM	Deep red; rounded, wrinkled leaves; prostrate habit
R. fortunei	2-4	5b	M	Pale pink to white; fragrant
R. haematodes	1-2	6b	EM	Dark red; oval, brown indumented leaves
R. insigne	1.5-3	6a	LM	Pale pink with red spotting; lanceolate, coppery indumented leaves
R. makinoi	1-2	5a	EM	Pink fading to white; narrow, white indumented leaves
R. maximum	1.5-3	4b	L	White
R. orbiculare	1-2	6b	M	Rose-pink; rounded leaves
R. oreodoxa	1.5-3	6a	EM	White to pink; rounded leaves
R. pachysanthum	1.2-2	6a	M	Pink fading to white; elliptic white to cinnamon indumented leaves
R. ponticum	1.5-3	6a	L	Reddish-purple to white

ELEPIDOTE RHODODENDRON SPECIES con't.

Species	Height (m)	Hardiness	Bloom Season	Description
R. pseudochrysanthum	0.6-1.2	6a	EM	Pink fading to white; elliptic, white to cream indumented leaves
R. rex ssp. fictolacteum	2-4	6b	EM	Pink to white, spotted red; huge, brown indumented leaves
R. roxieanum	1-2	6a	EM	Pink fading to white; very narrow, cinnamon indumented leaves
R. sanguineum	0.5-1	6a	M	Deep red; rounded, wrinkled leaves; prostrate habit
R. smirnowii	1-2	4b	LM	Pink fading to white; narrow, white indumented leaves
R. souliei	1.5-3	6b	M	Pink, white or soft yellow; rounded, blue-tinted leaves
R. strigillosum	1.5-3	6b	E	Dark red; bristly stems
R. vernicosum	1.5-3	5b	EM	Pink
R. wardii	1.2-2	6b	M	Yellow; round foliage
R. williamsianum	1-2	6a	EM	Solitary, pink; small rounded leaves emerge red; prostrate habit
R. yakushimanum	1-2	5a	EM	Pink fading to white; lanceolate, white to cream indumented leaves

ERICA (SPRING) CULTIVARS

Cultivar	Type	Description
Ann Sparkes	E. carnea	Orange foliage turning red in winter; rose-pink flowers
Arthur Johnson	E. X darleyensis	Mid-green foliage; pink to heliotrope flowers
Aurea	E. carnea	Golden foliage with orange winter highlights; rose-pink flowers
Beoley Pink	E. carnea	Mid-green foliage; heliotrope-pink flowers
Brian Proudley	E. erigena	Bright green foliage; white flowers
Darley Dale	E. X darleyensis	Mid-green foliage; shell-pink flowers
December Red	E. carnea	Mid-green foliage; pink to heliotrope flowers
Foxhollow Fairy	E. carnea	Mid-green foliage; two-tone pink flowers
Furzey	E. X darleyensis	Dark green foliage; lilac-pink to heliotrope flowers
Ghost Hills	E. X darleyensis	Light green foliage; pink flowers
Golden Lady	E. erigena	Golden-yelow foliage; white flowers
Golden Starlet	E. carnea	Yellow foliage; white flowers
Heathwood	E. carnea	Dark bronze-green foliage; lilac-pink to magenta
Irish Dusk	E. erigena	Dark grey-green foliage; rose-pink flowers
Isabell	E. carnea	Mid-green foliage; white flowers
Jack H. Brummage	E. X darleyensis	Yellow-orange foliage; heliotrope flowers
Jenny Porter	E. X darleyensis	Mid-green foliage; cream spring tips; lilac flowers
King George	E. carnea	Dark green foliage; deep pink flowers
Kramer's Rote	E. X darleyensis	Dark bronze-green foliage; magenta
Loughrigg	E. carnea	Dark green foliage; rose-pink flowers
March Seedling	E. carnea	Mid-green foliage; pale heliotrope flowers; late bloomer
Myretoun Ruby	E. carnea	Dark green foliage; magenta to crimson flowers
Pirbright Rose	E. carnea	Grey-green foliage; heliotrope flowers
Rosalie	E. carnea	Dark bronzy-green foliage; deep-pink flowers
Ruby Glow	E. carnea	Mid-green foliage; magenta flowers
Silberschmelze	E. X darleyensis	Mid-green foliage; white flowers
Springwood Pink	E. carnea	Mid-green foliage; pink flowers
Springwood White	E. carnea	Bright green foliage; white flowers
Startler	E. carnea	Dull green foliage; mauve to purple
Superba	E. erigena	Dark green foliage; shell-pink flowers
Vivellii	E. carnea	Dark bronze-green foliage; magenta flowers
W. T. Rackliff	E. erigena	Bright green foliage; white flowers

ERICA (SUMMER) CULTIVARS

Cultivar	Type	Description
Alba Mollis	*E. tetralix*	Grey-green foliage tipped in silver; white flowers
Birch Glow	*E. vagans*	Dark green foliage; rose-pink flowers
C. D. Easton	*E. cinerea*	Dark green foliage; magenta flowers
C. G. Best	*E. cinerea*	Mid-green foliage; rose-pink flowers
Caldy Island	*E. cinerea*	Dark green foliage; amethyst flowers
Cindy	*E. cinerea*	Dark green foliage; purple flowers
Con Underwood	*E. tetralix*	Grey-green foliage; magenta flowers
Corfe Castle	*E. ciliaris*	Mid-green foliage; rose-pink flowers
Cornish Cream	*E. vagans*	Bright green foliage; creamy-white flowers
David McClintock	*E. ciliaris*	Grey-green foliahe; bicolored white and megenta flowers
Dawn	*E. X watsonii*	Grey-grren foliage with yellow spring tips; deep pink flowers
Diana Hornibrook	*E. vagans*	Dark green foliage; dark rose-pink flowers
Eden Valley	*E. cinerea*	Mid-green foliage; two-tone white and lavender flowers
Fiddlestone	*E. vagans*	Mid-green foliage; cerise flowers
Golden Drop	*E. cinerea*	Golden summer foliage; red winter foliage; magenta flowers
Golden Hue	*E. cinerea*	Pale yellow foliage tipped orange in winter; amethyst flowers
Heaven Scent	*E. X griffithsii*	Grey-green foliage; lilac-pink flowers
Hookstone White	*E. cinerea*	Mid-green foliage; white flowers
Irish Lemon	*E. X stuartii*	Dark green foliage with yellow spring growth; mauve flowers
Irish Orange	*E. X stuartii*	Dark green foliage with orange spring tips; lilac-pink flowers
Jacqueline	*E. X griffithsii*	Grey-green foliage; cerise flowers
Kevernensis Alba	*E. vagans*	Bright green foliage; white flowers
Mrs. C. H. Gill	*E. ciliaris*	Dark green foliage; crimson flowers
Mrs. D. F. Maxwell	*E. vagans*	Dark green foliage; deep rose-pink flowers
My Love	*E. cinerea*	Dark green foliage; amethyst flowers
Ken Underwood	*E. tetralix*	Grey-green foliage; salmon-pink flowers
P. S. Patrick	*E. cinerea*	Dark green foliage; purple flowers
Pentreath	*E. cinerea*	Dark green foliage; dark magenta flowers
Pink Ice	*E. cinerea*	Dark green foliage; rose-pink flowers
Pink Star	*E. tetralix*	Grey-green foliage; lilac-pink flowers
Pyrenees Pink	*E. vagans*	Dark green foliage; dark pink flowers
St. Keverne	*E. vagans*	Dark green foliage; pink flowers
Stoborough	*E. ciliaris*	Mid-green foliage; white flowers
Valerie Proudley	*E. vagans*	Bright yellow foliage; white flowers
Velvet Night	*E. cinerea*	Dark green foliage; dark purple flowers
Windlebrooke	*E. cinerea*	Golden summer foliage; orange-red winter foliage; mauve flowers
Wych	*E. ciliaris*	Mid-green foliage; shell-pink flowers

KALMIA CULTIVARS

Cultivar	Height (m)	Description
Bridesmaid	1.2-1.8	Bright pink flowers with pale pink centre
Bullseye	1.5-1.8	White flowers with wide central band of wine-red
Carol	2-3	Red buds opening to pale pink flowers
Elf	1-1.5	Very pale pink; half-sized leaves
Firecracker	1-1.5	Red buds opening to pale pink flowers; half-sized foliage
Freckles	1.5-3	Light pink flowers with ring of dark wine spots near tips
Ginkona	1.2-1.8	Light pink flowers with ring of dark wine spots near tips; larger flowers
Heart of Fire	1.2-1.8	Red buds opening to pink flowers
Heart's Desire	1.2-1.8	Two-tone crimson and white
Kaleidoscope	1.5-2	Wine-red flowers with white edges
Keepsake	1.5-2.5	Dark purple-red flowers with deep pink edges
Little Linda	1-1.5	Red buds opening to pale pink flowers
Madeline	1.5-2.5	Double-flowered; two-tone white and pale pink
Minuet	1.5-2	White flowers with wide central band of wine-red; half-sized foliage
Mitternacht	1.5-2	Purple-black flowers with thin white edges
Moyland	1.5-2	Pink flowers with ring of dark wine spots near tips
Nipmuck	1.5-2	Red buds opening to light pink flowers
Olympic Fire	1.5-3	Red buds opening to two-tone pink flowers
Olympic Wedding	1.5-2	White flowers with narrow band of wine-purple near tips
Ostbo Red	1.5-2	Red buds opening to mid-pink flowers
Peppermint	1.5-2	White flowers with radiating central purple-red stripes
Pink Frost	1.5-2	Medium pink
Pinwheel	1.5-2	Mottled crimson to wine-red with pale pink edges and speckling
Pristine	1.5-2	White
Raspberry Glow	1.5-2	Deep pink
Sarah	1.5-2	Red buds opening to pink flowers
Silver Dollar	1.5-2	White
Snowdrift	1.5-2	White
Tiddlywinks	1-1.5	Light pink; half-sized leaves
Tinkerbell	1-1.5	Medium pink; half-sized leaves

LEPIDOTE RHODODENDRON CULTIVARS

Cultivar	Height (m)	Hardiness	Bloom Season	Description
April Gem	1-2	4b	E	Double white
April Mist	1-2	4b	E	Double light orchid-purple; purple-tinted winter foliage
April Rose	1-2	4b	E	Double reddish-purple; purple-tinted winter foliage
Arctic Tern	under 1	6a	M	White; dense rounded clusters
Balta	1-2	4b	E	Pink buds open white
Black Satin	1-2	5a	M	Light violet-purple; dark purple winter foliage
Blue Diamond	1-2	6b	EM	Purple-blue
Bluenose	1.5-3	6a	EM	Lavender-blue
Bubblegum	1-2	5a	EM	Mid-pink; purple-tinted winter foliage
Curlew	under 1	6b	EM	Yellow
Dora Amateis	1-1.5	5b	EM	White; deep green foliage, dense habit
Ginny Gee	under 1	6a	EM	Two-tone pink and white; domed habit; chocolate winter colour
Intrafast	under 1	5b	E	2-5 purple-blue flowers per truss; glaucous-blue foliage; mounding habit

LEPIDOTE RHODODENDRON CULTIVARS con't.

Cultivar	Height (m)	Hardiness	Bloom Season	Description
Isola Bella	1-2	5b	EM	Pale pink
Landmark	1-2.5	5a	EM	Fuchsia-pink; purple-tinted winter foliage
Malta	1-2.5	4b	EM	Light purple
Manitou	1-2	4b	EM	Light pink
Mary Fleming	1-2	5b	EM	Salmon and pink
Midnight Ruby	1.2-2.5	5b	EM	Reddish-purple; dark purple winter foliage
Milestone	1.2-2.5	5b	EM	Purplish-red
Molly Fordham	1.2-2.5	5a	EM	White
Northern Starburst	1.2-2.5	4b	EM	Pinkish-purple; purple winter foliage
Olga Mezitt	1.2-2.5	5b	EM	Bright pink; purple winter foliage
Patty Bee	under 1	6a	EM	Yellow; low domed habit
P. J. M.	1.2-2.5	4b	E	Lavender-pink; purple-tinted winter foliage
P. J. M. Elite	1.2-2.5	4b	E	Lavender-pink; purple-tinted winter foliage
Purple Gem	under 1	5a	EM	Purple; dense domed habit
Ramapo	under 1	5a	EM	Pinkish-violet; dense domed habit
Snow Lady	under 1	6b	E	White
Sugar Puff	1-1.5	5a	EM	White; dark green foliage
Thunder	1.2-2.5	4b	EM	Purplish-pink; purple winter foliage
Weston's Aglo	1.2-2.5	4b	EM	Bright pink; purple-tinted winter foliage
Weston's Pink Diamond	1.2-2.5	5b	E	Fuschia-purple
Windbeam	1.2-2.5	4b	EM	Light pink
Wren	under 1	6a	EM	Yellow; prostrate stems

LEPIDOTE RHODODENDRON SPECIES

Species	Height (m)	Hardiness	Bloom Season	Description
R. augustinii	2-3	6b	EM	Elliptical leaves; purple or lavender flowers
R. calostrotum	under 1	6a	M	Blue-tinted foliage; rich purple-crimson
R. campylogynum	under 1	6a	EM	Dark green foliage; tight dome; maroon-purple thimble-like blooms
R. dauricum	2-3	4b	VE	Semi-deciduous; rose purple or white flowers
R. fastigiatum	under 1	5b	M	Shiny dark green leaves; purple-blue flowers
R. ferrugeneum	under 1	5b	ML	Bright green foliage; tight habit; rose-pink flowers
R. hirsutum	under 1	5b	L	Bright green foliage; tight habit; pink flowers
R. impeditum	under 1	5b	EM	Small silvery-blue tinted foliage; tight dome; blue-purple
R. keiskei	under 1	6a	EM	Light green foliage; pale yellow flowers; 'Yaku Fairy' very dwarf cultivar
R. keleticum (calostrotum)	under 1	5b	M	Dark glossy foliage; deep purple-crimson
R. micranthum	1.5-3	6b	LM	Narrow dark green foliage; tight truss of white spirea-like flowers
R. minus	1.5-3	5b	LM	Thin leaves; pink flowers; relatively late blooming
R. mucronulatum	1.5-3	5b	VE	Deciduous foliage; pink to purple; early flowering; 'Cornell Pink' most popular
R. oreotrephes	1.5-3	6b	EM	Thin blue-green foliage; lavender-pink flowers
R. racemosum	0.6-1.5	6b	EM	Dark green foliage; bright pink flowers in tight truss
R. russatum	under 1	5b	EM	Dark green foliage; purple-blue flowers
R. sargentianum	under 1	6b	EM	Dark green fragrant foliage; white; 'Maricee' a selection with pale pink flowers

PIERIS CULTIVARS

Cultivar	Height (m)	Description
Bonfire	1-1.5	Red new growth; white flowers with contrasting red calyx; upright flower stems
Bonsai	0.3-0.6	Coppery new growth; small oval leaves; compact habit
Brookside	0.6-1.2	Chartreuse new growth; narrow, columnar habit
Brouwer's Beauty	2-3	Chartreuse new foliage; *japonica X floribunda* hybrid
Cabernet	1.5-2	Bronze new growth; deep pink flowers
Carnaval	1-1.5	Variegated; pinkish-red new growth turns green with white margins
Cavatine	0.3-0.6	Apricot new growth; compact habit
Cupido	1-1.25	Coppery-red foliage turns dark green; upright flower stems
Debutante	0.3-0.6	Dark green very glossy foliage; upright flowers; compact habit
Dorothy Wycoff	1.5-2.5	Coppery new growth; pale pink flowers
Fire N Ice	1-1.5	Variegated; red new growth becomes green with white margins
Flaming Silver	1-1.5	Variegated; red new growth turns green with white margins; more compact than 'Variegata'
Forest Flame	1.5-2	Red new growth turns creamy-pink then green
Katsura	1-1.5	Wine-red new growth
Little Heath	0.3-0.6	Variegated; coppery new growth turns green with white margins
Little Heath Green	0.3-0.6	Coppery new growth; small oval leaves; compact habit
Mountain Fire	1.5-2.5	Red new growth turns green
Passion	1.5-2.0	Pinkish new growth; cherry-red flowers
Prelude	0.3-0.6	Pink new growth turns green
Purity	0.5-1	Pink new growth turns green; later flowering than most *Pieris*
Ralto	0.5-1	Variegated; pinkish new growth becomes green with white margins; rose-pink flowers
Red Mill	1.5-2	Red new growth, turns mahoganey
River Run	1.5-2	Coppery new growth; desne white flowers; lace bug resistent
Rosalinda	1-1.5	Pinkish-red new growth; light pink flowers
Shy	1-1.5	Brick-red new growth; purple-pink flowers
Sincere	1.5-2	Red new growth
Temple Bells	1-1.5	Coppery new growth; stiff, almost whorled foliage
Tiki	1-1.5	Pink-tinted new growth; dense, upright flowers
Valley Rose	1-1.5	Pinkish-red new growth turns coppery then green; light pink flowers
Valley Valentine	1.2-2	Coppery new growth; deep rose-pink flowers
Variegata	1.2-2	Variegated; red new growth turns green with white margins
White Cascade	1.5-2	Pink-tinted new growth; large cascading flower clusters
White Pearl	0.5-1	Coppery new growth; dense, upright flower stems
White Rim	1-1.5	Variegated; pinkish new growth becomes green with white margins

INDEX BY LATIN NAME

INDEX BY COMMON NAME

IMAGE CREDITS

All photographs are by the authors, with the following exceptions:

ACKNOWLEDGEMENTS

My sincere thanks to all of my gardening friends and mentors, who have greatly influenced my passion for plants and gardens over the years. Their generous sharing of plants and knowledge inspired this publication and made it possible for me to photograph many of the superb plants seen in this book.

A very special thanks to Todd Boland for making this writing experience enjoyable. His phenomenal expertise in plants and gardens can be seen in his many publications. Thank you to Stephanie Porter and Iona Bulgin for keeping us on track and grammatically correct. A note of gratitude to Todd Manning for his excellent graphic design and layout and to Gavin Will and Boulder Books for taking on our publication.

Finally I would like to thank both my parents who instilled a determination, focus, and desire for accomplishment.

— **Jamie Ellison**

I would like to extend my appreciation to my editors Stephanie Porter and Iona Bulgin for their careful attention to the prose of this book. A special thank-you to graphic designer Todd Manning who created a book of beauty through his layout of the text and photos.

Jamie Ellison is one of the few people I know who is as passionate about plants as I am. We have dreamed about working on this book concept for years, and now it has finally come to fruition. It was so rewarding to work together on this venture.

Thank-you to the photographers who provided plant images missing from our photographic libraries. They are listed in the image credits.

Finally I would like to once again thank Gavin Will and Boulder Books for allowing myself and Jamie to share our love of plants and desire to share our knowledge with other gardeners.

—**Todd Boland**

Todd Boland is the author of *Favourite Perennials for Atlantic Canada, Trees & Shrubs of Newfoundland and Labrador, Trees & Shrubs of the Maritimes, Wildflowers & Ferns of Newfoundland and Labrador, Wildflowers of Nova Scotia,* and *Wildflowers of New Brunswick.*

Todd has written about and lectured on various aspects of horticulture and native plants internationally. He is a founding member of the Newfoundland and Labrador Wildflower Society and an active website volunteer with the North American Rock Garden Society.

Born and raised in St. John's, Newfoundland and Labrador, Todd graduated from Memorial University of Newfoundland with an M.Sc. in Biology and a specialization in Plant Ecology. Alpine and Asian plants are his longstanding outdoor gardening passion; indoors, he maintains an ever-increasing orchid collection. Photography and bird watching occupy any non-gardening downtime.

Jamie Ellison instructs in the Horticulture and Landscape Technology Program at the Nova Scotia Community College, Kingstec Campus, in Kentville, NS. Jamie holds a landscape horticulture technology diploma and a Bachelor of Technology in Environmental Horticulture from Dalhousie University. His employment experience includes a work term at Memorial University Botanical Garden in St. John's, Newfoundland, and at Jack Drake's Alpine Nursery in Scotland. Jamie has worked in many aspects of commercial horticulture and in 1994 he co-founded Bunchberry Nurseries, a specialty plant nursery.

Jamie's specialties include plant identification, plant garden design, and horticultural presentations on unique plants and gardens. Jamie is an avid photographer of plants and natural landscapes, has a passion for black and white photography, and is an insatiable plant collector focusing on alpines and *Ericaceae.* He has recently started to hybridize Rhododendrons where he lives and gardens in Canning, Nova Scotia.